IN SEARCH OF DR TANCRED FROM CORK

IN SEARCH OF DR TANCRED FROM CORK

THE 'JOYOUS ADVENTURER' OF THE OLD CAPE PARLIAMENT

BERNARD HALL

Matador
Unit E2 Airfield Business Park,
Harrison Road, Market Harborough,
Leicestershire. LE16 7UL
Tel: 0116 2792299
Email: books@troubador.co.uk
Web: www.troubador.co.uk/matador
Twitter: @matadorbooks

ISBN 978 1803137 230

British Library Cataloguing in Publication Data.
A catalogue record for this book is available from the British Library.

Printed and bound in Great Britain by 4edge Limited
Typeset in 11pt Minion Pro by Troubador Publishing Ltd, Leicester, UK

Matador is an imprint of Troubador Publishing Ltd

FOR MY MOTHER

Adeline Mary Tancred who during her eighty years of life drew every short straw on offer. Her abiding consolation was her pride in the memory of her father, Augustus Bernard Tancred, and his brothers, famous South African cricketers in their day, and the belief that we Tancreds come from an ancient family, which in a sense we do, though as it turns out not quite as she had hoped. Alongside the cricketers lurked a shadowy ancestor of whom she knew very little except for the fact that a very distinguished family in Ireland and Yorkshire came into the story. This book tells the true story of this shadowy ancestor. She would have been so disappointed. Sorry about that, Mum.

Great wits are sure to madness near allied,
and thin partitions do their bounds divide.
John Dryden, *Absalom and Achitophel*, 1681

Acknowledgements

In my quest over the last forty or so years to unwrap the parcel containing the life and times of Augustus Joseph Tancred, many people, professional and lay, have helped me along the way. It never was, nor could have been, a solo effort. Time has passed since I set out along the road, so inevitably this list includes the quick and the dead, both people and institutions.

It is customary to begin by admitting that 'all errors of fact or interpretation are entirely my own'. I am willing to go as far as 'most' but draw the line at 'all'.

I cannot do other than give a special 'thank you' to:

Diana Bricknell for the invaluable early research.
The ever-welcoming James Tancred at Boroughbridge.
Sue Newman, author of *The Christchurch Fusee Chain Gang* and *Christchurch Through Time*.
Geraldine Sowerby who travelled the early miles.
Lee McGovern, born Tancred in South Africa, now in New Zealand, who became tireless in the quest.
For early encouragement, Donal McCracken at the University of KwaZulu-Natal, Durban, and his father, J.L. McCracken.

Heinrich Schulze at UNISA, Pretoria, the legal brain behind our joint work on *Smith v Lindsay*.

Richard Parry, a proper South African historian, for encouragement and guidance. Not forgetting his expertise on early South African cricket.

My wife, Teresa, who was a travel companion on the journey, a constant source of wise suggestions and help putting the words in the right order to make a book. And for the use of her eyes when mine made progress difficult. Above all, thanks are certainly due to the late 'Dr' Augustus Joseph Tancred, D.D., whose extraordinary life and times provided the material in the first place and without whom many Tancreds would not have existed. R.I.P.

Many others made valuable contributions including:

Ireland: Henry McDowell; Lord Dunboyne (Butler family); Professor D.A. Webb; Paul Gorry; Edward Wallace, Cork Genealogical Society; Ann Marie Coghlan, independent researcher, Family, Past & Place Genealogy Services; Ita Gimblette, Archivist, Diocese of Cork and Ross; Margaret Lantry; Anna Porter, Archivist, St Patrick's College, Maynooth; Steven Skeldon, Cork City and County Archives (the source of the important information about Tancred and the Unitarian Church); the Unitarian Church, Cork City; Tony Harpur; Tom O'Leary; Fred Powell, UCC.

England: Conversations with Edward H. Burrows, author of *Hampshire Family, the Reverend Burrows and his progeny*; the staff at Christchurch Priory; Cornwall Record Office, when at Truro; Dorset History Centre, Dorchester; Essex Record Office, Chelmsford; Simon Fowler; Hampshire Record Office, Winchester; Kim Harris, Archive Assistant, Arundel Castle; Robert Harris; Peter Higginbotham; Naomi Johnson, Archivist of the Birmingham Diocesan Archives and Oscott College; James Levett; David Taylor.

South Africa: Heather MacAlister; Guy Barker; Brian Barnes; Dean McCleland, *The Casual Observer* of the history of Port Elizabeth and area; Marijke Cosser and William Jervois, Albany Museum, Rhodes University, Grahamstown; Mrs Duminy, Kimberley; D.N. 'Dot' Denoon Duncan; Liz Eshmade; Melanie Geustyn, Senior Librarian, Special Collections, National Library of South Africa; Zoe Kennedy (Tancred); Anne MacLean (Tancred); Lanthe Kat (Tancred); Erika Leroux, Western Cape Archives and Records Service; William Martinson, Border Historical Society; Mercia van Reenen; John Smith; Lenor Tancred; Mark Tapping; Paul Taylor; Koos de Wet.

France: Josephine Huet, *généalogiste*; Carole Jacquet, Head of Libraries and Archives, Centre Culturel Irlandais, Paris; Jenny Nitting (Tancred); Corinne Porte, Directrice, Archives Nationales du Monde du Travail, Roubaix.

Surveying this long list, I wonder how it can be that so many questions remain unanswered!

Contents

AFRICA

Introduction

Where did it all begin? Was it the belief that we descend from the French nobility, not any old scabby nobility?

My mother's father was in his time a famous South African cricketer. She was very proud of this but his death when she was only eleven years old made her frustrated and eternally sad. That left her with memories of him and the family name 'Tancred', of which she was proud. In 'the back of beyond' in the veld beyond Johannesburg, the fairytale story of the Tancreds' descent from the French nobility was a source of considerable comfort to her.

The reliability of the source of this belief system she viewed as cast iron. Somewhere in the forest of illusions, lies, distortions and false memories that litter the oral repository of years gone by, I recollect a tale of 'someone in the family' who 'did the ancestry' with the help of an expert while on a brief visit to London in the 1920s. Returning to South Africa, he brought back a handwritten family tree which proved conclusively that we descended from the Kings of France or, if not the Kings, then the Dukes of Orléans, if not the first Duke then perhaps the second Duke, certainly no lower than the third Duke. By the time I became curious about these things the document had disappeared and we had buried anyone who might have remembered the identity of the man who went to London, or how any of it might connect to our Tancreds, a detail my mother had overlooked. But she never failed to remind herself, and anyone else with ears to hear, of the incontrovertible fact of our descent from the French nobility.

In the 1920s it may have been relatively easy for a visitor from a far corner of the empire, gold coins jangling in his pockets, to hire an expert in London to trace a family tree to order. It is possible that the social standing of the resulting ancestors might sometimes appear to correlate positively with the ability and willingness to pay the researcher. Not that I am suggesting that all genealogists are bent, just that one or two, here and there, may have succumbed to temptation, nudged a name here, smudged a date there. Some genealogists may have experienced hunger, cold or an addiction to drink. Things are, of course, different now.

ALAS, WE DO NOT DESCEND FROM THE FRENCH NOBILITY

Later, when I looked into this version of the family history, it very quickly became evident that there was not a word of truth in the French nobility story. The 'research' in London was all pure, unadulterated hokum, with not a single sighting of a Tancred strolling down a Baron Haussmann boulevard, with an independent air or otherwise. Perhaps fortunately, it was not until after my mother's death that I discovered we were not in line to hang out with the French nobility. An invitation to a weekend house party at Versailles was no longer a prospect.

But if we did not descend from the kings of France, or their underlings, then to whom could we trace our exalted lineage? This turned out to be a very good question. Fortunately, my mother had ready answers to most questions and in this case it was that we owned a ruined castle in Yorkshire. One day we would have enough money to reclaim the title that went with the castle before rebuilding the castle. Yorkshire might not be France but what of our relation, the Baronet, who had usurped our ruined castle?

OUR RUINED CASTLE IN YORKSHIRE

When I turned my genealogical research guns on this fortress, disappointment awaited. There are indeed castles in Yorkshire, not all of which are ruined but, as it turned out, none are part of our birthright. There is a Tancred baronet in Yorkshire but I have found no conclusive evidence that we are members of his tribe. Family history research is so often the last resting place of false hopes.

SAVED! A SURVIVING OBITUARY

When I was nine or ten, or thereabouts, I became aware of a typed copy of an obituary buried away in a sock drawer. At the time I took no interest in it whatsoever. After all, what was an obituary? Nothing but boring words about dead people. I was finding living people difficult enough.

Fortunately, unlike the family tree, the obituary survived and circulated quite widely in the family. In time people came to believe all it said about the deceased, one Dr Tancred. We now had an ancestor to justify those moments when we swelled with public pride.

'My ancestor, you must have heard of Dr Tancred?'
'No.'
'I am surprised.'

But with the obituary's timeline of the most significant events in his life here was a family historian's dream come true. He was from Ireland, and a member of an ancient family. He was awarded a doctorate in Divinity from Trinity College in Dublin. He was Rector of Christchurch in Hampshire. He had married a relative of Sir William Molesworth. He was a central player in a notorious case, *Smith v Lindsay*. Whatever was that all about? And what were his 'many failings'? The questions went on and on. Perhaps our ruined castle was in Ireland. And our baronetcy?

Decades later I started to flesh out and check some of the details and plug some of the gaps in the obituary. I had no idea then what an extraordinary man my researches would reveal as I hunted him low, and hunted him high, in Ireland, England, France and South Africa. I confirmed some of the 'facts' in the obituary but found many instances where old Tancred had been very economical with the truth. There was always something more beyond the obituary, *plus ultra*.

In the beginning I wanted to know where the story began. What follows is what I have come to know about the life and times of this extraordinary man, his family, and the places and times he inhabited from his birth to his death sixty-two years later.

I sometimes wonder what my mother would have made of it all.

'Piffle!' perhaps. It may have been enough for her to know that her father, the famous cricketer, was from proven stock even if it fell short of the French nobility and the English gentry.

EUROPE

1

A NATIVE OF IRELAND

The deceased, as far as we are acquainted with his history, was a native of Ireland, and the descendant of an ancient family. Born in 1802...
Obituary, *De Zuid-Afrikaan*

So far, so vague. What was this 'ancient family' from which Dr Tancred descended? At first glance the obituary was a good place for me to begin the search for the answer but little did I know then that the knowledge that an ancestor 'was a native of Ireland' is often the last resting place of many a hope of tracing an Irish family. Although not a large island, it is not so small and thinly populated that a cursory glance is enough to reveal who lived where and when. It is a land of counties, farms, cities, towns and villages, as well as people and leprechauns. Not knowing *where* has caused many an overconfident researcher facing this, the very first hurdle, to fall to their knees howling with frustration.

Fortunately, my distant early searches unearthed a paper trail of clues that led to County Cork, the largest county in all Ireland, and then to Cork City.

*

Augustus Joseph Tancred's life story begins in Cork, so it is about a Cork man. A character in Lisa McInerney's novel *The Rules of Revelation* about goings-on in Cork observes: 'Cork is a very male place. But then I suppose isn't that the way of history? It's all fecking men.'

The reader may wish to bear this gentle 'gender awareness warning' in mind: whether in Ireland, England, Belgium, France or Africa, my account of Tancred's life and times is mostly about men. It seems that in some ways little has changed in the two centuries since his birth.

*

Augustus was indeed 'a native of Ireland', and not only that, for it now proved possible to pinpoint where in Erin's Isle. But where in Cork City? And who were his parents? They, after all, were the gateway to the 'ancient family'. I needed to know more about his early days in Cork.

*

At this juncture good fortune seemed to smile on me when in 1985 a new job in London involved regular visits to Ireland and, not just to anywhere in Ireland, but to University College Dublin, Trinity College Dublin, and University College Cork. Tancred being a Cork man, and a graduate of Trinity College Dublin, I would be able to combine business with genealogical pleasure.

My first visit to Ireland took me to Cork and where

4

better place to start my search than in his birthplace. Or so I thought.

The plane landed and I headed for a taxi, remembering to put on my listening ears for the taxi ride into the centre of town. I am convinced that taxi drivers everywhere sing from the same hymn sheet be they in London, Dublin, New York, Cape Town or Cork, or anywhere in between. The journey allowed enough time for me to learn that there was much wrong with the Irish body politic. The word 'corruption' occurred, frequently, as did the word 'politicians', with evident disapprobation, not forgetting the derisory phrase 'political parties'. The republican Fianna Fail, the liberal-conservative Fine Gail, were one as bad as the other.

'The Irish Labour Party?' I asked. Snort of derision. Or was it disgust? Well, that proved to be a stupid question.

Leaving aside the detail, it really did sound like the England I had just left behind. Perhaps taxi drivers should rule the world? Who is to say they might not make a better job of things?

At University College Cork (UCC) I met warm, friendly, richly talented people in a lively university. Not everyone knows this, and I certainly didn't, but George Boole, the first professor of mathematics at UCC, developed Boolean algebra that would later make computer programming possible. I was fed, watered, and accommodated in splendid accommodation but, and it was rather a big 'but', attempts in my downtime to find one iota of information about Augustus Joseph Tancred led absolutely nowhere.

At which point cue taxi to the airport and, yes, the

story was the same, the country was still going to the dogs, perhaps more so than a week earlier.

Failing to advance my knowledge of Augustus Joseph in Cork, I returned to London knowing that searching on the ground was not a promising way forward. I would have to resort to traditional searches and for that London was as good a place as any.

*

So it was that after several fruitless years aided by professional genealogists in Ireland, a local man in Cork found and shared a church record that opened a window from which much else came into view, revealing that on 30 August 1804, the baptism of 'Augustin' Joseph Tancred was registered at St Finbarr's Roman Catholic Church in Cork City. Throughout his adult life he used 'Augustus' as his first name. The baptismal record identified his parents as Moses and Mary Tancred. From this moment on the floodgates of information opened.

*

St Finbarr's is a city centre parish on the south side of the River Lee, bounded on the north by Oliver Plunkett Street, and to the south by St Patrick's Road. The parish stretches from St Maries of the Isle to Albert Road. It is the oldest (1766) Roman Catholic church in the city still in use to this day, replacing an earlier church on Douglas Street. St Finbarr's was built with the help of donations from local Catholic families.

John Hogan's fine sculpture (1832) of the dead Christ, the outstanding feature in the interior, is sited below the altar. A near contemporary of Augustus, Hogan was born in 1800 in Tallow, County Waterford. His father was a carpenter and builder resident in Cove Street in Cork. His mother, Frances Cos, was a great-granddaughter of Sir Richard Cox, Lord Chancellor of Ireland (1703–1707). Marrying beneath her station, as the family saw it, she was disinherited. Cove Street is not very far from St Finbarr's and the Tancred family home in Hanover Street. The dictates of class, and the realities of economic status, were alive and well in the Cork of the time. At the same time the natives, voicing their displeasure at their political, religious and economic circumstances, were restive with rebellion in the air, but that is another story.

PARENTS AND SIBLINGS

Looking into the background of the mother of Augustus, Mary Tancred, showed her to have previously been Mary Power, but born Mary O'Sullivan. It looks as if she first married a Mr Power, who presumably died, leaving her free to marry again, this time to Moses. The marriage record at the church shows that when Moses and Mary married on 23 November 1803, at St Finbarr's, they were both of Hanover Street, Cork City. The witnesses of their marriage were Robert French and Elizabeth Long. Robert was a professional man holding a Diploma in Civil Engineering from Queen's University in Ireland.

Mary was born in 1781, the daughter of Tad O'Sullivan and Mary Long. It seems that two children had been born to her first marriage, Agnes Power baptised in 1800, and Thomas Power in 1801, half-siblings of her Tancred children with Moses.

If Augustus descended from an ancient family the key to this door was most likely to be found in the pocket of his father, Moses. But who was Moses? This question dogged the enquiry for almost all of the following thirty or more years. Moses, it turned out, was and remains something of a mystery man.

Augustus, the eldest child of the marriage of Moses and Mary Tancred, was followed into the family in Hanover Street by two brothers and three sisters: a John Tankard (transcribed as born in Hane Street, but probably Hanover Street), baptised on 28 September 1805, Thomas on 24 August 1806, Eliza on 12 October 1807, Mary Anne, who died in infancy and was baptised in 1809, and a second, perhaps replacement, Mary Anne (Tankard) in May 1810. Only Eliza, possibly, and Mary Anne appear later in the known life of Augustus, both in England; Mary Anne in Christchurch in 1834, and Eliza in London in 1839 and 1840.

The marriage of Moses and Mary, and the baptisms of all these children, apart perhaps from John, are given as from Hanover Street. John and the second Mary Anne are given as Tankard. A name variation such as 'Tancred' or 'Tankard' is not unusual and, although it may indicate different families, this seems unlikely in this case.

THE FAMILY IN CORK SOCIETY

The best clue to the social background and family circumstances of the Tancreds in Cork lies in the occupation of Moses as revealed in the local trade directories. *West's Cork Directory* for 1809–10 lists Moses Tancred, a breeches-maker, of Hanover Street. *Connor's Cork Directory* in the 1812 edition lists Moses Tankard as a stay-maker at Hanover Street; the 1826 edition lists Moses Tancred, a glover, at 17 Hanover Street, Cork, as well as a James Tancred, also a glover, who may have been a relation, in Cockpit Lane. Pigot & Co. in their 1824 *Directory* have Moses at 17 Hanover Street and James at 12 Cockpit Lane, both as glovers. Moses, clearly, fits neatly into the merchant class. In *Aldwell's General Post Office Directory of Cork* in 1845, James is a glover at No. 29 Grand Parade, an upmarket shopping area, suggesting that he had moved up, or started higher, in the world.

BREECHES, STAYS AND GLOVES

At first glance, living in Hanover Street in Cork, a father in trade, suggests quite modest origins for Augustus. 'Breeches-maker', 'stay-maker' and 'glover' sound rather lowly occupations. Moses was 'in trade' and, hence, fell short of the gentry level, yet was a man of independent means not employed by others. Furthermore, these were luxury trades and, in the case of glovers, had their own professional guild in London, formed in 1349 and incorporated by a Royal Charter in 1638.

Stay-making as a trade, making a comparison with the trade in England as a guide, was typically a man's occupation, usually a separate business or one incorporated into the tailoring trade with a long history:

> The Stay-Maker is employed in making Stays, Jumps and Bodices for the Ladies. He ought to be a very polite Tradesman, as he approaches the Ladies so nearly.
>
> *The London Tradesman ca. 1747*

Glove-making as a formalised trade with its own guild dates from the fourteenth century in London, although the roots of glove-making in Britain lie further back. A glove, according to an old saying, should be dressed in Spain, cut in France and sewn in England, although the adage no longer served once France beat most other countries out of the field. Nonetheless, the English glove trade was historically of great importance; in the fifteenth century it had become one of the staple occupations of the country with foreign importations strictly prohibited. In other centres, including Dublin and Cork, glove manufacturing flourished.[1]

Nor was glove-making in Ireland restricted to Dublin and Cork for:

> Limerick was celebrated for a very beautiful glove, made from the skin of very young calves, lambs, or kids, and so fine that a pair might be enclosed in a walnut-shell; they had the further merit of rendering the wearer's hand smooth and delicate.
>
> *Fine Art Registry*

---

1   Mairead Dunlevy, *Dress in Ireland*, Cork, The Collins Press, 1989, 134; Irish Rural Life and Industry, *Glove Making in Ireland*, Dublin, Hely's Limited, 1907, 193; Mike Redwood, *Gloves and Glove-Making*, Shire, 2016.

This begs the question, 'How did these trades fare in Cork?' The answer is found in the reign of Elizabeth I and an act of 1569 giving power to the Lord Deputy, advised by the Queen's Council in Ireland, to appoint places where it would be lawful to tan leather. Cork was very probably one such place. A subsequent grant a few years later shows that members of the Company of Glovers in the city were licensed to tan leather. This and subsequent grants by the sovereign show that shoemaking, tanning and glovemaking, all dependent on the tanning of hides, were early trades on the Cork commercial scene and ones which came before the brewing for which Cork later became more famous.[2]

It seems reasonable to conclude, albeit with some caution, that in the early nineteenth century Moses Tancred and family occupied a modestly respectable position somewhere in the merchant class in the Cork social order, successful enough to have an entry in the local trade directories of the time. They do not appear to have been elected or appointed to any positions in society in the tiers above them. Once again, the boasts by Augustus about his eminent family origins seem, put politely, to have tended to exaggeration with this one perennial caveat: the unknown origins of Moses, father of Augustus.

Breeches seem to have been something of a Tancred specialism. John Watson Stewart's *The Gentleman's and Citizen's Almanack for the Year 1814* lists 'Tancred and Sons' among the merchants and traders in Dublin as

---

2   William O'Sullivan, *The Economic History of Cork City from the Earliest Times to the Act of Union*, Cork University Press, 1937, 64-5.

'Breeches-makers at 78, gt. Britain-street'. Was Moses perhaps related to this Dublin family?

THE FATHER OF MOSES

In his adult life Augustus made the startling claim that he was related to the English baronets of Boroughbridge in Yorkshire. He went beyond that, to assert that he might one day become the Baronet. If this claim was valid, it would provide an incontrovertible link through his father, Moses, to the Boroughbridge family. But was it true? The answer could only lie in the paternal branch of the family tree, and the antecedents of Moses who were... and that is where the trail ran cold.

If Augustus was related to the Boroughbridge Tancreds, and the Baronet, then this must have been because his father, Moses, was related to that family. In his genealogical history Moses therefore holds the key of the door. Unlocking and opening the door would depend only on identifying his father as a member of the Boroughbridge Tancred family. This should have been easy but, and it is a big 'but', Moses' key does not appear to fit in the lock of that door. Four decades of work by genealogical locksmiths have failed to fashion a working key.

There were occasional glimmers of hope along the way. A branch of the Boroughbridge Tancred family tree showed that Judith Tancred, the wife of Sir Thomas Tancred, the 4th Baronet, was Irish. She was born Judith Dalton at Grenanstown, County Tipperary, and married Sir Thomas in Yorkshire in 1740. This ticked both the distinguished Tancred box and the Ireland Tancred box.

Surely Moses, and consequently Augustus, descended from this union?

Or did he? A closer look at the tree showed that Sir Thomas died in 1759 and Judith in 1781. There is no evidence that they had a child called Moses or that Augustus was related to them or any other member of their family.

In 1989, the late Henry McDowell, a leading Irish genealogist, researched the Tancred–Dalton families but in spite of his exhaustive searches the traditional genealogical brick wall remained intact. Finding no possible connections between Judith Tancred (born Dalton) and Augustus, McDowell could only suggest that someone in Judith's family might have hung around in Ireland for a while and given birth to the missing link. However, exploring this possibility produced no results.

With this promising line of enquiry at an end the search continued in new directions. But where to begin? Although the registers of St Finbarr's in Cork show the marriage of Moses and Mary Power and the baptisms of their six children, nowhere in all of Ireland has there been found any other known mention of Moses, his birth, death, or any other hint as to his origins. He is indeed a man who seems to have no hinterland. Was he born in Ireland, the record obscure, or perhaps an arrival from England or France or elsewhere, who set up in trade in Cork?

THE BOROUGHBRIDGE TANCREDS

If Augustus did descend from this Tancred family, whether or not he stood to inherit the baronetcy, he could reasonably claim to be, in the words of the obituary, 'the descendant of an ancient family'. On the other hand, a moment's reflection prompts a reminder that 'ancient' refers not only to distinguished families for, in the ultimate sense, so are we all, going way back to whatever living thing first crawled out of the primeval slime.

The Tancreds of Boroughbridge are indeed 'an ancient family' of distinction, they are of the class that inhabit Debrett's and Burke's Peerage. Alas, no mention of a Moses Tancred can be found in these august collections, nor in the detailed family tree compiled over the years by the family. On this basis alone it seems unlikely that Moses belonged there. One Moses Tankard does show up in Yorkshire but without a link to the Boroughbridge or Cork families. This is a Moses remembered mainly for his frequent appearances before the Leeds magistrates – and subsequent periods of residence 'at Her Majesty's pleasure' in the local prison.

THE COVENT GARDEN TANCREDS

In the records of the Boroughbridge family there is reference to a branch of the family who lived and worked in Covent Garden in the eighteenth century. Could this be the missing link?

Two of these Tancreds, in a family of four brothers and four sisters, were 'in trade' in Covent Garden: Walter Tancred, a draper, and his brother John who was described more specifically as a woollen draper. Walter was under twenty-five in 1748 and recorded as active in trade in Covent Garden in 1765, 1770 and 1775. He later became guardian of his brother John's son Thomas, known in the family as 'Thomas of Liège'.

John, who was also under twenty-five in 1748, married Mary Bodenham in 1760. He was still in Covent Garden in 1765. Then, for no known reason, he headed to Dieppe, either directly or perhaps stopping off elsewhere en route, and lived in Dieppe from 1769 till his death, a widower, in 1773. There are hints at John being an irresponsible character. When he married Mary Bodenham, her father Charles paid him £2,000 in a marriage settlement, a significant sum at the time, and an apparent act of generosity. In his will, though, her father included this caveat: 'the said John Tancred agrees that whatever I should give or leave unto my said daughter Mary his intended wife should be for her sole and separate use'. John, it seems, was not trusted by his father-in-law.

Apart from Walter and John, there were two other brothers: Charles (intriguingly also 'alias Robinson'), who died in 1745 and is buried at St Paul's, Covent Garden, and Thomas who died in 1740 and is also buried at St Paul's, Covent Garden. These four men and their four sisters, Elizabeth 'of Liège', Henrietta, Ann and Barbara, were the children of Thomas Tancred and Frances Gazaine.

And what of Thomas 'of Liège', the son of John Tancred and Mary Bodenham? He was baptised on 17 June 1762, in Lincoln's Inn Fields Roman Catholic Church, was later in Bruges 1771 to 1773, and then in Liège from 1773 to 1777.

Might Moses have descended from one of these Tancreds? Might this be the link Augustus claimed to the baronets at Boroughbridge? Did one of the Cork Tancreds baptise a child, Moses, perhaps hoping for reasons unknown to lie below the sight of the authorities and achieve a degree of anonymity? Answers came there none.

FUGITIVES FROM JUSTICE

There is a further twist to the story of two of the Covent Garden Tancreds for, or so the Boroughbridge family story goes, at a certain point they encountered financial headwinds which eventually overwhelmed them. History does not record the names of these two men. It seems they fled to Cork rather than appear in a debtors' court in England. Might John above be one of the men who scarpered to Cork? One apparent success story in Cork, possibly a relation, is a John Tankard who is shown as a Freeman of the City (of Cork) 'free gratis', the date unspecified, and neither his family connections nor why he was honoured in this way are known.

Although Covent Garden provides by far the strongest leads connecting the Boroughbridge family to Moses, no proof has yet been found. Yet, a moment's thought gives cause for hope. Paul Blake, in his book on insolvent ancestors, recounts how easy and frequent it was for nimble debtors with sufficient funds to evade the court system by escaping to another jurisdiction. It was not an avenue open to all but would have been an option for the Covent Garden Tancreds, a solution they may have embraced. The Isle of Man and France (including Lady Emma Hamilton in Calais and Beau Brummell in Paris and Caen), as well as other nearby countries, were popular destinations beyond the reach of the law.

The possible link between Moses and the Covent

Garden Tancreds certainly merits future research. For the moment the quest has led into clutching-at-straws territory.

But there was one more straw.

A DEATH IN LONDON

It was at this stage of the enquiry that one further line of enquiry presented itself when I discovered a 'Moses Tancred' in a 'births, deaths and marriages' search in England. His death certificate shows he died of a liver complaint in 1838, a 'Gentleman' aged fifty-eight, at 21 Webb County Terrace, in the sub-district of Saint Mary Newington in the County of Surrey, now part of metropolitan London. His daughter, Elizabeth Verling, was present at the death. His age at death makes him born in or about 1780 which could be consistent with Moses in Cork. If so, could Elizabeth be the same person as Eliza, baptised in Cork in 1807, a daughter of Moses and a sister of Augustus? Did Eliza, or Elizabeth, Tancred marry a Mr Verling?

Elizabeth Verling did not long survive her father for she died two years later in central London from inflammation of the lungs. Her death certificate shows one Margaret Tancred present at the death. But who was Margaret? This was yet another clue that would merit further research.

Could these be more than mere coincidences: a Moses dying in London, his daughter present at his death, a woman with the same family name who was present at her subsequent death, also in London? All these snippets of possible 'evidence' were tantalising, although in the end, for the present, they merely added to the lengthening list headed 'perhaps' or 'what if?'.

2

TRINITY COLLEGE

*… he was in his earlier years placed under the best
teachers, and at the age of 20 (he) entered Trinity College
as a student of divinity. After the completion of his studies,
and obtaining his degree of D.D., he…*

Obituary, *De Zuid-Afrikaan*

THE BEST TEACHERS

No details are known of the childhood of Augustus apart
from the obituary statement that 'he was in his earlier years
placed under the best teachers'. This suggests that he, and
probably his siblings, or perhaps only the boys, benefitted
from a significant measure of basic education, enough
to proceed to an institution offering higher education,
something not always available to Catholic children
in Ireland at the time. Education at even the basic level
generally indicated a family in reasonable circumstances,
or an education provided for those less well off by the
Church or a voluntary agency.

The second report of the Irish Education Inquiry of

1824, published in 1826, shows that there were charity schools in Cork. The Blue Coat School founded in 1780, better known as St Stephen's Hospital, was one such school for which registers survive, although no Tancreds have been found therein or in any other early records.

Nano Nagle, from a wealthy Catholic family, identified with the harsh conditions affecting poorer Catholics living under the Penal Laws passed against Roman Catholics in Britain and Ireland after the Reformation. These laws penalised the practice of the Roman Catholic religion and imposed civil restrictions on Catholics. There were no Catholic schools and the law forbade Catholic parents from having their children educated abroad. Nano's parents sent her to France for her education despite these laws.

Among Nano Nagle's charitable acts were the schools she set up in Cork and elsewhere so that deprived children could benefit from a basic education regardless of their religion. Her pioneering work was continued after her death in 1784. It is conceivable that a Catholic boy like Augustus may have been one of the beneficiaries. Against this is the fact that the Tancreds did not come under the 'deprived' umbrella. Tantalisingly Augustus later baptised his third child Oswald Finbar *Nagle* Tancred. Finbarr is the patron saint of Cork, and the Nagle reference unmistakeable, so these names are at least a clear acknowledgement of his Cork origins and, just possibly, an acknowledgement of his debt to Nano Nagle.

What is beyond doubt is that his early education must have formed a sufficient foundation on which to build his subsequent higher education. In adult life he trumpeted his knowledge of the Bible, classical authors such as Homer in the *Iliad* and *Odyssey*, and Virgil in the *Aeneid*, as well as Horace, Juvenal in the *Satires*, and many others besides. His first language was English in which he demonstrated a high degree of competence in grammar and literature. He later claimed to be fluent in the Irish language. He was also at home in ancient Greek and Latin, French and Dutch. By the time he reached adult life he was certainly a highly educated man.

The boy from Hanover Street in Cork had done well. But where? The obituary pointed to his higher education at Trinity College.

TRINITY COLLEGE

Trinity College is the sole constituent college of the University of Dublin. Founded by Queen Elizabeth I of England, the last of the Tudor monarchs, in 1592, it is historically a European university of high repute.

A few months after my visit to Cork, I found myself in Dublin and, after the usual political update from the taxi driver, arrived at Trinity College where I received as warm a welcome as on my earlier visit to Cork. I immediately leapt at the opportunity to confirm that Augustus was one of their graduates, a Doctor of Divinity, no less. Where better to begin than in the college records? I did not, and still do not, sing, dance, whistle or perform conjuring tricks, any more than I am a skilled genealogist, but here I felt on the verge of an important discovery as I marched down Grafton Street to College Green, before crossing the road to the main entrance to Trinity, as fine a campus as I have seen anywhere.

Conscious that I was treading in the footsteps of a host of great alumni including Bram Stoker, Edmund Burke, George Berkeley, Jonathan Swift, Oscar Wilde and Samuel Beckett, among others, in my mind I added to the list Dr Augustus Joseph Tancred, D.D., a lesser luminary I admit, but my distinguished great-great-grandfather nonetheless.

Mindful of the college motto *Perpetuis futuris temporibus duraturam*, which translates approximately as 'it will last into endless future times', and anticipating a significant discovery, I advanced to meet the keeper of the college records. Proudly announcing that my great-great-grandfather was a Doctor of Divinity, no less, of this august institution, I was nonplussed when a search of the records by the archivist found no entry for anyone of that name. Could this be correct; might she have missed something? Did the information in the obituary count for nothing?

I should of course have paused at this stage to remember that he was a Catholic, not a Protestant, a crucial distinction in Ireland at that time, and later. Trinity was a Protestant institution and entry to its hallowed halls by Catholics was by no means straightforward. Just as people frequently changed their religion to advance their careers or protect their property rights, so too did they change their religious horse to enable entry to the stable labelled education. This was known as 'passing'. The Tancreds, belonging to the merchant class, would have been able to pay the college fees and maintenance costs.

My host for the day introduced me to some of his colleagues over lunch, with conversation turning to my Tancred ancestor. I noticed nervous glances across the room to a Professor Webb who was said to be the college historian as well as a distinguished botanist. But my fellow social scientists were in awe of this man and after much 'Shall we, dare we…?' it was decided that it would take a braver man or woman than those present to approach the great man.

After lunch, explaining to my host for the day that I was short of ready cash, having fallen foul of the strict rules governing Irish banks cashing visiting English cheques, he took my arm and said, 'Let me walk you across the road.' We strolled into the ornate Bank of Ireland, once the historic Parliament House building, and bypassing queues of customers marched up to a teller with a grim visage counting bank notes and a sign on the counter in front of him announcing CLOSED. Without pausing for any preliminaries my host said, 'My friend from England just wants to cash a cheque.' In an instant it was a done deal, a cheque hastily written, the notes handed over. 'I was at school with the fella,' my host explained as we walked back into the street. So here I was in Ireland, home of my great-great-grandfather, who, it seemed, was not an alumnus of Trinity, though the natives were proving friendly. Fortunately, I had not needed to mention my apparently undistinguished Irish Tancred as proof of entitlement to the teller. A trump card can so easily turn into torn shreds of cardboard flapping around on the pavement in gusts of wind. But I had learned a valuable lesson: the natives were approachable – if one went about it the right way and knew the right people. I was beginning to understand Ireland.

Encouraged by these insights based on experience, and undeterred by the negative result in the archives, I returned to England feeling emboldened to write to

Professor Webb, the man who was said to know everything there was to know about the college records.

The reply, when it came, was unambiguous:

> I'm afraid that a thorough search of our records gives no grounds for thinking that anyone called Tancred was ever connected with this College. Moreover, the idea that he got a DD of ANY university as a curate is fantastic. In those days it was primarily an indication of STATUS and there must have been very few aged less than about 45.
>
> *Letter from Professor D.A. Webb, Trinity College,*
> *to Bernard Hall, 17 January 1990*

With the seat of learning identified by the obituaries having nothing to do with him, might the obituary refer to another 'Trinity'? But no, Trinity Colleges, in Oxford, Cambridge and elsewhere, professed no knowledge of him either.

If not Trinity, then where? He certainly looked like a Catholic young man who attended a Catholic institution. Initial enquiries at St Patrick's College, Maynooth, a Catholic seminary, drew the same blank response. One other possibility, Carlow College, also denied knowledge of him. As one door closes, another door opens, or so it is said. Typically, in the quest for the life of Augustus, as one door closed, I would soon discover that another door closed seconds later. Where did he receive his higher education? At this point the trail went cold for a number of years.

ORDINATION

The silence lasted until an internet search of the British Newspaper Archive (British Library) yielded this information in *The Cork Constitution* of 10 January 1828:

> ORDINATIONS. – On Tuesday, the Roman Catholic Bishop, Right Rev. Dr. Murphy, conferred Priests orders upon the Rev. W. Delany, Rev. Austin J. Tancred, and the Rev. J.F. Drinan.

This was a lightning flash moment; next came the need to know more. Surely an enquiry to the Bishop of Cork and Ross, the diocese of his ordination, would reveal records of his training and subsequent career as a priest? Alas, it proved not so, for once again a promising lead sank into the quicksand when the response to an enquiry to the diocese showed there to be no records of a priest called Tancred. As was so often the case that left a further question: where did he prepare for his ordination, and where was he engaged as a priest? The Cork and Ross Archivist pointed to a publication containing the *Maynooth Student & Ordination Index (1795–1895)*, by Patrick J. Hammell. This, she thought, might help. An earlier enquiry to Maynooth had proved negative. Perhaps this would be different? And it was.

MAYNOOTH

The index in Hammell's book includes this entry:

Tancard Augustine
25-8-1824
Rhetoric
9087

So it was that St Patrick's College, Maynooth, the Roman Catholic education and training college, now replied to my enquiry with a positive result. In the words of the archivist:

> Augustine Tancred, of the diocese of Cork, completed his matriculation examination on 25 August, 1824, and joined the Rhetoric class in St Patrick's College, Maynooth. 9087 was his student number. Usually students started in the Humanities class, the fact that Augustine skipped this and went straight into Rhetoric implies that he had a good standard of education when he joined the college.

The archivist went on to set out a likely scenario covering Tancred's case. Apparently, young men would usually follow a course of study that consisted of one year each of Humanity, Rhetoric and Logic, perhaps with a year or two of Natural Philosophy (Science). Logic and Natural Philosophy were somewhat interchangeable in the curriculum. These earlier courses were always followed by three to four years of Theology. The entire course of preparation for the priesthood normally took seven years.

This seemed to be exactly the sort of education that would infuse the later writings of a literate, educated man, well versed in the scriptures. Augustus would have matriculated in 1824, aged about twenty. He would then have completed the course in four or five years by 1828 or 1829. This is consistent with his ordination in 1828 if, as was apparently not uncommon, he was brought back by the Bishop from college early when the diocese experienced a pressing need for more priests. Augustus was ordained after only four rather than five years in Maynooth, which may reflect well on his earlier education.

Having completed his pre-ordination training he now returned to Cork for his ordination and, one would assume, his work as a parish priest. Yet, the diocesan archivist had found no records of Tancred, in spite of his ordination by the Bishop as reported in *The Cork Constitution*. The archivist did, however, suggest a further possibility: he might have joined a religious order. If so, which order? Here again the trail petered out. The apparent lack of any church record of this phase of his career remains a mystery.

His parents were no doubt proud to see their son established in a career in the Church, his achievement perhaps involving financial sacrifices on their part. The future would look promising. Their son Augustus was on course to a modest but financially secure and respected position in the community. There might be sacrifices ahead, not least the requirement for celibacy. For some this proved a vow too far. Might the commitment of Augustus, like that of many another priest, wilt when faced with this challenge?

In all of this there remained another unanswered question: which institution awarded him 'his degree of D.D.'? Later, when he strutted his stuff in Africa as 'Dr.

Tancred', no one seems to have questioned his right to use the title 'Doctor'. Whatever else, it had not been awarded by Trinity College Dublin. If it was not a title protected by law, perhaps he like anyone else was free to call himself 'Doctor'.

And a further niggle remained: according to the obituary, he held the Anglican rectorship of Christchurch, Hants, 'up to the period when he resigned it, somewhere between 1835 and 1840'?. If he was ordained as a Catholic priest in Cork in 1828, when and why did he change horses from Catholic to Protestant?

The intriguing reasons behind his journey from Cork in Ireland to Christchurch in England, from Catholic to Protestant, lay long buried in the history of his early career in Cork. The obituary had proved a diversion; what events lay behind this abrupt change of career?

*

My quest had begun to feel like it was making progress. Now I suddenly faced many more questions than answers. Where and what next?

3

EARLY CAREER

*After completion of his studies, and obtaining his degree of
D.D., he was appointed first to one curacy, then to another.*
Obituary, *De Zuid-Afrikaan*

Leaving aside for the moment 'his degree of D.D.', if the
obituary is to be believed, on completing his studies
Augustus was appointed 'first to one curacy, then to
another'. This is vague in the extreme. The knowledge we
have which is set in stone records that he was ordained in
Cork in January 1828, and yet the Cork diocesan archives
can find no trace of him working there as a priest. The
answer lay sleeping for almost two centuries in documents
now held in the Cork City and County Archives and
provided for this research by Steven Skeldon.

TANCRED THE UNITARIAN

The sequence of events unravels in a letter from Mrs
Kirkpatrick, of 48 George's Street, Cork, dated 25 July
1831, to the head of the Unitarians in Cork. A prominent
member of the Unitarian Church, she was staunchly anti-

Catholic. The Bible Christians (the Unitarian Church) believe that the Christian God is one entity, whereas most other branches of Christianity believe in the Trinity with God in three persons: Father, Son and Holy Spirit. Unitarianism and Catholicism are incompatible. This letter shows that Augustus approached Mrs Kirkpatrick intending to join the Unitarians.

Was it his behaviour that saw him expelled from the priesthood, or did he walk away because he came to embrace a view of Christianity at odds with Catholicism? All the evidence suggest that it was his behaviour rather than a doctrinal conversion that came into play at this point. Everything in his later writings confirms that he was perfectly comfortable with a belief in the Holy Trinity.

The consequences of the imbroglio were life-changing. As a practising Catholic priest, leading a celibate life, he might have continued in his career and been well regarded in the church and community, and in all probability remained in Cork till the end of his days, baptising, marrying and burying his flock, spouting his sermons to a captive audience; he would surely have remained the family's pride and joy. And then everything changed.

Thanks to the letter from Mrs Kirkpatrick there can be no doubt that it was the celibacy requirement that proved his undoing. Announcing her startling news, as well as her hopes as to where it might lead, she began her letter:

Dear Sirs,
    Subject: Augustus Tancred
    To the secretary of the British and Foreign Unitarian Society, the intelligence that a Roman

Catholic Priest has turned Unitarian will be valuable to a high degree.

She then revealed, no doubt based on the gist of the story as provided by Augustus himself, how a Jesuit priest had impeached him to his bishop for 'immorality' and 'incontinence'. After a trial before a Roman Catholic bishop, he claimed to have come off triumphant. Boasting to her about his qualifications, he claimed to have had examinations at Trinity College Dublin, and to hold a 'Certificate of Capability' from an archbishop in France. Added to these, though bald on detail, was an 'RC Scholastic Course' he had completed with credit. Was France the location of some earlier training that could account for the acceptability of his foreshortened time at Maynooth? None of the documents that would have confirmed and added details to these claims is known to survive.

And what of the impact this development may have had on the family? Mrs Kirkpatrick's letter goes on to report how his mother had been on her knees begging him to repent. His parents had stopped his private income. Clearly things had gone badly wrong in his personal and family life. As an aside Mrs Kirkpatrick even marked his card socially observing he was 'a member of *only* (author's italics) a respectable tradesman's family'. Inconsequentially, however, as if to compensate for this deficiency, she noted that he had 'a good sonorous voice'.

But what did the Unitarians stand to gain from a Catholic priest changing sides? Mrs Kirkpatrick was clear on the matter: a Roman Catholic priest turned Unitarian would be valuable to them to a high degree. Ireland, if not the whole of the British Dominions, would ring with the news of a Catholic priest converting to Unitarianism. Newspapers and journals would give widespread currency to the story. This may have been fanciful but there is no doubt that she believed it.

What was the outcome? Alas, Mrs Kirkpatrick found her high hopes disappointed when she learned that he hoped to escape from Cork to England. At first she was sympathetic to his plight and, feeling sorry for him, offered him £5 which he graciously refused. However, he subsequently accepted a loan of £10 from her, a loan he did not repay. By then she had lost patience with him. Perhaps by now she had heard a version of the story from a different source, for she observed, 'the Unitarian Church is well rid of him… after heading for London, he is by now in the Church of England in the Diocese of Winchelsea'. She refers of course to the Diocese of Winchester which includes Christchurch. Winchelsea was not a diocese.

*

Surely the local Catholic bishop at the time of these shenanigans would have a record of such unusual events? Apparently not, for a further enquiry by me to the Bishop of the Diocese of Cork and Ross, Bishop Murphy, once again yielded a reply from his archivist stating that there was no record of the matter. This is beyond puzzling. Augustus had been ordained in Cork with priest's orders conferred upon him by the local Roman Catholic bishop and, though later he apparently fell foul of the church authorities, no record of these events seems to have survived. Had he been deleted from the church records in an attempt to detoxify them and remove all traces of a sin perpetrated by one of their number? Unlikely, but if not this, then what?

INSOLVENCY

At about the same time a second misfortune was about to befall the Tancred family.

Whatever success his father, Moses, had enjoyed up till then was not to last, for on 19 November 1831, four months after Augustus' conversations with Mrs Kirkpatrick about joining the Unitarians, the *Southern Reporter and Cork Commercial Courier* announced news of the financial downfall of Moses Tancred taken from the *Dublin Gazette*:

> 1831 INSOLVENT DEBTORS
> TO BE HEARD AT CORK ON Monday, the 21st
> Day of November, Instant. At nine o'clock in the
> forenoon.
> Moses Tancred, Glover

If, as Mrs Kirkpatrick was told by Augustus, the family had stopped his income, this may have been at least partly due to the financial crisis affecting his father's business. Or did the indiscretions of Augustus involve costs to Moses and cause the collapse in his business and hence the financial security of the family? Alternatively, the two events may of course have been unconnected.

This must, unquestionably, have been a desperately difficult time for Moses and Mary, parents of Augustus. The sacrifices they had almost certainly made to support the expense of his education and training, the high hopes they no doubt held for their eldest son, were now in the past. It is not difficult to imagine angry and depressed feelings tumbling around in the family, drawing in the siblings as well as the parents.

What followed six months after the insolvency may have dealt another hammer blow to the family fabric.

MARRIAGE

This marriage announcement was carried in newspapers in Dublin, Limerick and Mayo in May 1832:

> MARRIAGES
> The Rev. August Joseph Tancrede, to Evelina, second daughter of the late Joseph Senior Lattey, Esq., Collector of Kilkenny.

The newspapers all include the identical information. Somewhat unusually there is no indication as to where, on what date, or in which church the marriage took place, nor a list of those present at the wedding. No marriage register entry, and no press report, of the marriage has been found apart from this bald announcement, perhaps inserted by Augustus. Not to put too fine a point on it: were they ever actually married and, if they were, did her family, the Latteys, give it their blessing and attend? Her father 'the late Joseph Senior Lattey, Esq.', Collector of Excise at Kilkenny, had died in October 1829. Did her mother approve of the union? And what of his family?

Was a pre-marital sexual relationship with Evelina behind the 'immorality' and 'incontinence' of which he had been accused as a priest? Had he now made an honest woman of her? Whatever the truth of it, he would never again work in the Catholic Church. But what was the truth in the obituary assertion that *he was appointed first to one curacy, then to another*?

PREACHING IN TIPPERARY AND DUBLIN

Augustus may have been down but he was certainly not out. Two years later, in 1834, he published a book containing two sermons which, on his own ever modest admission, he 'preached with great success to the cause of pure and undefiled Religion in Tipperary and Dublin, and at Christchurch, Hants, in the diocese of the Lord Bishop of Winchester'. (Two Sermons, by the Reverend Augustus J. Tancred, D.D., James Nisbet, Berners St, London, MDCCCXXXIV (1834).)

It is not clear from this alone whether he was now marching under a Catholic or Protestant flag, although the best guess is that, having burned his boats with Rome, he was now sailing his leaking craft in Protestant waters. But in which churches in Tipperary and Dublin did he preach, and how long did he spend at either location? Were these the one-off sermons of an itinerant preacher or the result of settled periods of employment?

Though he was by then long gone from Ireland, a later circumstantial clue points back to a Tipperary connection in the Irish Equity Reports, 1845, with this 1844 reference to a financial settlement regarding certain lands in Tipperary, subsequent to the marriage of one John Power to Frances Lalor, in which Augustus acts with another man as a trustee:

Whereas, under and by virtue of the aforesaid settlement I am seised of a reversion in fee, expectant upon the decease of my said wife Frances without issue by me, of and in the lands of Clonomockogemore, situate in the barony of Eliogarty in the county of Tipperary: Now, I do hereby leave, devise and bequeath the same, after the decease of my said wife Frances, to my friend and nephew Robert Barry of the city of Cork, merchant, and the Reverend Augustus Joseph Tancred, and the survivor of them and his heirs, upon trust to the use and behoof of my son William Power and his assigns, for and during the term of his natural life, and from and after his decease to the use and behoof of the child or children of the said William Power lawfully to be begotten, as tenants in common and not as joint tenants; and for default of such issue to my own right heirs for ever.

The testator then devised other lands to the plaintiffs, his grandchildren, the issue of his son John. He afterwards (on 16 July 1832) made a codicil to his will. The will (1831) and codicil (1832) correspond with the time when Tancred may well have been in Tipperary, although in 1844 he was in the Cape Colony.

Perhaps William Power in the will was a relative of Mary, mother of Augustus, through her first marriage to a Mr Power. The will does add credence to the idea that Augustus may have spent at least part of the missing months or years in Tipperary. Although there is no evidence for it, he may also have been in Dublin for a while. It is not, however, possible to fully account for the time between his leaving Cork in 1831 and arriving in Christchurch in 1834.

ARRIVAL IN ENGLAND AT EWHURST

Before his time in Christchurch there is more or less rock-solid evidence of his first steps in England. An online search in the British Newspaper Library yielded a report of 'The Testimony of an Esteemed Man in Hampshire'. The esteemed man is of course Augustus.

This item in *The Record*, a newspaper based in London and founded in 1828, which later, after mergers, became the *Church of England Newspaper* or *Church Family Newspaper*, included an item in praise of Tancred by 'An Observer'. Reprinted in *The Cork Constitution* on 23 November 1833, it describes the manifold merits of a Mr Tancred who was 'indefatigable in the good work he has undertaken'. The author 'heartily congratulates the Bishop of Winchester for having patronised such a man', who is moreover 'considered a first-rate linguist, of profound learning and sincere piety, who, unknown to the world, is unaffectedly labouring with real humility to extend Christ's kingdom on earth'. This would be all the more impressive were it not for the fact that the style of the writer is remarkably akin to that of Tancred himself such that there can be little doubt that he is the author, were it not for the slight doubt arising from the fact that here he uses the title 'Mr' and not 'Dr' Tancred. If this was the first time he used the device of anonymity to publicise his views, and his merits, it was certainly not the last.

Augustus being as ever verbose, there was more to tell, and the article continues with a tale of his persecution as a Catholic in Ireland, of such menacing severity that he was forced to leave Ireland following several attempts on his life, all in spite of his converting to the Protestant faith 'quietly and unostentatiously, without noise or show or bustle', and having 'sacrificed all emoluments in the Roman Church and all expectations from his friends'. How this contrasted with, he commented, the favourable treatment afforded to those who transfer from the Protestant into the Catholic faith.

Thanks to the good offices of the Bishop of Winchester, he continues, this virtuous man, clearly Augustus, now preached twice on Sundays to the poor flock in the 'obscure village of Ewhurst' in Surrey, and during the week 'spares neither labour nor exertion to improve the morals and inculcate the true principles of the Gospel'.

Allowing for Mrs Kirkpatrick's confusion between Winchelsea and Winchester, this ties in with her assertion that he had reached a diocese in the south of England. Winchester with its bishop lay equidistant between Ewhurst and Christchurch and, according to the obituary, Christchurch was his next port of call. Why, and on the basis of what information, did the Bishop ride to the rescue of Augustus? Did family connections play a part?

According to the obituary, after graduating Augustus was appointed to one curacy and then to another. These remain unspecified. Cork may have counted for one, Ewhurst for the other. Preaching in Tipperary and Dublin may have also been on the list.

*

His career had been fast sinking when he headed for the nearest shore away from the old sod. After reaching England he never seems to have set foot back in Ireland. Was he aided in his flight by family or friends? As so often in his life there is the unanswered question: where did the money come from?

The obituary shows him rapidly climbing high in the ecclesiastical tree as Rector at Christchurch in Hampshire, a very prestigious position in a substantial church, before resigning sometime between 1835 and 1840. How did he come to be employed there, what did he achieve, why did he leave, and where did he go next?

Christchurch had to be my next stopping point; I felt that here at last I would find him back on the road to a successful career. Wrong.

4

CHRISTCHURCH

*After completion of his studies, and obtaining his degree of
D.D., he was appointed first to one curacy, then to another,
and eventually held the rectorship of Christchurch, Hants,
up to the period when he resigned it, somewhere between
1835 and 1840.*

Obituary, *De Zuid-Afrikaan*

The obituary conveniently skipped lightly over the period
between completing his studies and serving in more
than one curacy before reaching Christchurch as Rector.
He may, understandably, have wished for it to remain
thus, confident in the belief that no one would ever dig
deeper into his past. If this were the case, he was due for
a disappointment. Amongst his descendants were those
seeking to unravel his life story, warts and all.

Having failed as a Catholic priest in Cork, his
subsequent rise to Rector at Christchurch within three
years was nothing short of remarkable. In fact, it turned
out to be remarkably untrue.

*

At the time Christchurch was part of the county of Hampshire; in 1974 it became part of the county of Dorset and then, in 2019, part of the unitary authority of Bournemouth, Christchurch and Poole. To some this signalled the march of progress.

Founded in the seventh century, the town is situated between the sea and the two rivers, Stour and Avon, which flow into the harbour. If Augustus left Ireland at a time of political turbulence, Christchurch, scene of his rectorship, was far from being the bustling, prosperous, peaceful town it later became.

When he arrived in the 1830s poverty was the norm for the majority of the inhabitants. The approaching agricultural revolution was already destabilising lives and livings. Now, nowhere could people feel safe from the forces of change. In the countryside around Christchurch there was predictable resentment against the new machines introduced by the local landowners, the threshing machines which reduced the wages and employment opportunities of agricultural labourers. It was farewell to the world of Gray's *Elegy* (1751) and even of Cobbett's *Rural Rides* of the 1820s. No longer would as many of Gray's ploughmen plod their weary homeward way after a hard day's work in the fields.

In 1830 the 'Swing Riots' in the counties adjacent to Hampshire scythed through any sense of complacency among the landed gentry as alarm, then panic, spread through their ranks as displaced farm workers set about destroying the new farm machinery, more expensive to purchase but more economical to employ than human labour. As machines were destroyed and hayricks and other farm assets set on fire, fear crept closer to Christchurch, bringing unforeseen threats to the income and wealth of the propertied class. The forces of law and order were organised to calm the situation.

In these unruly times 'the church in Christchurch was crowded with nearly all the landowners and tenant farmers in the parish'.[3] When some of the alleged protesters were taken before a special assizes at Winchester the Chairman of the jury was none other than Sir George Henry Rose, MP for Christchurch, whose impartiality must have seemed questionable to the defendants. The punishments meted out were severe, ranging from those sentenced to hang (later reprieved), and transportation to Australia or Van Diemen's Land (Tasmania). Not surprisingly, these measures did not entirely extinguish the unrest.

Against this background there lived the many distressed townspeople of Christchurch, still a poor town with only two trades of note: the illicit smuggling which was active along the entire south coast and reaching into all ranks in society, and the licit (legal) fusee chain-making trade. Fusee chains were delicate components used in the manufacture of timepieces. It was the manufacture of these chains that provided the only significant legitimate employment in the town.

Tremors were now rumbling not only against the wealthy citizens and landed gentry but also against the Church with its tithes and tracts of land not available for the peasantry to grow food on. The grievances did not end there. The corrupt system for electing members of Parliament,

---

3   Sue Newman, *The Christchurch Fusee Chain Gang*, 51.

and resentment at taxation, added to the aura of discontent which contributed to the pressure for political reform. The resulting changes, including the 1834 Poor Law Amendment Act, met some but certainly not all the demands on the table. The 1832 Reform Act had led to the construction of a network of workhouses across the country – with one of which Augustus would, before long, become acquainted.

*

This was the backdrop to the world of the Church when Augustus arrived in town. As Rector at the Priory church between 1835 and 1840, he would no doubt have risen above these mere material matters, and may even have spread balm in and around Christchurch. It was a time when a good rector, in a position of spiritual and moral authority, would step forward and assuage the concerns of rich and poor alike.

It seemed reasonable to expect that, as Rector, he would leave in his wake a trail of documentary evidence detailing his years in Christchurch, how he became aware of the vacancy, his qualifications for the job including his licence to preach, the source of his doctorate, as well as a reference or two explaining his suitability for the post. When he moved on to his next appointment some years later there would be paeans of praise for his work in the parish, as well as heartfelt good wishes for his next and, no doubt, more senior appointment. His manifold achievements would attract the attention of the local newspapers; he was, after all, thanks to his position in the Church, a local bigwig of high status.

Except that the records did not show anything at all like that.

*

The Priory church, constructed in the eleventh century A.D., is the longest parish church in all England, larger than twenty-one of the English Anglican cathedrals.

It was time for me to visit. Walking through the town till I stood facing the welcoming main door, I remembered the keen anticipation I had felt on my approach to Trinity College Dublin the year before. Trinity had let me down, the Priory church, I was sure, would not disappoint me.

Once inside I scanned the lists of rectors and curates on the boards on the walls but was forced to conclude that they contained no mention of a Tancred. Surely there must be some mistake? Or perhaps not. My assumptions based on 'when he was Rector' were beginning to morph into 'if he was Rector'. It was the 'if' word once more; surely not another Trinity experience?

Nil desperandum, the family history researcher's rallying cry when faced with the proverbial stone wall barring further progress. Spotting a curate wafting at speed down the aisle, his black clerical garb flowing like a sail behind him, I approached and proudly, in spite of my now draining confidence, barred his progress and asked about my noteworthy great-great-grandfather whose towering presence had once graced this fine church. But to say that this cleric was not interested is an understatement for, pointing to the boards of names on the wall, he was curtly dismissive of my enquiry. As overwhelmed by the demands of God's work as he was underwhelmed by my great-great-grandfather, he was far too busy with God to spare a smidgeon of his valuable time to stop and talk to me. I persisted. There are people who are able to spend ten or more minutes telling you they are too busy to answer a simple question when, in half the time, they could easily answer the question. Here was one such who, like the character in Chaucer's man of law's tale, 'seemed busier than he was'.

I was, though, silently wondering if the obituary had lied to me once again. Did Dr Tancred ever exist at Christchurch? Was I facing a disappointment equal to that at Trinity College Dublin?

Grudgingly the divine creature led me to an inner sanctum where in a locked cupboard the registers of baptisms, marriages and funerals were stored. The 1830s, was it? Yes. When the page for 1834 opened my eyes fastened on the name TANCRED. Just as I had begun to doubt his very existence, here was enough proof to dispel my uncertainty. Relief. He did exist here, and once upon a time he was employed in the Priory church, even if it was a year earlier than I expected from the obituary.

The register entry showed that on 22 April 1834, Dr Augustus Tancred officiated at the marriage of William Witcher and Eliza Strickland. Then, on 12 May 1834, Dr Tancred and Evelina Tancred attended the marriage in the Priory church of Mary Ann Tancred and Charles Henry Baker, a lieutenant in the Coast Guard Service. The Rector, a man called Burrows, presided at the marriage ceremony. Dr Tancred and Evelina signed the marriage register as witnesses.

No doubt Evelina was the wife of Augustus and Mary Ann Tancred was his sister, born in Cork in 1810. A year later the Bakers had a daughter, Elizabeth Victoria, born on 3 May 1835 at Haven House, Mudeford Quay (Christchurch).

Research following my visit to the town revealed further details of the life of Augustus at Christchurch. James Lemmon, the Parish Clerk, kept a cryptic daily *Journal of Events*[4] for a couple of years after 1833. His spelling may have been anarchic, his disdain of punctuation all too evident, but he did make notes in 1834, a crucial year in the Augustus story. He confirms an arrival, most probably from London, as follows: 22 February 1834, The Revd Dr Tancred came by *Independent* coach.

The *Independent* set off from the Spread Eagle public house in Gracechurch Street and then the Bull in Aldgate, both in London, on or shortly after 7am every day. It went via Hounslow and Staines to Basingstoke, Winchester and Southampton and was operated by J. Nelson & Co. and W. Chaplin & Co. I have not been able to discover if it went on from Southampton to Christchurch and Poole or involved a change to a local coach in Southampton. Sadly, few nineteenth-century coach timetables survive and, when they do, are not always comprehensible.

1836 was the peak year for stagecoach travel with ten million passenger journeys. The decline, when it came, was catastrophic. Steam power, James Watt, George Stephenson and the coming of the railways all had a great deal to answer for in the eyes of one observer:

---

4   MS record of the Priory church made by the Parish Clerk, October 1833 to March 1835.

... they will ruin the breed of horses, as they have already ruined the innkeepers and the coachmen, many of whom have already been obliged to seek relief at the poor house, or have died in penury and want. *The Times*, 1839

Lemmon only mentions Augustus on four further dates:

2 May 1834, Doctor Tancred read prayers in a very great hurry.

22 May 1834, Dr Tancred read prayers and finished the reading without giving time for the boys to sing the evening Hymns. He also preached in the evening.

22 May 1834, Dr Tancred preached from (Chapter Verse details omitted in the original, perhaps because of difficulty identifying the Bible reference). After the Sermon he gave a Lecture to those whom he saw misbehaving themselves.

Then there is Lemmon's final mention of Augustus:

On 28th June 1834, Dr Tancred left Christchurch by *Pilot* Coach.

There are no subsequent mentions of him in the Priory church after this date, either by Lemmon or in the parish registers. Thereafter he was gone. After four brief months as a curate he was not, as the obituary stated, there until

1840, and he never did become the Rector, the top man at the Priory church. He had preached sermons, conducted one marriage service, been a witness at a second, but officiated at no baptisms or funerals.

Fortunately, it was the local newspapers of the day which yielded some clues shedding light on events during his four months at Christchurch. Reporting on events at Christchurch in the edition of 28 June 1834, the *Hampshire Advertiser and Salisbury Guardian* broke the story:

> The duties of the curacy for three months past have been to the pleasure and consolation of a very numerous and respectable portion of the inhabitants performed by the Rev. Augustus J. Tancred, D.D.; but circumstances not under the control of the Rev. Gentleman have caused his departure, to the deep regret of himself and a large portion of the church congregation, which was expressed to their spiritual teacher in the subjoined address, signed by sixty-seven respectable masters and heads of families.

The 'subjoined address' referred to appeared in the newspaper dated Christchurch, 16 June 1834, twelve days previously. It contained the same theme and specifically the 'serious and deep regret' of those who were 'about to be deprived of your most valuable services'. His ministry had been 'crowned with success, by drawing together a larger congregation than usual, and that in the face of a confirmed, strong, and powerful dissenting interest'.

The reference to the powerful dissenting interest may

reveal what was at stake here: Augustus, their 'spiritual teacher', had supported the doctrinal approach of those opposing the dissenting interest. Does this explanation help us understand why his position as curate may have become untenable?

What was the dissenting interest? Divisions within the Church of England (Anglican) had emerged in the eighteenth century, notably with John Wesley and the Methodists. The following century witnessed the growth of the Oxford Movement, the name deriving from its origins in the University of Oxford where John Henry Newman, Edward Bouverie Pusey and others opened a rift within the Church of England following the publication between 1833 and 1841 of Newman's *Tracts for the Times.* This expressed their wish to restore a Catholic orthodoxy in place of the Protestant traditions that had prevailed since the separation from the Roman Catholic Church in 1534. In time this led to the distinction between 'high' church which veered toward Anglo-Catholicism, and 'low' church which continued the Protestant tradition.

The 'low church' supporters favoured an evangelical approach and disliked the trappings of the 'high church' with its emphasis on ornaments, vestments, candles, incense and more formal ceremony. The views expressed by Tancred's supporters seem to suggest that these differences of doctrinal opinion were in the air at Christchurch at the time. Given his Catholic origins it comes as no surprise that his sympathies, and those of the more conservative parishioners, would have pointed in the high church direction. The authorities at the Priory church, who, in the words of the parishioners supporting Tancred, supported the 'confirmed, strong, and powerful Dissenting interest', would have had the final say in the matter. Feelings often ran high at the time. Had Augustus backed the wrong side?

Characteristically, on 18 June (published in the newspaper on 28 June), he replied at length in fulsome praise of his supporters. On reading this it rapidly becomes apparent that brevity was not Augustus' strength.

In summary, the 'Rev. Gentleman's answer' to the respectable and intelligent members of the congregation who had offered 'approbation of my conduct' had given him 'the highest possible gratification and pleasure of mind'. He invokes Matthew 10: 11-14 in the matter, 'And into whatever city or town he shall enter, enquire who in it is worthy,' before deciding that 'whosoever shall not receive you nor hear your word, when ye depart out of that house or city, shake off the dust of your feet'. This almost reads as an injunction to check out the citizens in any new town and, if you find them wanting, then leave them behind for you are in a bad place, the fault theirs not yours. For which read Christchurch?

Poignantly perhaps, for the rest of his life would not turn out as he hoped at that moment:

> I shall look to this day that you present your address to me as an epoch of my life, and from it, I trust, be able to date many a happy occurrence. One thing I am convinced of, I will always look back to it with a feeling of gratitude...

The next comment by his supporters in the same newspaper shows that the parishioners had now come to accept that his departure was inevitable:

The feelings expressed by such a numerous and respectable portion of the inhabitants, had encouraged a hope that the Rev. Gentleman would have remained; but it being otherwise, a subscription for a superb box, with a suitable inscription, was entered into, and it has been presented to him by a deputation of the following gentlemen: Captain Lyte; Mr Collins, R.N.; Messrs. John Bemister, Stephen Groves, and Samuel Bayly.

Presented to
The Rev. AUGUSTUS J. Tancred, D.D. (1834)
By the Members of the Church Congregation of
Christchurch, Hants,
In testimony of their admiration of the zeal and talent
Evinced by him during his short
Ministration among them.
1834

The silver snuff box is fully hallmarked. It was made by Nathaniel Mills in Birmingham with the date mark for 1825–6. Miraculously, it survived in his possession throughout his turbulent life. After his death it passed on down in the family, somehow surviving unscathed.

There was one final sighting of his involvement in local church matters when the *Hampshire Advertiser and Salisbury Guardian* reported that various sermons were preached on Sunday 22 June 1834, for the promotion of the objects of the Church Missionary Society. The Reverend Augustus J. Tancred, curate of Christchurch, and fifteen other reverends from far and wide, including the Isle of

Wight, were present at numerous meetings, morning and evening, in the National School Rooms. This was in connection with various missionary objectives as well as the associated extension of 'the knowledge of salvation to the uttermost ends of the earth'.

*

But what were the 'circumstances not under the control of the Rev. Gentleman' that 'caused his departure'? Why was he departing, given his regret, and that of 'a numerous and respectable portion of the inhabitants'? Was there something untoward the inhabitants did not, or did not yet, know? Or was it just that the church authorities supporting the dissenting interest were more powerful than Tancred's admirers who wished to follow the established view? If that was the case the authorities would have had the final say and may have seen the doctrine as more important than the financial and spiritual benefits of a larger congregation.

Was it as simple as that or were other factors at play?

5

THE REASONS WHY

'Events, my dear boy, events.' A century later this famous remark was made by Harold Macmillan, the British Prime Minister from 1957 to 1963, who, when asked what was most likely to knock his administration off course, quoted the existence of things unpredictable. The life of Augustus provides many examples of unexpected events causing him to make a decision, or accept a decision by others, that faced him with an abrupt change of direction. As a Catholic priest in Cork his future must have seemed settled, until events intervened. As a curate at Christchurch his career surely appeared secure, were it not for events. But what were these events? Tensions between the 'high' and 'low' church factions at Christchurch may have played a part but this, on its own, always felt a wafer-thin explanation. If word of his Catholic background in Ireland, his training, his disgrace as a priest, and his false claim to a doctorate from Trinity College, reached Christchurch, we have no evidence for it.

Fortunately, intermittent research over three decades gradually exposed some other possible and more plausible explanations for the departure from Christchurch.

AUGUSTUS THE SMUGGLER?

In addition to the local industries of fishing, brewing, fusee chains, straw bonnet- and chair-making, smuggling was the major industry along most of the English south coast. Many of the townspeople were involved, including some amongst the great and the good.

Was Augustus a party to this profitable trade? Was it, as in Kipling's poem, a question of 'brandy for the parson' and 'baccy for the clerk'? The possible connection lies hidden in the marriage of Mary Anne, his sister, whose wedding he and Evelina were witnesses to in May when she married Charles Henry Baker. It seems that before their marriage the courting couple would walk out together in the local area, as one Benjamin Joy Tucker recounted:

> Dr Tancred, with his daughter, lodged in a house by the river. In a store adjoining were a lot of tubs secreted. A revenue officer courted Miss Tancred, and in walking round the garden with her passed the store, and for some time the door was open, but love being blind, no seizure of the spirits was made.[5]

The quote raises a number of questions. Although the newspaper article was published in 1933, almost a century after the events described, Benjamin Joy Tucker (1825–1912) was aged nine in 1834, but would have heard the story as an adult. The reference to Augustus lodging with 'his daughter' must be incorrect as the available evidence has him in

---

5   'Stories of the Past: the memories of Benjamin Joy Tucker', *Christchurch Times*, 2 September 1933.

Christchurch with his wife, Evelina. Mary Anne, probably his sister but certainly not his daughter, may have lived with them for a while. Perhaps it was just that memories of Dr Augustus seeped down in the folklore of Christchurch, draining them of factual accuracy over the years.

And yet Baker was a revenue officer so there may be some truth in the smuggling story. As a Royal Navy lieutenant in the Coast Guard Service based at Christchurch, the man courting Miss Tancred would have found himself in a difficult position witnessing his intended bride's brother involved in handling contraband when, as a revenue man, he was employed to prevent the vigorous illegal trade in goods, notably liquors such as gin and brandy, as well as laces and silk, and tea, smuggled from the Continent.

Should he report his future brother-in-law to the civil authorities, perhaps adversely affecting the outcome of his courtship? Or did he perhaps report Augustus to the church authorities? Or, as Tucker suggests, turn a blind eye?

Had it become known publicly that Augustus was involved in smuggling, the church authorities might have felt duty-bound to intervene. But then, what if the church authorities were themselves up to their necks in this profitable trade? Although townspeople at all levels in society were active in the trade, a wise man would not get caught or, if worst came to worst, would enjoy the protection of those that mattered, not least the magistrates. The big boys, the streetwise, all knew about that. Augustus may well have been naïve in these matters. Curates being poorly paid, Augustus dipping his toes into the waters of illicit trade is certainly a possibility. Even Burrows, the Rector, forever short of money, may have been involved.

There is also a more honourable explanation: might Augustus have disapproved of smuggling and hence been shocked to discover the churchwardens and gentry with their hands in the trough? There is a good deal of evidence, viewing his life overall, that he was more than capable of mounting a moral high horse on an issue of principle and pursuing it to the end when all around him were keeping their heads down. If this happened, Augustus might have paid no regard to the consequences for himself or his family. There is later evidence that there were times when he did just that.

AUGUSTUS AND THE NUN IN THE BED

What nun? I see no nun. But there is the nun's story. Over eighty years later, Ralph Kilpin, once Clerk to the Cape Parliament, described this version of the aftermath of the departure of Augustus from Christchurch, when his friends in the Christchurch congregation had apparently been shocked to learn that:

> … he had eloped with a nun. Thereafter misfortune
> dogged him and his family…[6]

Kilpin is the only source of the eloping with a nun story. Augustus had been dead for half a century when Kilpin penned these words and we cannot know if this gem originated with Augustus himself, or someone knowledgeable about his earlier circumstances. After

---

6 Ralph Kilpin, 'Dr A.J. Tancred, M.L.A., the tragi-comedy of an eccentric divine', *Cape Argus*, Christmas edition, 1918.

Tancred's days in the House, Kilpin became Speaker of the Parliament and would have been aware of any parliamentary gossip swirling around in Cape Town. This story has long been remembered and repeated. There is, however, no corroborative evidence of a nun in the life of Augustus, although a scandalous liaison with, and marriage to, Evelina may have seen her upgraded to a despoiled nun. The story never lacked a pair of legs. It is possible that Evelina, aged twenty, may have married Augustus, aged twenty-eight, without her family's permission or blessing.

AUGUSTUS VERSUS THE POWERS THAT BE

There were multi-layered church authorities from the bishops of Winchester and Salisbury down to Burrows, the then Rector of the Priory church, and his staff. Was it no more than coincidence that the departure of Augustus followed shortly after the visit by the Bishop of Salisbury, who, Lemmon, the Parish Clerk, noted, attended the services on 8 June when Augustus 'did the whole service of the day'? Why did the curate, rather than the Rector, conduct the whole service of the day? Three weeks later he left Christchurch. Was he being inspected, perhaps investigated, prior to dismissal?

And what of Burrows? The Reverend William Francis Burrows was inducted into the vicarage in 1830 and remained in titular charge even after his departure from the town till his death in 1871. Perhaps of some significance, anticipating the Augustus episode, were the events in 1833 when Burrows:

… was licensed as perpetual curate of Corhampton, a minor church sinecure, and the Bishop's secretary immediately informed him that this appointment rendered his living at Christchurch void. Faced with the prospect of being deprived of income, he threw himself on his parishioners who rallied to his side and collected £80; then the Bishop relented and made an exception and allowed him to remain at Christchurch.[7]

Was Augustus wheeled in as a replacement for Burrows, whether temporary or permanent, before the Bishop relented only for Augustus to be sent packing when Burrows was back in apparent favour? This seems unlikely in the light of other information surrounding Augustus' departure, though it may have been in some degree connected.

I contacted a direct descendant of Burrows who wrote a book about his ancestor and family. Surely Burrows, in charge while Augustus was a curate in his church, would know the background to the story and, hopefully, tell all. But no, wrong again, for neither the book nor the author was able to provide any enlightenment. Burrows apparently spent most of his ministry wandering around the area painting pictures of local scenes. His writings contain very little about the life of the church, either secular or theological.

The biography by his descendant does identify two features of Burrows' life that are of interest and possibly relevant here. Firstly, he was short of money for most of his

---

7   Edmund H. Burrows, *Hampshire Family, the Reverend Burrows and his progeny*, 2000.

life. With a growing family to support he turned to ways to supplement his parish stipend, including running a small boarding school. The 1841 Census shows ten boys aged nine to thirteen living in the vicarage with the Burrows family and their maid.

Secondly, although he matriculated at Oxford (admitted to the university in 1820), he did not obtain a degree at a time when a bachelor's degree was the normal requirement for ordination. Bishops of southern dioceses such as Winchester had usually studied at Oxford or Cambridge and preferred candidates for ordination who had followed this route. Augustus spent no time at all in Oxford or Cambridge and certainly never held an Oxford degree.

Did Augustus offend one or more of the men in the town who were more powerful than Burrows, the Rector? He later showed a fine talent for falling out with important people and this may have happened at Christchurch just as it did at later stages of his life. The local MP, Sir George Henry Rose, was one such, a man with his finger in many a pie. Yet it is hard to imagine how Augustus might have found time to fall foul of him. In the world of the Church it was the Bishop of Winchester who had the ultimate power over those beneath him. Again, there is no evidence of his intervention.

Or was it that his face just did not fit in the world of the Priory church and the town, this opinionated Irishman with a sonorous voice who came from modest origins in Cork? Or was it something to do with patronage, at that time very often the key to doors leading to appointments or promotions?

WHERE NEXT?

The *De Zuid-Afrikaan* obituary recounts only that after leaving Christchurch where 'his prospects of preferment were bright; but having, by his resignation, given great offence to his relatives, he retired to Belgium, where, after a residence of three years, he determined, with his wife, to join the Roman Catholic Church. Some time after this he determined to emigrate to this colony, which he reached in 1844.'

There is something missing here. What evidence was there that he went to Belgium for three years and how did he spend the other seven years implicit in the obituary? And why did he want to join the Catholic Church in which he had been baptised and ordained as a priest and which he had left in disgrace?

Fortunately, his next two steps yielded readily to my further enquiries.

6

DOGS WELCOME IN COGGESHALL

Surely, after the setbacks in Cork and Christchurch, things could only get better? Or worse, perhaps. Time would tell, or not. The obituary had been silent on his priesthood in Cork, his fall from grace, the reasons behind his briefest of brief stays as a curate, not Rector, at Christchurch. After Christchurch the obituary had fallen silent for a very long time.

Augustus Frederick Tancred, the first child of Augustus and Evelina, was born on 16 July 1834, in London. From what can only be described as an inauspicious beginning, the infant Augustus Frederick rose from the travails of his early life to later become the Town Clerk of Kimberley in diamond rush days, an auditor of the De Beers accounts, and the father of the South African 'cricketing brothers Tancred'. He died in Kimberley in 1894. His eldest child, Augustus Bernard, was the grandfather of the author.

Augustus, the subject of our pursuit, was once again in need of a fresh employment opportunity. Struggling to find something equal to his expectations, his finances must have seen him in a parlous state. The obvious assumption is that his income depended on his employment, rather than a private income.

On an unknown date in 1834 he wrote to the Bishop of London seeking employment in his diocese. Only the Bishop's intriguing reply has survived:

East Cowes Castle. IOW
10 Oct 1834

Dear Sir

Your letter has been forwarded to me at this place. It is not easy for me to advise you whether to accept the Bishop of Exeter's offer. The Curacy which is proposed to you seems to be an eligible one; certainly better than you have any prospect of obtaining in my diocese. On the other hand you are the best judge of the nature of those difficulties to which his Lordship alludes and of which I have never heard before. Discreet and judicious conduct will I suppose ensure your continuation in the Curacy referred to and conduct of another kind would render doubtful your continuance in any Curacy.

If Mr Smith is on the continent, you may probably have two- or three-months' employment at Coggeshall but I have no distinct prospect of a permanent Curacy to hold out to you.

I would not have you to make any change in the accustomed Church services at Coggeshall but continue to perform this duty which was done by the late Curate.

If you accept the Bishop of Exeter's offer you must give due notice to the Churchwardens to procure other assistance.

The letter is very revealing. The Bishop of Exeter has offered a curacy in his diocese to Augustus who seems to have then asked the Bishop of London for advice on whether or not he should accept. He appears to have been at best lukewarm about Exeter's offer and to have asked the Bishop of London for a job in his diocese, showing his clear preference for London. The Bishop of London, however, is either not able or not willing to make an equivalent offer, apparently because he has no knowledge of the difficulties to which the Bishop of Exeter alluded. These it seems are referred to by Augustus in his letter, all the more reason why it would be very helpful to have sight of that letter.

The Bishop of London is, however, able to offer Augustus a temporary curacy in Coggeshall provided he does not make any changes to the accustomed services. Might this, perhaps, point to the current need for those of the low church persuasion to guard against the appointment of men taking the high church view? Needs must, however, and Augustus grasped the Bishop of London's offer of temporary employment as a curate for 'two or three months' at Coggeshall, with no prospect of a permanent post beyond that.

Lying some sixty miles north from London, Coggeshall in the 1830s was a small market town between Braintree and Colchester on the old Roman road, Stane Street. Its listed buildings make it attractive to visitors to this day. In earlier times its wealth derived from the trade first in wool, then cloth, silk and velvet. Later came brewing. Local hostelries such as the White Hart Hotel, a staging post between Colchester and Braintree, offered liquid refreshment for travellers and residents alike.

Augustus made his reluctant way to Coggeshall and was there long enough to conduct two baptisms, two burials and one marriage, all in October 1834. There is no other mention of him in the church registers. He was only passing through, a temporary curate, a locum.

I headed next for Coggeshall, where I visited St Peter-ad-Vincula, the Church of England church. A prominent notice beside the main door advised those about to enter the church that it was dog friendly, with dogs always welcome at church services. I liked that, but then I like dogs. The sun shone and the few parishioners going about their various tasks in the almost empty church mingled with visitors admiring the architecture. One kindly parishioner advised me that the church was dog friendly, dogs always being welcome at the services. I did not like to say to him that I had read the notice at the door. But had it proved Tancred friendly, I wondered? Was an Irish curate, once a priest in Cork, welcome? The answer was, not for long.

The customary list of clergymen displayed on the wall unsurprisingly makes no mention of Augustus. It reveals that Percy Smith was Vicar from 1834 to 1835 when he was succeeded by Arthur Capel Job Wallace. Smith was referred to in the Bishop's letter: 'If Mr Smith is on the continent'. The circumstances in which Mr Smith was able to take time away from his flock are unclear. Was he on holiday, or perhaps recuperating from an illness?

After leaving the church I followed Augustus back to London. There, on 17 October 1834, young Augustus Frederick Tancred was baptised at St John's, Smith Square. On the baptismal certificate Augustus is given as 'Clergyman' and the address as 7 Wood Street.

At this moment the only employment offer to Augustus was still the one from the Bishop of Exeter, a curacy in Redruth in Cornwall. He faced no realistic options other than acceptance. The family were once more on the move. Might this be the time when he would settle into a financially secure job with a prospect of long-term stability?

But why had Exeter offered him a job in Cornwall?

7

REDRUTH

*(Augustus) had been married... to a near relative of the
late Sir William Molesworth.*
Obituary, *De Zuid-Afrikaan*

The obituary makes no mention of Cornwall, although it
does refer to the Molesworth family in connection with
Evelina. Was she 'a near relative of the late Sir William
Molesworth'? Was it no more than coincidence that 'give
me a job' Augustus turned up in full-time employment in
Redruth in Cornwall in 1834, the year of his brief curacy
in Coggeshall? Did he last longer as a curate in Cornwall?

A NEAR RELATIVE OF SIR WILLIAM

If Evelina was related to the Molesworths, then there
must have been a link between the Molesworths and
the Pittars, Evelina's mother's family, or the Latteys, her
father's family. There are no reasons to suppose a Lattey
connection. Such evidence as there is connects to her
mother, Frances Pittar, who was a sister of Samuel John

Pittar, born 1777, both of whom were born in Ireland. Samuel married Mary McNeil of Larne, Co. Antrim, in June 1809 but when she died, he married again in 1817 to Elizabeth Waring, a widow. Elizabeth had a daughter by her previous marriage, and it was this daughter who in 1833 married St Aubyn Molesworth, son of the Reverend John Molesworth, the second son of the 5th Baronet of Pencarrow, Cornwall, and the grandson of Sir John Molesworth, the 4th Baronet. So, in a roundabout way, there was a tenuous family connection through marriage. However, on this evidence, Evelina was by no means a 'near relative' of the Molesworths.

One other snippet of information hangs in the air: when Evelina died, Augustus claimed that he arranged for her remains to be interred in Devonshire, 'from which county she came'. Was this playing the Molesworth card? There is only one problem: beyond question she came not from Devonshire but from Tullamore in Ireland.

A later writer compounded the problem of Evelina's family origins by naming her as 'one of the Butlers':

> She is said to be one of the Butlers, a family of great distinction in Ireland, and related to the Molesworths, but is not mentioned in Burke's Peerage.[8]

Thanks to the kindly assistance of the Butler family (Lord Dunboyne), it became readily apparent that Evelina was not 'one of the Butlers'.

---

8   Ralph Kilpin, *ibid.*

The Molesworth heartland lay in their estates in the counties of Cornwall and Devon, the two counties comprising the diocese of the Bishop of Exeter whose offer of a job to Augustus was referred to by the Bishop of London in his letter to Augustus of 10 October 1834. Redruth is a mere thirty miles from Pencarrow, the fine Molesworth house and gardens in Cornwall, where the family have been in residence since Elizabethan times. The hunting on the Devon estate was said to be better.

Like many a family of their class and wealth they had at one time owned land in the West Indies. Hender Molesworth, Lieutenant-Governor of St Katherine, Jamaica, was created a baronet in 1688 only to die without issue in 1689. In 1670 he had owned 2,480 acres of land in St Catherine (or Katherine). In his will he left the plantation known as Cow Park to his wife for life and then to his brother, Sir John Molesworth of Pencarrow, the 2nd Baronet, who developed the family estates in Cornwall and Devon. The 2nd Baronet died in 1716 and was succeeded by his eldest son, Sir John Molesworth, the 3rd Baronet.

In Cornwall the family were involved in local matters, including the church, and may well have had considerable influence in appointments to St Euny, the Church of England parish church in Redruth.

Down the years, many in the family were also much involved on the canvas of national life. In 1834, when Augustus arrived in Redruth, Sir William Molesworth (1810–1855), the 8th Baronet, was a radical politician who later served in the coalition cabinet of the Earl of Aberdeen from 1853 until his death in 1855, first as Commissioner of Works, then Colonial Secretary, where his remit included the Cape Colony.

Sir William was as radical in his views on religion as he was on politics and, after repudiating the Christian theology, he declared himself to be an agnostic. This 'was viewed unfavourably by the land-owning gentry in his constituency' and caused friction in the family.[9]

AUGUSTUS AT REDRUTH

By the end of 1834 Augustus had left Christchurch, spent a few weeks in Coggeshall, and arrived in Redruth. How did he become aware of the vacancy, and how and why was he chosen to occupy the post? Was it only ever a short-term appointment or did he or his church employers see it as something more permanent? What was the source of the family income between his episodes of employment? These questions arose throughout his life. The answers, when they came, were few and far between.

Was this now the moment from when he would live a life of decorous behaviour, personal and religious, so that the family might look forward to a comfortable and secure living in the sheltering arms of the forgiving Church? Did he bear in mind the Bishop of London's injunction that 'discreet and judicious conduct will I suppose ensure your continuation in the curacy referred to and conduct of another kind would render doubtful your continuance

---

9   Alison Adburgham, *A Radical Aristocrat: Sir William Molesworth of Pencarrow*, 1990.

in any curacy'? Did he think to himself, 'I must be more discreet and judicious in my conduct'?

For a while Augustus and John Molesworth, M.A., were both involved in St Euny, the parish church in Redruth. John Molesworth was Rector from 1833 to 1836. John had succeeded a younger brother, Hender Molesworth, B.A., who was Rector from 1822 to 1833. Hender later succeeded to the Clowance Estates in 1844. The first outbreak of cholera in the area occurred during Hender's incumbency. He built the Chapel of Ease in Chapel Street which was closed in 1916. The Chapel of Ease is now deconsecrated and used as a store, a store which unusually houses an altar. When I visited the town, a parishioner confided in me that the continued existence of the altar was most irregular and hence not generally known; I promised him that the secret was safe with me. The Clowance Estates are now a time-share development.

As I expected, I found no traces of Evelina among the graves in the churchyard here, nor in the churchyard close by the Molesworths' Devonshire seat at Tetcott.

*

The Exeter diocesan records in the Devon Record Office list the curates in the diocese between 1831 and 1835, including Tancred, Aug. Jos., in the Parish of Redruth. On 12 November 1834 he was granted a licence and with it the authority to perform the office of Stipendiary Assistant Curate in the Parish Church of Redruth with a yearly stipend of £150 paid quarterly 'for serving the said cure'. This was a comfortable living at the time for a family man in a country town. His post was described as having a 'clerical status' and his residence given as 'Parish'. The licence gives his qualification as 'D.D.' (no doubt Doctor of Divinity) but leaves blank the boxes for his university or college or the relevant year of his degree or qualifications; not for the first or last time, for this proves commonplace in his career, surely a regrettable lack of what would now be called 'due diligence'.

Augustus, no doubt accompanied by Evelina and the baby Augustus Frederick, had moved with their possessions to Redruth, at that time a rough-and-tumble sort of place in a Cornish copper and tin mining area. Augustus may not have liked the idea of moving away from London but he had run out of options. Until that moment Evelina, not least, must have viewed their plight as little short of desperate, with her very young child and a husband fast shredding his career in the church. For her husband, the curacy must have seemed very much more attractive after the Bishop of London slammed shut the door on a job in the London diocese. Not for the first time, Evelina must have hoped that they would at last find stability and security. Once again Augustus seems to have been shoehorned into a job with few if any questions asked about his qualifications or previous employments. Did no one ask or did he just fail to answer? Or was a Molesworth connection sufficient?

Now, in spite of all that had gone before, he was poised to resume his career in the Church.

*

In November 1834, he conducted his first baptism and burial services at Redruth, signing the registers with his name and the designation 'Curate', the designation he uses in the burial register till 8 January 1835. From December onwards the parish registers indicate his participation in a steady stream of births, deaths and marriages for about a year: on 8 December 1834, he conducted his first marriage service. After 8 January 1835 he starts to sign the burial register with his name only; for some reason he drops the designation 'Curate' which he had used since his first entry in the register. By September his handwriting has deteriorated markedly in the burial register. Was this significant? Did he perhaps tackle his paperwork aided by a drop to drink? On 18 November he conducted his last marriage service at Redruth.

In all he conducted twenty-four marriage services (about two per month), including three in one day on 2 March. The weddings are spread fairly evenly over time, although he did none in November 1834 or in January, August, September or December 1835.

Until 14 December 1835 John Molesworth signed the marriage register as Rector when he officiated but thereafter, from 17 December, as 'Vicar of Crowan'. On 20 December Molesworth signed the Crowan burial register 'J. Molesworth, Vicar' for the first time. Thereafter various others officiated on what was no doubt an interim basis. Molesworth may have been otherwise engaged or away for quite large stretches of this time.

Augustus' current spell in permanent employment was running out but there was a hopefully joyful event in compensation when their second child and only daughter, Evelina Tancred, was born on 21 December 1835. A pattern was beginning to emerge with Evelina becoming pregnant followed by Augustus losing his job, a stressful combination, not least for Evelina.

On 21 December, the day of his daughter's birth, Augustus conducted his last baptism and burial services at Redruth. In all he conducted 117 burial services. Perhaps he was the burials specialist, a job that others allowed to pass them by.

Then, on 25 December, there is an entry in the burial register by Molesworth. Times had moved on; Augustus' days in Redruth were at an end with no known reason. If his performance proved inadequate, at least no whiff of scandal wafted down the years. Perhaps it was just that the Molesworths now needed the employment opportunity to provide a living for a younger son. The area was in fact awash with Molesworth relatives in Anglican livings. At various moments in the first half of the nineteenth century the roll call included: Sir William's uncle, yet another William, who was Rector of the parish of St Breocke, as well as the incumbent for St Ervan; the Reverend Paul William Molesworth who was Rector of Tetcott, the family seat in Devon; the Reverend John Molesworth who was Rector of Redruth and Crowan while his brother Hender covered St Erney and Redruth; and Hugh Henry Molesworth, Sir William's first cousin, who was Rector of St Petroc Minor, at Little Petherick near Padstow. It was almost a family firm.

When, thirty or more years ago, I visited Pencarrow, walking in the gardens I found myself wondering if Evelina had ever known this beautiful place. I wanted to believe she might have done but knew just how unlikely it was.

Unless a Molesworth connection was behind the sojourn at Redruth there is no known explanation of how and why Augustus went to what was otherwise an apparently random choice of a small town somewhere on the map of England. For this or any other reasons unknown the hard fact remained: a year after his appointment he was once again unemployed. By the end of 1835 Augustus and the little family were on the move once more.

The infant Evelina was not baptised until 30 March 1836 in London, like her brother, at St John's, Smith Square. Their address was given as 8 New Street. The Tancred family was back in London.

WHERE NEXT?

That Augustus had still not given up hope of a position in the London area is shown in this letter from his old correspondent, the Bishop of London:

Fulham   25 May 1836
(To) The Rev. Dr. Tancrede

Dear Sir,
I have received your letter and am sorry that I cannot give you a favourable answer.

It is not without sufficient reason that I now finally decline licensing you to officiate in my Diocese – I told you, from the very first, that you could not be licensed to a curacy and although I afterwards permitted you to officiate for a few Sundays at Coggeshall I made subsequent enquiries which confirmed me in my first determination.

I remain, Rev. Sir. Your faithful servant.

CJ. London [Bishop Blomfield]

The reference to the 'subsequent enquiries which confirmed me in my first determination' is frustrating because no trace has been found of the Bishop's enquiries or the results. The news reaching the Bishop was clearly uncompromising. Did it contain details of the untoward events in Cork that preceded the ignominious departure of Augustus in 1833? Did it refer to events in Christchurch in 1834? It would hardly be surprising if the Bishop had stumbled into something critical of Augustus sloshing around in the ecclesiastical system.

Coggeshall and Redruth account for some of the time missing from the obituary. This still left a gap between his leaving Redruth in December 1835 and the obituary account of his spending two or three years in Belgium before departing for the Cape.

Frustratingly, at least one other tantalising gap in my knowledge of this period remained: the obituary mentions three children but up to now only two had made an appearance, Augustus Frederick and young Evelina. A third child, a boy named Oswald in the obituary, had yet to enter the world. Attempts to find the family in Belgium drew a blank. It took a chance search in a library on a rainy-day visit to Edinburgh to unlock the next door, the one leading to the remaining events in the lives of the family before their departure for the Cape Colony, including the birth of Oswald.

8

DR TANCRED'S RAVINGS

For a number of years I had been intrigued by my discovery in a book of his letters to Earl Grey, Secretary to the Colonies in London, which he published at the Cape in 1851, in which he complains about it being said 'that I was a little cracked, and it was instantly caught up by my enemies and sent around'. He mounted a defence, though, for 'in England I have had frequently to visit the assembled insane of 42 Parishes, and report on their condition'. The logic was impeccable: how could anyone who visited the insane be himself insane? On the other hand, trumpeting what was being said about him in his book can only have had the effect of broadcasting the story to an audience well beyond his immediate 'enemies'. It also contains a hint of paranoia. His state of mind was already emerging as a significant issue, for when the original letters were received at the Colonial Office in London an official wrote on them: 'The enclosed are a continuation of Dr Tancred's ravings'.

Looking back from 1851 he was clearly recalling an earlier period of his life. Might this include part or all of the missing years between Redruth and Belgium? But if he was visiting the insane, in what capacity did he visit them, and where were the forty-two parishes located? If in England, where in England? In what institution were the insane assembled? For how long was he thus employed?

It looked like a locked door that would never open and there my questions lay fallow for a number of years. Frustratingly, if only I could identify a diocese with forty-two parishes, I could identify his missing location. I failed in this partly because Augustus had made a mistake with the number of parishes.

Occasionally a chance event leads an amateur genealogist to stumble through a door in the proverbial family history brick wall after the experts have tried but failed despite their best efforts.

Then I went to Edinburgh.

EDINBURGH IN THE RAIN

On a wintry afternoon in Edinburgh some years ago I was intent on visiting a regimental museum in the castle to investigate details of an episode in Tancred's later life at the Cape. Dismayed at finding the museum closed for refurbishment, and with cold rain sheeting down and stinging my face in the gusty wind before trickling down inside my collar, I first tried hiding in one of the closes and wynds along the Royal Mile that leave entrances between the shops and pubs like the gaps left by extracted teeth in an ageing mouth. But in that unashamed street of shops selling tourist trinkets, tartan-clad dolls and a chance to locate your clan history on a chart hanging up at the door, there was little chance of shelter. Should I follow the tourists into one of the cash-hungry bars or coffee shops? Edinburgh in winter seemed horribly familiar, for I had been a student here many years before.

Remembering dodges and wheezes from my student days, I sought refuge from the weather in the nearby National Library of Scotland. I loped across the road to where, once inside that building, austere from the outside, all welcome warmth and dryness on the inside, I posed as an earnest visitor bent on high literary purpose. Idly looking through a collection of compact discs in the era before internet searches transformed family history research, I noticed that one disc contained Palmer's Index to *The Times* 1790–1905. I tapped in the word 'Tancred'. Expecting a brusque statement that the CD contained no references to anyone of that name I was more than a little surprised when this intriguing entry for 13 September 1838 appeared on the screen:

BASFORD POOR LAW UNION –
case of Dr Tancred

The words 'Poor Law Union' could only mean one thing: *the workhouse*. But was this 'my' Dr Tancred, my Augustus Joseph? Was he now in a workhouse? 'Tancreds' are reasonably rare and Dr Tancreds even more so. From that moment on I was confident my quarry was in my sights. He was still using the title 'Dr' but, I wondered, was he still a 'Reverend', still a practising cleric or, after his malfeasances to date, had he been reduced to penury and the charity of the Poor Law? How had he come to be in Basford, at that time a village on the outskirts of Nottingham? From this point onwards the answers came tumbling down at my feet, like ripe fruit from a tree at the end of summer. My subsequent searches showed this to be the location of the '42 parishes' where he visited the insane and reported on their condition. He had apparently not been admitted as a lunatic pauper. But why was he there, some 150 miles from London?

This was how a chance event dependent on a visit to a city hundreds of miles from my home with a different purpose, a rainy day, and a student memory, led to a significant breakthrough by an amateur family historian. I only wish I could have been that lucky more often.

*

Basford led me to the correct location, although the detail proved far from straightforward when I discovered that Augustus, escaping the financial bondage of unemployment, now had two paid jobs: one as chaplain at the workhouse in Basford[10], the other as curate in the little parish church a mile and a half away in the neighbouring village of Bulwell. Both Basford and Bulwell are now engulfed as suburbs in the urban sprawl of the city of Nottingham. He was still bearing the Church of England flag. It is not known how he got wind of these appointments or, as was so often the case, whether anyone had checked his qualifications or past history.

His appointment at Bulwell, and the additional appointment at Basford, arose from the somewhat confused circumstances surrounding the departure of his

---

10 Peter Higginbotham, *Workhouses of the Midlands*, 2007. Chapter 5, Nottinghamshire.

predecessor, a man by the name of Banks. The records of the Guardians of the Basford Poor Law Union show that before the arrival of Augustus, the Reverend T. Banks held the curacy at Bulwell Rectory, as well as serving as chaplain to the Basford Workhouse employed by the Basford Poor Law Union, with a salary of £25 per annum, since 3 May 1836.

On 18 October 1836, the minutes of a meeting of the guardians, the statutory officials responsible for the management of the workhouse at local level, recorded the decision that he (Banks) 'be requested to attend the sick poor in the Workhouse once each week and oftener if requisite'. This can only have been a rebuke for his failure to attend to this duty. Faced with this criticism, or perhaps for some other unknown reason, Banks resigned shortly afterwards on 29 November. He had been in post at the workhouse for a little over six months.

In his resignation letter Banks wrote to the guardians:

Bulwell Rectory, Nov 29 1836

Gentlemen

As I am about to leave Bulwell soon after Christmas, I beg leave to give notice of my intention to resign the Chaplaincy of the Poor House on the 26th December. I continue to hold this curacy till the Spring, and no permanent successor is likely to be appointed for some months who could apply for the Chaplaincy; in this case, if it meet the approbation of the Guardians, the gentleman who takes my duty here for 3 or 4 months might be engaged to take the duty at the House likewise; and then the clergyman who takes this Curacy might have the opportunity if he chose of applying for the Chaplaincy.

The guardians having received his letter of resignation accepted it unanimously. When Banks resigned the chaplaincy at the Basford 'Poor House' (Workhouse) from 26 December, he predicted it would take some months to appoint a successor. The Workhouse would soon need a temporary chaplain. After a few further months the church at Bulwell would be without a curate. He suggested that after his departure from Bulwell his successor there might take on the duty at the Workhouse in a permanent capacity. And who should somehow become aware of these forthcoming ecclesiastical openings in Nottinghamshire? Step forward Dr Tancred, a jack-in-the-box once again in need of a job. After what appears to have been a very casual selection process, he would in due course secure both employments. The guardians agreed (6 December 1836) that 'the curate who officiates for Mr Banks during the remainder of Mr Banks' curacy may attend to his duties in the Basford Poor House'. Later, in a letter from Tancred at the Bulwell Rectory to the Poor Law Commissioners in September 1838, Tancred writes, 'Since the first of January 1837 I have been performing the duties of chaplain at the Basford Union Workhouse.'

Those who selected him as chaplain at the Workhouse, like those who appointed him as curate at Bulwell, would come to regret that their selection processes had not been more rigorous.

The inmates of any workhouse would include a proportion of men and women, of different ages, the halt and the lame, the insane, and generally speaking the poor who were and are 'always with us'. Here were assembled 'the insane of forty-two parishes'.

Things seem to have begun to everyone's satisfaction, for on 4 April 1837, Augustus was officially appointed by the guardians to the post of chaplain to the workhouse at a salary of £24 per annum. The Chairman was requested to inform Dr Tancred of his appointment and, surprisingly given the letter to Banks regarding his failure to visit the sick poor in the workhouse, to express to Tancred the great satisfaction the board felt in the service of Mr Banks, the man who had been with them for only six months before departing following a rebuke from the guardians. Be that as it may, they no doubt hoped to find satisfaction in their new appointment. A man claiming a doctorate from Trinity College Dublin probably seemed the next best hiring to an Oxford man. Tancred was up and running again.

*

In the background the national mood was buoyant with the accession to the throne of Victoria in June 1837, although the men, women and children in the workhouse may have had less cause than most to celebrate.

Having seen his known previous appointments slip through his fingers, in Cork, Christchurch and Redruth, Tancred might have been expected to make every endeavour to make a success of his new opportunities.

The door to a London appointment had been slammed shut by the Bishop of London so there was no point in him continuing to hanker after an appointment there. Surely, this time, he would ensure that nothing would go wrong?

Things began well. He is seen on the payroll of the Poor Law Union on 18 July 1837, when it was proposed by Mr Falconbridge and seconded by Mr Brown:

> ... that the salaries of the Union for the Quarter ending June 25th, 1837, with the exception of Mr Pogson's, be paid.
>
> (includes £6.00 to The Revd Dr Tancred, Chaplain).

THE CHANGING OF THE GUARD

It is unclear whether or not Banks remained at Bulwell till the spring or, if so, how active he was at this time. The Bulwell Parish baptismal register suggests he soon lay dormant in the shadows, for on 1 January 1837, J. Banks, Curate, undertook his last baptism. The first baptism undertaken by Augustus J. Tancred D.D. at Bulwell was on 7 January 1837.

It seems that, in his untidy resignation, Banks continued to draw his stipend, first overlapping with and then making way for Tancred. On 14 February 1837, Tancred signed himself 'Minister of Bulwell' when sending a copy of one John Jennison's baptism certificate to the Jennison family at their request. Nothing untoward is known of his early days as curate at Bulwell.

With her husband once again in secure employment, and the family housed, Evelina must surely have felt hopeful that the rollercoaster ride that had been their lives since leaving Ireland might have juddered to a halt. Was she thrilled or despondent to find herself pregnant again?

The birth of Augustus and Evelina's third and final child, Oswald Finbar, had long eluded discovery. Now I found his birth record in Nottinghamshire, thus completing the set of Tancred children born to this marriage. The Bulwell baptismal registers show:

> 25th September 1837: baptism of Oswald Finbar Nagle son of Augustus Joseph and Evelina Tancred of Bulwell;
> *Augustus Joseph, Curate, St Mary's Church, Bulwell*

'Finbar' and 'Nagle' clearly represent a nod to Tancred's roots in Cork, Ireland. Yet even this simple record contains a curiosity: a note in the register explains that 'This child was named Alfred but the entry was altered by A J Tancred several months afterwards. See Clause 14 of the Act at beginning of this Book.'

The entry is, however, puzzling. Tancred, who not only performed the baptism ceremony and made the initial entry, was also responsible for the subsequent alteration. And why 'Alfred'?

This aberration aside, once again, so far so apparently good. It now only needed Dr Tancred to settle diligently into his relatively leisurely, undemanding work at the heart of village life, baptising, marrying and burying villagers, and supplementing these occasional events by a weekly sermon on Sundays.

Events at the Basford Workhouse, however, would soon take a turn for the worse. Next came the now familiar question, 'What went wrong?'

9

GÖTTERDÄMMERUNG

If the steady job that came with a house, and the birth of Oswald in September, meant rejoicing in the family, storm clouds were already gathering in the skies above Nottingham. Things were about to get a whole lot worse.

By 7 November 1837, Tancred seems to have been short of funds when asking the Poor Law Union for clothes from the stocks held for the destitute or insane inmates, for his personal and family use. On that date it was agreed, in what appears to be a reasonable decision by the guardians:

> That the Clerk do write to the Revd Dr Tancred and inform him his application has been taken into consideration viz (requesting to have a Bag out of the Workhouse with suitable clothing) the Clerk was directed to inform that they could only furnish such articles of clothing as is provided for the use of the poor.

A proud and irascible man, Tancred no doubt felt

humiliated at the need to ask, doubly so at being rebuffed. With the winter approaching were he, Evelina and the children short of adequate clothing?

Tancred was no god, Germanic or otherwise, except perhaps in his own eyes, and it may well have been his vain and deluded self-belief that drove him through these twilight years towards self-destruction. One of the striking features of his actions and personality had always been his ability to bounce back from adversity; he was a great survivor. Yet, at this moment, he stood on the edge of a rotating vortex into which he would soon be helplessly sucked.

For trouble was bubbling below the workhouse surface and eight months after the clothing incident a communication to the Chaplain, echoing the earlier entry for the attention of his predecessor, Banks, was entered in the chaplain's book on 24 July 1838:

> The Board wishes to know why the sick women's ward is not regularly visited by the Chaplain.
> *signed H Smith Chairman*

Was a reluctance to visit the sick women a common failing among workhouse chaplains, or did it only apply to Banks and Tancred? Was there something uniquely repellent about the Basford sick women's ward? Were these guardians particularly zealous in this regard?

Two aspects of this communication seem to have annoyed Tancred: firstly, the bureaucratic nature of the reprimand and, secondly, because according to him, it was not true. He responded to the Chairman's entry with an entry of his own in the chaplain's book on 7 August, robustly defending his performance of the required duties.

His lack of contrition did little to endear him to the guardians who, faced with what they regarded as insubordination, launched an investigation into his conduct. By now allegations were starting to fly on both sides. The guillotine was about to fall. Tancred tendered his resignation less than a month later. Although he subsequently disputed that he had resigned, the guardians lost no time in ridding themselves of their turbulent priest. At a special meeting on 21 August 1838, they accepted his resignation and wrote to inform him of the fact. For Evelina, the one who looked after the children and the home, their material security was once again crumbling about her.

Tancred's later denial that he had resigned is somewhat unconvincing. It seems more likely that he acted impulsively, in anger, later thought better of his intention to quit, and tried to undo the harm he had done to himself and the family. But from this moment on he was undone, thrashing around in the water, struggling to remain afloat but all the while sinking further beneath the waves.

His next step was to contact the Poor Law Commission (PLC) in London with overall responsibility for the operation of the Poor Law and powers over and above those of the guardians.

In his letter to the PLC the Reverend Dr Augustus J. Tancred of Bulwell Rectory appealed against what he claimed to be the injustice of his 'dismissal' from the Basford Poor Law Union Workhouse. He rested his case on a number of factors: his previous good conduct; the insulting and inaccurate entry regarding his failure to visit the sick women's ward in the chaplain's book; a claim that his actions prevented the murder of the workhouse Governor six months previously; the failure to inform him of the decision to appoint another chaplain in his place; and the fact that he never did intend to offer an 'absolute resignation'. The distinction between an 'absolute' resignation and the alternative, presumably a 'partial' or 'temporary' resignation, is obscure. Whatever Tancred had in mind, the guardians were clear on the matter: a resignation was a resignation.

There is no record apart from his assertion here that Augustus prevented the murder of the Governor. If there was some such incident one can only speculate that one of the residents became overexcited, threatened the Governor, and Augustus then intervened. If this event did take place Augustus no doubt expected it to have attracted the good will of the Governor. Apparently, the Governor felt under no such debt of gratitude.

Hoping the Poor Law Commissioners, on hearing his side of the case, would side with the force of his arguments, Augustus requested that they issue orders to the Board of Guardians for him to be retained as Chaplain. Alas, it was not to be; the commissioners sided with the guardians, who moved with alacrity to go public with the news of a new appointment. An advertisement duly appeared in the local press, the *Nottingham Journal* and the *Mercury*, seeking a chaplain for the Union Workhouse and offering a salary of £24 per annum for the duties prescribed by the Poor Law Commissioners. At the time this was a significant salary in return for relatively little work, certainly something Tancred could ill afford to flounce away from.

On 11 September, avoiding any chance that Tancred might sneak back in, the guardians appointed the Reverend J. Austin to replace him as Chaplain at the workhouse from 30 September, and then wrote to the Poor Law Commissioners in London for their approval.

On 12 September the powder keg was now well and truly alight:

> The Clerk (to the Board of Guardians) received a notice to call a Special Meeting from Mr T Potter and Mr Wm Parr, to take into consideration the propriety of increasing the salary of the auditor, and also the Chaplain's (Tancred's) answer to a minute entered in the Chaplain's Book by the Chairman of the Board of Guardians on July 24th 1838.

The meeting fizzled with outrage at Tancred's temerity in questioning the validity of the actions of the board. He had clearly failed to recognise his lowly station in Nottinghamshire society. Now he would have to be punished.

All was not lost for Augustus, however, as he was able to retain his post as curate of the church in nearby Bulwell. The family could at least rely on the house and income that came from that position. A well-ordered man might at this stage have licked his wounds and settled for this diminution in status compensated for by the security still available to his family. Whether he was dismissed from the workhouse chaplaincy, as he saw it, or had resigned, as the guardians saw it, he could have continued his life in the area for a while longer as curate at Bulwell. A wiser and more stable person might have settled for that, but not Augustus. It was not in his nature to let matters rest, accept that he had blundered, lost the argument, and settle for second best. He did not so much harbour grudges as clasp them to his chest as an emotional springboard for his continuation of the fight. So it was that just as things could scarcely get worse, they did.

*

The controversy went nationwide when a letter from an anonymous 'correspondent', undoubtedly Augustus himself, appeared in the London *Times* on 12 September 1838. Under the heading 'The New Poor Law Again' the correspondent quotes 'another instance of a clergyman being grossly insulted by some of the conceited upstarts who, wielding a little brief authority as guardians of the poor, conceive themselves the mighty men of the earth'. More at fault, though, than these men were the men in Parliament who passed an act conferring on them 'the power of acting as they do'. There followed extracts from the guardians' remarks in the chaplain's book and Dr Tancred's reply. Clearly, no meeting of minds would ever occur.

Not content with this broadside the same 'correspondent' was back in the paper the following day pointing out that 'Dr. Tancred is a gentleman well known for his literary talents, and for the exemplary manner in which he discharges his duties as a minister of the Church of England.' The writer contrasts this with the qualities of the Board of Guardians of the Basford Union who are 'thick-headed blustering Radicals, whose principal qualification for the office they hold is the talent of gabbling loudly and incessantly'. Like all Radicals they suffer from 'an officious, busy, meddling spirit, and a continual and uncontrollable desire to interfere in matters with which they have no manner of concern'. Worse still, they meddle in matters which they do not understand and, in this instance, they 'kick up a dust' to attack Dr Tancred who, as a representative of the clergy of the Church of England, these thoroughbred Radicals so detest.

Having shown these men to be lesser mortals than the author of these considered words, he was quick to point out that the Chaplain at the workhouse, as well as 'the poor wretches' who were the inmates, was at the mercy of these incompetent, vindictive men, 'the clodhoppers, the old-clothes-men, the tallow-chandlers, and the snips' who are in charge of the workhouse. These men, in his opinion, superior by birth, wealth, social status and education, ruled the lives of the paupers who could do nothing to appeal against the injustices they suffered. Their abuse of power did not end there, for it extended to tormenting Dr Tancred, who, as a clergyman of the Church of England, apparently deserved it all.

The diatribe continued as he pointed to 'the policy of the men who abuse the confidence reposed in them by a young and innocent Sovereign' to attack the Church of England and insult and annoy the clergy. These ideas and values, he continued, came from higher up the social and political ladder than the local guardians. It is these unseen people whose many tentacles reached into the various organs of the administration of the nation, including those in charge of the workhouses. The more people like the guardians 'can vex and harass the clergy the greater will be their claim for promotion'.

In concluding, his view altered focus to reveal a changing world, one in which 'this state of things is widely different from what it was some years ago', with this due to 'the advancing intelligence of the age' which brooked no opposition. Hence 'we must submit to wear the yoke which this advancing intelligence lays upon us, until it becomes too oppressive, too galling to be borne'.

When things reach this sorry state the people of England will rise:

> … like giants refreshed with wine, and shake off the chains and the fetters of their despotic taskmasters, asserting their determination no longer to submit to the tyranny imposed by a Ministry bound in the bonds of a Popish demagogue. We shall see them cast off those men who have dared to tamper with the church, those men who are the champions of the New Poor Law – those men, in short, who have joined the ranks of the people's foes. We shall, ere long, hear the people of England, with a voice like thunder, shout "Down, down, with the enemies of the church!" Thousands, and tens of thousands, will join in that cry, and thousands, and tens, and hundreds of thousands, will also exclaim, "Down, down, with the Poor Laws!"

In this overflowing revolutionary fervour, it is far from

clear what he is revolting against, or in favour of. He is certainly for the monarch, Victoria, against those who he sees as the enemies of the Church of England. He is vehemently opposed to the influence of the landed gentry and professional men. He is for the oppressed, as he sees them, the men and women lower down in the social scale.

This extraordinary outburst – the complete diatribe is some 2,000 words in length – was certainly a novel, if counterproductive, way of winning friends and influencing people. Or not. There can be little doubt that Augustus was the author, but how was he able to reach and then be published in *The Times*? By what connections was he able to place this lengthy article while working as a minor cleric in a provincial Poor Law workhouse? What was his connection, his route as a rural chaplain to publication in what was even then one of the grandest organs in the land? He always claimed to be socially well connected as a member of the Tancred family of Boroughbridge, but was he? Or was it through Evelina's supposed link with the Molesworths? It was certainly not to do with the Tancreds of Hanover Street in Cork.

Reading the detail, it is easy to unravel Tancred's transparent views on many aspects of the society of the time: he was against the Poor Law, the legislators who brought it into being, and those whose responsibility it was to administer the relevant statutes. Whatever the rightness or otherwise of any of his views so freely expressed in this form, it was singularly injudicious from his employment point of view to air them in this way.

He continued to poke his nose into workhouse affairs. He would later claim that on 13 September, he was physically assaulted by the Governor of the workhouse and, as a result, was unable to ride his horse and had to be 'bled' by a doctor.

He now chose to fire one more shot at the guardians by reminding them how, before his own appointment, they had found cause to reprimand his predecessor, Banks, for an identical failure when he had been 'requested to attend the sick poor in the workhouse once each week and oftener if requisite'. His observation fell on deaf ears. As he moved into an all-out attack on the guardians they seemed to suffer from collective amnesia about the earlier incident with Banks and could only recall that when Tancred was appointed 'so far from the Board having any fault to find with, as suggested, the manner in which the previous Chaplain, the Revd T Banks attended to his duties, a notice had been appended to the appointment conveyed to Dr Tancred'. To emphasise their point they expressed to Dr Tancred 'the great satisfaction the Board has received in the services of Mr Banks.' Moreover, they pointed out, they had in 'all cases treated Dr Tancred with the consideration due at all times to a clergyman and, through their Chairman, with the consideration due to their own character and, therefore, they distinctly deny any act or wish to treat Dr Tancred otherwise than as a Gentleman.' It was an argument Tancred was never going to win.

In the further words of the board, the minutes referring to Tancred's assertion state:

Without referring further to the previous conduct of the Chaplain, the Board desired distinctly to state that his conduct, language and remarks since his resignation have been such as to tend materially to insubordination and bad conduct. In these circumstances they believed that credit was due to the Governor for keeping the paupers in order under the exciting language used by the Chaplain.

By now the guardians, with the support of the Poor Law Commissioners, faced no further obstacle in confirming their appointment of a replacement chaplain. They had, however, one more knife to insert into their late employee, 'as to the remarks in the Public Papers it might not be impertinent to enquire if Dr Tancred has any cognizance of the statement in the *Times* Papers of the 12th September headed "The New Poor Law again"'. In other words, the board were saying, we know you wrote it.

Nonetheless, Augustus, a man who seldom hesitated to fight a battle he had little or no hope of winning, was not done yet. He now lobbed another mortar into the debate, alleging that two of the inmates of the workhouse had suffered serious assaults. After investigating these complaints, the guardians met once again on 21 September and recorded their findings.

They found that Polly Rose, an inmate, had disobeyed the instructions of the Governor and alarmed the Matron to such an extent that the Governor had no option other than to use the degree of force which caused discolouration on her arms. The force had been necessary and not excessive.

They further found that another inmate, William Smith, a schoolboy, had deserved severe correction as a punishment for his conduct and, in the interests of all the children, it would serve as an example. Smith had in fact been to their enquiry, admitting that he was not much hurt and had played Stag in the yard after the beating. The scratch near his eye was purely accidental. This rather suggests that Smith knew his future best interests lay in the *mea culpa* direction. Based solely on this evidence the guardians found no case for censuring the Schoolmaster; quite the contrary, for the board expressed their entire satisfaction with the general manner in which the school was conducted – promoting the morals and learning of the children, and with very few cases meriting physical punishment.

It was now a fight which Augustus would pursue, showing scant concern for the material consequences either for himself or for his family. If only he had ever said, in words that survived, why his opposition to corporal punishment mattered so much to him. The corporal punishment of children survived in England until 1986 in state schools, and 1988 in fee-paying schools, and was generally supported by parents and teachers for whom, in many instances, it was a necessary tool of their trade if discipline was to be maintained. The practice also long survived Augustus with near universal support for the physical punishment of juvenile offenders, and in the army and prisons.[11] Why, one wonders, did he not only feel so strongly against it, but be prepared to put his reputation and material position at risk in opposing it when he witnessed it. There is nothing to show that he

---

11 Ian Gibson, *The English Vice*, 1978.

campaigned against it on a broader canvas, just that in the known instances when he came across it in action, he felt bound to act against it.

Time would prove that this was not the last time that Augustus set forth, sword in hand, in the cause of someone experiencing physical punishment. But would it ever extend more broadly to civil rights in general?

10

ASSAULTS!

The next act in the multi-act Tancred drama saw him emerge as the prosecutor in a prosecution he brought before the court in Nottingham. Not for the first time, questions abound. Where did he learn the administrative steps necessary to institute such an action? How did he come by the required skills and knowledge to prosecute the case? How did he fund the venture?

Like Don Quixote, he was never one to give up without a futile fight. Did he bring cases against the workhouse Governor and Schoolmaster because of his hatred of injustice, or was it a way of getting back at the workhouse Board of Guardians? Perhaps it was some amalgam of both of these.

He appeared on Saturday 15 September 1838 in the County Hall, Nottingham, bringing three cases before Colonel Rolleston, MP, Colonel Coope and Thomas Nixon, Esq. It was a bold move and certainly ill-advised. The three gentlemen were the sort of citizens, based on class and income, who could have formed the bench in any magistrates' court in the land. The status of this court is not altogether clear. Given it was not a criminal prosecution we must assume it was a private prosecution. If Tancred had drawn the matters before the local forces of law and order then, not surprisingly, they no doubt sent him away with a flea in his ear. It would have taken a good deal more firepower than he possessed to enlist support in an action against worthy citizens in the form of the workhouse Governor and Schoolmaster. The Board of Guardians, wishing to protect their own reputations, would undoubtedly side with the accused.

THE TRIAL

The *Nottingham Review* of 21 September 1838 reported the cases in considerable detail.

TANCRED V. JOHNSON

In the matter of *Tancred v. Johnson* (the workhouse Governor), the Reverend Augustus Tancred, Clerk and Doctor of Divinity, of Bulwell, appeared as the prosecutor 'against James Johnson, Master of the Basford Union Workhouse, charging him with having inflicted corporal punishment on the 1st of September, inst., upon Polly Rose, an adult poor person in the workhouse, and that he did abuse, ill-treat, and otherwise ill-use and misconduct himself towards her, whereby he had forfeited not exceeding £20, pursuant to the statute'.

The evidence was to prove contradictory with the residents of the workhouse often unable to articulate what they had observed or maintain a consistent line, often in the face of forceful cross-examinations. Mr Nixon had seen a livid mark on the back of Polly Rose's neck but he was quick to point out that 'she was a person of weak intellect, incapable of taking care of herself, and had been there for years'. Mr Williams, who appeared on behalf of the defendant, cross-examined Tancred who described a visit to the workhouse to see Polly Rose as a result of information received from an unnamed pauper. Tancred confirmed that she was a person of weak intellect, incapable of taking care of herself, who had been an inmate there for some years.

Referring to entries in his own handwriting in the chaplain's book, Tancred then described the events leading up to the prosecution. On 5 September he had visited the sick women's ward and seen Polly Rose with 'marks of cruelty and ill-treatment on her'; these marks it was said had been inflicted by the Governor. On the same occasion he had visited the sick men's ward where he had spoken to a boy named Hodges who 'complained of being struck by the Governor in the face'. According to Tancred his face was 'much swelled under the eye'.

He next visited the itch room where he found a boy called William Samuel Smith lying 'in a wretched condition with scarcely any covering' and with a cut over the eye and on the cheek. Smith stated to Tancred that he had been 'cruelly beat by the schoolmaster, until he broke the stick on him, and then he kicked him on the back and about the ribs, and afterwards took a strap, and continued beating him; while beating him about the head, the blood gushed from his mouth and eyes'.

Back in the men's ward he listened to some of the men complaining that 'they cannot be spoken to by the Governor without much cursing and swearing on his part'.

On the following day Tancred returned to see young Smith in the itch room and found him still lying 'in a wretched condition' and stating that black ointment was rubbed all over his body to hide the marks of ill-treatment.

Mr Williams, defending, then attempted to explore the motives that had led Tancred to bring the prosecution, but Colonel Rolleston remarked that 'the magistrates had nothing to do with motive'.

Pressed by Williams, Tancred explained that he knew Polly Rose was of weak intellect, though he did not know exactly the strength of her mind when he examined her relative to this case, although she had answered directly that she had received a blow upon the head with a broom stail (handle) the previous day.

Under further cross-examination, Tancred added to the written evidence in the chaplain's book explaining how on looking at the right arm of Polly Rose he had found it badly marked between the elbow and the shoulder. It was black and blue, the result in his opinion of very heavy pressure and violence, most likely as a result of blows.

The cross-examination of Polly Rose herself and the evidence of other witnesses then followed. When 'called to the table' Polly stood throughout her own evidence and then during the contributions of witnesses with evidence bearing on her alleged assault. The newspaper account provides a compelling picture of a woman at sea in an unfamiliar world: 'her appearance and manner evidently indicated that she was of weak mind, and though aware that the inquiry was about her having been struck, she did not seem interested in the proceedings, or capable of comprehending the nature of them'.

Mary Hudson, a pauper 'belonging to Arnold', and resident in the workhouse was then called to give evidence. She said she had seen the Governor strike Polly Rose three times with a broom stail at the top of the stairs at about eight o'clock on the night of Saturday 1 September. Polly was struck on both her arms but Mary did not know why she was beaten. She did not hear Mr Johnson say anything. Polly screamed out after the event and then went to bed. When Mary went into Polly's room next morning, she found Polly still in bed, crying bitterly, complaining that her arms hurt her. Mary insisted it was truth she was saying, and God's truth.

Cross-examined by Williams, Mary's evidence began to crumble. Asked if she was allowed to go into the kitchen when the former governor was at the workhouse but not under his successor, she was at first flustered, and then annoyed when asked perhaps provocatively if she was 'on all occasions most temperate and quiet'. When she replied 'in a loud hurried tone' asking, 'I wish you would hear me', Colonel Rolleston was quick off the mark: 'My good woman, we are hearing you: answer that gentleman's (Mr Williams) questions.' A further question from Williams seems intended to confuse Mary: 'Were you not in partnership with Mary Gibbs, and did not you advise her to practise falling into fits?' Mary denies this as a false report but Williams persists: 'Then it is not true that you went about defrauding the public in that way?' Mary denies this before Williams gets to the heart of the case: 'Well, where was the first blow struck?' Mary, clearly rattled, insists the Governor struck Polly three times but then announces she 'shan't be cross-questioned' on this at which point the magistrates told her she must answer the questions. As the cross-examination continues Mary insists that she did not see Polly struggling with Johnson, the Governor, but insists 'he struck her with a besom stail over her right arm'.

A succession of witnesses followed whose evidence is dealt with in less detail, although the sequence of alleged events becomes more complete. Mary Tilson, a pauper, 'was at the bottom of the stair-case, and saw the governor beat Polly Rose'. She went immediately and told Sarah Thompson what she had seen. She did not notice Mary Hudson at the scene nor hear any words. Cross-examined she said she did not know anything of Polly refusing to go to bed and did not hear a cry of murder by Mrs Johnson. Nor did she hear that Polly flew at Mrs Johnson. Although she knew of Polly as 'a woman of weak intellect' she could not speak of her as being violent. Coming to the crux of the matter she too claimed that Polly had been struck 'very violently with a heavy besom stail'.

The events leading up to the alleged assault are beginning to emerge as a result of some dispute between Polly and the Governor's wife. One thing is clear however, the assault by the Governor on Polly is confirmed by a number of witnesses who it seems are unlikely to have been coached to repeat the same story.

But there are discrepancies in the stories: Elizabeth Hopewell, also a pauper, saw Rose struck twice in her room, as she sat on the bed, partly undressed; Mr Johnson struck her twice on the back. Elizabeth could not say who else was in the room, only that several others were present; it was on Saturday night, about eight o'clock. She reported that the stick was something like a walking stick and that Mr Johnson, the Governor, had said he would take her to the dark hole. She did not hear anything pass between the Governor and Polly before he struck her. Polly had been 'doing something', as she understood, to Mrs Johnson, the Governor's wife. Elizabeth knew nothing about the first time that the Governor struck Polly, nor did she hear anything said about it. There were marks on Polly's back, on one arm, and across her shoulders; she saw them the next morning. The marks reached from one shoulder to the other; she could not say how many she saw in all, only that they were black and blue. It was not a besom stail. Polly Rose did not say that she had frightened Mrs Johnson into fits, but somebody had observed Mrs Johnson in a fit in the kitchen, and it was said this was 'due to the conduct of Polly Rose'. In this version Polly is assaulted in her room rather than at the top of the stairs as in Mary Hudson's account.

At this point Mary Hudson was recalled and said she did not see Hopewell, nor any black marks upon Polly's back. Furthermore, if there had been any marks upon the back, she would have seen them when she examined Polly's back and arms on Sunday morning. She did, however, maintain that although both Polly's arms were black she only saw Mr Johnson hit her on one arm.

Further clarification was then sought when Mary Tilson was recalled. Like Mary Hudson she did not see any marks on Polly's back but confirmed the marks on her arm.

Ann Shooter, a pauper, heard Polly scream, but not louder than usual. She said she had not seen Polly the next day. Polly, she said, 'is very violent sometimes'.

Next up was the defendant, Johnson, the Governor. In answer to the charge, he said in evidence that, 'there was great confusion, as one woman had been beating another with a broom stail. Polly Rose was ordered to bed.' When Polly refused to go to bed he took hold of her at which point she tried to bite and kick him so he 'seized her by both arms and held her flat'. He said she was very violent and he 'would have placed her in confinement, but was called away from her to Mrs Johnson, who was in a fit'. He had the besom stail in his hand, which he had taken from a woman, but did not strike Polly with it. The marks upon her arm were occasioned by being held, and not from blows. He denied having struck her in her bedroom, as sworn to by one of the witnesses.

Hannah Keetley, an inmate in the workhouse, was in the shop in September, and heard the Matron, Mrs Johnson, tell Polly to go to bed, which Polly refused to do. Directly afterwards Mr Johnson took Polly by the shoulders and put her out of the room. She then heard Mrs Johnson call out for Mr Johnson. She did not see the besom stail, nor Mr Johnson strike Polly which she would have done had he struck her at the bottom of the stairs.

Cross-examining her, Dr Tancred asked if before these events Hannah had been living along with the rest of the paupers but was now keeper of the sick room. In other words, had she been rewarded for saying that which suited the defence? This was denied.

Next up was Mary Foster, a pauper, who was employed in the kitchen on 1 September and had seen Mrs Johnson in a fainting fit.

Mr Butler, surgeon, had examined Polly Rose, but

could find no marks upon her back or shoulders; those upon the arm proceeded most likely from pressure. There was no mark upon her head; had she been struck violently a mark or marks would have appeared. He would take upon himself to say that he thought she had not been struck with a thick stick. Cross-examined, Butler said that he saw her on 7 September and could say that a blow, if not a severe one, might have been inflicted, and not leave a mark till that day. He would swear that these were distinct marks of the fingers, though he did not count them. They had the appearance of arising from pressure.

The magistrates then heard from Mr Ashton, Clerk to the Board of Guardians, who knew Mr Johnson although he had only been appointed Governor six weeks ago. He had been selected on the basis of his testimonials; the board had not interviewed him. He came recommended as a humane man. As proof of this Ashton produced letters from the Colonel and several officers of the 6th Enniskillen Dragoon Guards, in which Mr Johnson was Troop-Major; he had served twenty-four years, and was recommended most highly as a temperate, sober, honest, humane man. The officers expressed their regret at him leaving the regiment. Ashton said he had known Polly Rose for years; she was of weak intellect and, if contradicted, would immediately become very violent, and give anyone a slap in the face. As for Mary Hudson, he said he would be very sorry for any person convicted upon her testimony as she was violent in her conduct and language, opening her mouth with a curse and closing it with the worst possible language. She would swear black's white for half an ounce of tobacco.

As if to prove the point Mary Hudson, who was at the

other side of the room, on hearing this became turbulent, and cried out, 'that's like you; you are the biggest rascal that ever lived', following up with 'several other exclamations', which seemed sufficient to Mr Ashton to believe his point proven for he riposted, 'there, you have a specimen of her now'.

Mr Farrands, one of the guardians, followed stating that he frequently visited the workhouse and believed Mr Johnson to be kind and humane and incapable of the alleged act. When visiting the paupers, he had not up till now heard a complaint. Similarly, Mr Brown, another guardian, had twice gone round to see the paupers and not heard any complaint. He believed the marks on Polly arose from pressure. He too believed Mr Johnson incapable of the violence described.

The magistrates then retired to consider their verdicts. If Tancred's hopes were riding on a successful outcome they were about to be dashed, for:

'… after returning into court, Colonel Rolleston said, the charge was two-fold; first, that corporal punishment had been inflicted, and next, that an assault had been committed. The magistrates were of the opinion that on the first point Johnson had not been guilty of inflicting corporal punishment within the meaning of the act; on the second point, they were bound to convict, but they considered that the assault was occasioned by over excitement, arising from Mrs. Johnson having a fit, and, therefore they should only impose a nominal fine of one shilling upon the defendant'.

Given the confused and often contradictory nature of the evidence the verdicts are not surprising. Polly Rose was an awkward inmate, the Governor was inexperienced, and his wife was possibly terrified by some of the inmates she had to deal with in the positions to which she and her husband had so recently been appointed. A fracas which, handled differently, might have been prevented had got out of hand and the Governor had tried to enforce order while his wife fell apart in the background. When taken together with the two remaining cases heard that day, there does, however, remain cause for a degree of disquiet.

TANCRED V SPENCER

Next up was a case in which Dr Tancred accused William George Spencer, the workhouse Schoolmaster, of ill-treatment of a boy named William Samuel Smith, aged eleven and an inmate in the workhouse.

It appeared that on 1 September, Smith, a scholar in the school, had been talking to another boy in the school, for which he was beaten with a thin stick. Spencer was charged with not only beating him, but also with cutting his cheek with a strap and kicking him. It was claimed that Smith went afterwards to play, and appeared as usual. He had a mark upon his face, and another boy, William Tilson, said that he saw blood come out of the boy's nose and mouth but could not prove whether the blow on the cheek was or was not accidental.

Spencer made a written submission in his own defence:

The boy, William Samuel Smith, is usually very disobedient and troublesome, on Saturday, the 1st inst., while at School, I saw him talking to another boy, I called to him to be still; he looked at me with great impudence, but continued talking. I went and gave him a few stripes with a stick, and it broke. I then gave him a box on the ear and a kick over the bottom. I had scarcely sat down again, when a boy, who sat opposite to Smith, told me he was laughing at me, I had repeatedly seen him laugh at me before. I then took a small strap, and commenced giving him a severe beating, which I thought he deserved; he lay down upon his back, that I might not hit him. I took hold of his arm, to make him get up, I suppose with resisting he struck his head against the corner of the form he was near to, and scratched the side of his eye. I saw no blood gush out of his mouth or eyes, he did not seem unwell, but repeated his spelling, staid (sic) the usual time at school, walked round the garden with the other boys, eat his dinner and went to play in the yard. In the afternoon he was undressed, to go into the bath, when the Governor found he had got the itch. I went to look at him, but saw no marks or wails on his body, only the scratch or cut on the side of the eye.

W.G. Spencer,
Schoolmaster, Basford Union Workhouse

This proved sufficient for the magistrates who found that the charge was not proved and so dismissed the case.

ASSAULT UPON DR TANCRED

ASSAULT UPON DR TANCRED

The third and final case involved the alleged assault by Johnson, Governor of the workhouse, on Dr Tancred, the workhouse Chaplain.

Dr Tancred now requested the magistrates to afford him protection on the following day (Sunday) while he was discharging his duty at the Basford Workhouse claiming that on the preceding Thursday he had been attacked and assaulted by the Governor and had, as a result, been obliged to be bled in the arm.

Colonel Rolleston said he did not think it necessary to comply with the request believing that no violence would be offered, adding that if an assault had been committed, the magistrates were ready to hear the case if he thought it proper to apply to them.

Dr Tancred needed no second invitation and immediately applied for a warrant and then, upon oath, charged Mr Johnson with having, on Thursday last, forced him out of a room, and struck him. He admitted he had no witnesses to prove his case but stated that as he was about to enter a room, he heard the Schoolmaster call out, 'turn him out; he has not business there'. Tancred alleged that the Governor went up to him, grasped him by the left arm and forced him out by throwing him off the step into the yard while striking him with his other hand in the heart, and saying, 'if you don't leave this immediately I'll make you leave it very uneasy'. Tancred said he then left the yard and went to the schoolroom where he found the door had been locked. When he demanded to be admitted the Governor went up to him and said, 'if I had seen you when you were coming in, I'd

110

have put your nose under the front door'. He then followed the Doctor into the avenue, saying, 'your visits to this house tend to no good and you'll see what I'll do for you'.

Mr Walker, a surgeon, was called to visit Dr Tancred at eleven o'clock that night, and bled him, in consequence of inflammation, arising in his opinion from extreme violence inflicted on the side. Cross-examined, Walker thought that in his opinion riding would not have caused the inflammation.

The Governor denied striking Dr Tancred saying he merely locked the door to prevent him from going into the wash-house to which Tancred responded saying that Johnson had 'no right to seize hold of me in any manner'. Spencer, the Schoolmaster, swore that the Doctor was not struck and that Mr Johnson had only acted to prevent him entering the wash-house. Mary Higginbottom, a pauper who was in the wash-house, swore that she did not see Mr Johnson strike the Doctor; if he had struck him, she must have seen it.

The magistrates decided that the case was not proved, and dismissed it.

Finally, 'Colonel Rolleston called the poor people up, and told them that order must be kept, and the authority of the officers must be supported, at the same time the magistrates would protect them from cruelty; after a suitable admonition all the parties left the hall.'

THE AFTERMATH

Might a more effective prosecutor than Tancred, perhaps someone independent of the guardians, workhouse and Governor, have achieved a different result? If ill-treatment did take place it was not proved; if it did not then the verdicts seem appropriate. Tancred had gone to extraordinary lengths, including almost certainly some expense, to seek justice as he saw it. In doing so he had exposed himself to likely ridicule. Why had he gone so far out from his role as the workhouse chaplain? Was he a cleric who saw the rights of others as part and parcel of the role? Was he simply using events to get at the workhouse staff and, ultimately, the workhouse guardians and the Governor?

With a coincidence in the name Smith, Tancred would, several years later, go on to fight a battle with many similarities against the British Army in the Eastern Cape: the case of *Smith versus Lindsay* in 1846. Smith, a civilian, had been flogged by the army for refusing to obey an order. Once again Tancred put his reputation and the family finances at stake. Clearly corporal punishment was something he felt strongly about.

Meanwhile, back in Nottingham things were moving on outside the courtroom. Tancred had made many enemies; the family was now poised on the brink of disaster, his self-made enemies ready to pounce. Had he paid out of his own pocket? Had he hoped to win his court costs?

11

ENTER FRIEDRICH ENGELS

On 30 September the Reverend Austin commenced his duties at the Basford Workhouse. For a while longer Tancred lingered as the curate or, in his own designation, 'Minister at Bulwell'.

In the absence of living witnesses, or their contemporary written accounts, it seems fair to conclude that life in the Basford Workhouse went on much as before. If the regime was imperfect then this was far from unique in workhouses at that time. The demands on the foot soldiers providing care to those relying on the welfare of the state were onerous indeed, combining, as they did in the best practitioners, a number of complementary attributes: kindness, tolerance, a caring attitude, practical and people skills, as well as mental and physical stamina. Workhouses were staffed by men and women with varying abilities and little or no training, perhaps often selected with little attention to suitability, and certainly paid modest amounts. Always in the background were the ratepayers either questioning the need for charity or, at the very least, grumbling at the expense of it all.

*

Tancred's failure at Basford is beyond doubt. His allegations concerning the treatment of the inmates in the workhouse at Basford were settled in the outcome of the court case he fought and lost. One or two lingering doubts remain, however, not about Tancred's conduct in the matter, but about conditions in the Basford Workhouse. Unseen by Tancred, his departure did not see an end to public attention alighting on events at the Basford Union. These must be seen against the background of events in such institutions in other parts of the country and, not least, the reliability and independence of the evidence.

Over time a number of scandals in various parts of the country reached the newspapers. On 22 March 1841, three years after Tancred's departure from Nottinghamshire, and nine months before he left for Africa, workhouse conditions were the subject of a debate on the Poor Law Commission in the House of Commons. One of the workhouses discussed was none other than the Basford Union, with Colonel Rolleston, MP, whom Tancred would have remembered as the Chair of the magistrates who heard the case he brought against the Governor and Schoolmaster, active in the debate in defence of his own actions, some might say inactions. The case had hit the headlines and Basford was once again in the limelight.[12]

While absent from the Commons, Rolleston had heard that the member for Finsbury had mentioned his name in connection with an incident at Basford. Rolleston

---

12 HC Deb 22, March 1841, Vol. 57, 460–509.

expressed his regret that the matter had not been drawn to his attention sooner as he had knowledge of the matter. As a result, misunderstandings had arisen, with the blame for what went wrong now being 'attached to the wrong quarter': none other than Rolleston whose speech sought to clear his own name and point an accusing finger at the right quarter.

In Rolleston's account his role in the affair had been exemplary. As an ex-officio guardian of the Basford Union he considered it his duty to attend to the 'business of the board', ensuring its smooth running, rather than merely visiting the workhouse occasionally. However, when he heard of the incident he attended a meeting of the board to establish the facts, only to find that it had already been discussed with a resolution passed calling for the case to be investigated.

Rolleston was keen to point out the true circumstances of the case in question in which a pauper had, allegedly, died in 'the most distressing circumstances' as covered in a most frightfully inaccurate report in the newspapers. The investigation in Basford revealed a different story. The deceased, 'this unfortunate man', had been taken to the workhouse at five o'clock in the evening when 'exceedingly ill' and in the 'most inclement weather', the temperature being ten or fifteen degrees below freezing point, and, though receiving attention, he never rallied and died the following morning in spite of the best efforts of the 'inferior servants'.

Rolleston explained how he had lost no time in taking aim at the Medical Officer who, when interviewed, described how he had prescribed 'some water-gruel and tea, and something warm &c'. When Rolleston observed that '&c' was vague in meaning the medical man replied, 'something warm of that sort; nothing but warm tea or water-gruel'. Rolleston had asked if in a case of 'extreme debility' then 'something more calculated to sustain life, or more stimulating' was necessary.

Rolleston outlined his astonishment when the Medical Officer said that yes, he would 'most assuredly have given him warm wine or spiced wine, or something of that sort, but had no power to do that' when this 'would have been contrary to the Act and the rules and regulations of the Poor Law Commissioners, as against the common feelings of humanity'. The Medical Officer had apparently believed that only orders from the guardians, with their powers, would have enabled him to take such an action.

In the course of the investigation, it was revealed that the Chairman of the board had ordered the Medical Officer not to 'apply stimulants of this sort' without first gaining a special order from the board. Was this a question of cost, or from a concern that wine on the premises might be abused if available in the workhouse? Although the Medical Officer had applied four or five times for such an order to be made, he had been met by refusal each time. So, who was to blame? Not, it seems, the Poor Law Commissioners, although one of their number was present at the investigation into the incident but taking no part in the proceedings. The guardians? The Medical Officer? Colonel Rolleston himself? No, certainly not he.

Rolleston's version of events seems to have been crumbling at this point, the Medical Officer's account gaining traction, but no, the matter could not be allowed to rest there.

The serious nature of the event had required the circumstances to be brought before the magistrates who decided that further investigation by a higher authority would be appropriate. Brought before a court of law the judge advised the jury that no more than a misdemeanour applied when the Medical Officer and the Overseer sent 'this poor unfortunate man' to the workhouse in an open cart in atrocious weather. The jury found the defendants Not Guilty.

Rolleston, critical that the indictment had referred only to a misdemeanour rather than manslaughter, concluded by telling the House that the 'proper authorities' were still investigating the case, in pursuit of where the blame lay: he was certain it did not lie with him or the guardians.

FRIEDRICH ENGELS AND BASFORD

Coincidentally, another insight into conditions in the Basford Workhouse at about the same time comes from none other than Friedrich Engels. In his investigation into the condition of the working class in England published in 1845, when discussing the attitude of the bourgeoisie towards the proletariat, he writes:

> In the workhouse at Basford, an inspecting official found that the sheets had not been changed in thirteen weeks, shirts in four weeks, stockings in two to ten months, so that of forty-five boys but three had stockings, and all their shirts were in

tatters. The beds swarmed with vermin, and the tableware was washed in the slop-pails.[13]

Higginbotham, an authority on workhouses in England, takes a more sympathetic view of conditions at Basford some six years after Tancred's departure:

> In 1844, the *Nottingham Review* printed allegations of incompetence and corruption at the workhouse. Although proved to be unfounded, and probably the work of Chartist opponents of the New Poor Law, the accusations generated much publicity and a much-exaggerated version was included by Engels in his 1845 work, *Conditions of the Working Class in England.*[14]

But where is the corroborating evidence one way or another? Was a visit by an 'inspecting official' acting on behalf of Engels, the source of the information, or misinformation, or did Engels merely parrot an article in the local newspaper? While it may be the case that the 1844 allegations in the *Nottingham Review* were unfounded, where is the proof? Perhaps it was the work of Chartist opponents of the New Poor Law but once again, where is the evidence? Further research might throw light on the matter.

What is beyond dispute is the fact that in some workhouses conditions were deplorable yet generally hidden from public view by an understandable reluctance on the part of those in the know to act as whistle-blowers.

---

13 Friedrich Engels, *Conditions of the Working Class in England*, 1845.
14 Peter Higginbotham, *ibid.*, 66.

Despite society's general ability to turn a blind eye to unpalatable truths, examples of ill-treatment gradually came to public attention. Among the most notorious were the events surrounding conditions at Andover in Hampshire 'where in 1845 starving paupers were discovered eating rotting marrow from the bones they were meant to be crushing'.[15] In the end it was thanks to the press and resulting public indignation, rather than the Poor Law Commissioners or Parliament, that such instances were exposed.

Right up to the present day, conditions in which the elderly or infirm or mentally ill are cared for are sometimes scenes of gross abuse. This is hardly surprising: carers may be carelessly recruited, poorly trained, managed and badly paid, for work with some of the most difficult and vulnerable members of society. It is work which most of those in search of employment choose not to do. It also requires a commitment of significant resources.

*

By the time of the publication of Engels' investigation Tancred had long since moved on. He arrived at the Cape in 1842. By then hardly anyone would have remembered the allegations he gave vent to before the magistrates and in *The Times* – not Colonel Rolleston in the House of Commons, nor the inspecting official quoted by Engels. It will never be known for certain whether or not the injustices alleged by Tancred occurred. The Governor and

---

15 Simon Fowler, *Workhouse*, 2007, 7.

the Schoolmaster may have been entirely innocent. But if not, as Engels observed of members of the proletariat, '... his poverty... casts him off from legal redress against any caprice of the administrators of the law; for him, therefore, the protecting forms of the law do not exist... (it is) evident how little the protective side of the law exists for the working man, how frequently he has to bear all the burdens of the law without enjoying its benefits'.[16]

There is undoubtedly some truth in the old saying that 'English justice is the best that money can buy' and a nagging doubt remains. Tancred behaved idiotically but in the case of the Basford Workhouse, did the powers that be simply leap to the defence of the staff rather than the inmates of the workhouse? Was James Johnson, the Governor, still in charge, one wonders, when the 'inspecting official' visited Basford Workhouse? Was William George Spencer still the Schoolmaster? I added these questions to the list of 'things worth further investigation'.

---

16 Engels, *ibid.*

12

PETER PEEPER

Ripples from the Tancred affair were lapping around the county. A meeting of the Board of Guardians of the nearby Nottingham Poor Law Union was held on Monday 17 September 1838 and reported at length in the *Nottingham Review* on 21 September.

Most of the business of the meeting seems to have been concerned with a continuation of an earlier discussion concerning the proposed appointment of a chaplain for the Nottingham Workhouse. The events at Basford had not gone unnoticed. Perhaps it would be better to do without a chaplain? Mr Hind, observing that 'his object was simply to do good', brought a motion for the appointment of a salaried chaplain for the workhouse. Mr Sutton argued that there was no need to 'tax the whole town' in order to pay a chaplain for the workhouse when the town already had an 'excellent supply of religious instruction'. This limited view of the chaplain's role, to 'instruction', is interesting. Clearly the pastoral care of the paupers was not seen as relevant. Mr Sutton was also firmly in the camp concerned to keep down the cost of poor relief, which fell on the worthy and wealthy citizens, to a bare minimum. This opposition to expenditure from the public purse for the benefit of the needy was typical at the time.

Not surprisingly, recent events at Basford intruded into the arguments for and against the appointment of a salaried chaplain at Nottingham. Mr Sutton quoted the example of the way in which the 'system of communicating religious instruction, by means of a salaried chaplain' worked in the neighbouring Basford Union. He had no doubt 'they had all heard of Dr. Tancred'. Although two members then expressed the wish that 'a solitary case might not be referred to' Mr Sutton returned to the fray, arguing that he knew of no other example of a chaplain being appointed in the area and 'it should be remembered that Dr. Tancred was the only candidate for the situation of Chaplain in the Nottingham Union'. It seems that having lost out at Basford, Tancred was now in the running for the chaplaincy of the workhouse at Nottingham. The Board of Guardians, however, had seen that one coming and knowing of his reputation were not minded to appoint him. His behaviour had strengthened the resolve of those not wholly sympathetic to the workhouse ethos in general, and to the value of a chaplain in particular. As Mr Sutton observed, not unreasonably, the appointment of a chaplain in the Basford Union 'had not worked well'. This was something of an understatement.

After further discussion the motion went to a vote with opposition to the appointment of chaplain winning by ten votes to five. Mr Close, one of those who voted against, argued that he did so as he believed the ratepayers were opposed to a salaried chaplain. He then observed, somewhat paradoxically, that although he was voting against it now, if he were returned as a guardian at the next election he would then most probably vote for a chaplain. Was this apparent inconsistency perhaps because Tancred would by then be off the scene?

'ONE OF THEIR SERVANTS'

The same issue of the newspaper contained an astonishing diatribe, over 2,000 words in length, pouring scorn on Dr Tancred. This anonymous piece, penned by one 'Peter Peeper', provided a savage coda to the affair, indicating the extent to which Tancred had got under the skin of the local bigwigs with his excoriating comments about them in the London *Times*. It must of course have been obvious to anyone with eyes to see that Tancred, though not mentioned by name, had been the author. Now in response came a catalogue of seemingly well-founded counter-allegations. Peter Peeper no doubt expended much time and energy in crafting this scathing outburst. It was a fine piece of vituperative writing, dripping with sarcasm, cruel and clearly intended to hurt. Through this spokesperson the local bigwigs were taking their revenge on Tancred while quoting salient facts which aid our understanding of events at the Basford Workhouse as well as offering insights into the personality of Augustus.

The Chairman of the Basford Board of Guardians, Colonel Rolleston, MP, Peter Peeper pointed out, might be only a country gentleman yet he is 'the managing partner in the oldest established bank in Nottingham, a churchman and a Conservative, of a family that in many generations has furnished members of Parliament to the town, the nephew of a Peer of the realm, and married also to the daughter of an Earl'. How could a man like this, Tancred's 'thick-headed blustering Radical', coming from such modest lineage, be expected to know 'the etiquette of making a communication to a clergyman and gentleman'? On the other hand, surely a clergyman, a Doctor of Divinity no less, should both believe and practise the catechism he teaches?

After taking exception to Tancred's piece in *The Times* newspaper, Peter Peeper turned to matters of substance, beginning with Tancred's entries in the chaplain's book. Surely, if those in charge of the workhouse had cause to doubt that 'one of their servants' was neglecting his duty, there was an obligation to enquire into the matter? Was it not strange that if the Chaplain had concerns regarding the conduct of various officers of the workhouse, he did not mention these concerns to the guardians? In any event, though, these allegations were not borne out by the facts 'as proved before the magistrates at the County Hall' in the actions brought by Tancred.

Surely the Board of Guardians, be they 'clodhoppers, old clothesmen, tallow chandlers, or snips', on searching through the minute-book, and noticing Tancred's errors and omissions, had a duty to draw them to his attention? In view of his 'intemperate reply, just allow poor Peter Peeper gently to admonish you'. Tancred was about to receive some of his own medicine, the prescription now coming with a stronger dosage.

Turning to specifics, the writer could think of no good reason why, if Tancred had visited the female ward, he never made an entry recording the fact. Furthermore, he has clearly 'violated the rule printed at the beginning of the chaplain's book, which says that therein "he shall insert the date of each of his attendances" at the workhouse'.

Moreover, the instructions in the chaplain's book contained a written requirement 'to examine and catechise the children at least once every month, and after each of such examinations to record the same, and state the general progress and condition of the children, and the moral and religious state of the inmates generally, in a book to be kept for that purpose'. This book, which must include the date of each attendance at the workhouse, should be laid before the Board of Guardians at their meetings.

Worse, if that were possible, was to come, for on four Sundays in 1837 – 11 May, 23 July, 6 August and 13 August – there were no services of any kind in the workhouse. On five other Sundays in the same year the services were performed by other clergymen. Then there was the school, and a litany of dates when Tancred made no recorded visits, so when and how could he have examined and catechised the children? And surely a Doctor of Divinity should be able to spell the names of the parishes which form the union. Tancred, it seems, had been prone to error on this too.

As to the printed instruction to record 'the moral and religious state of the inmates generally', again apparently there was silence. And although he claimed to have visited the female ward there were, as yet, no entries to this effect.

His veracity seemingly shot to pieces Tancred was left without the proverbial leg to stand on. His humiliation was complete. And Evelina? Sadly, history records virtually nothing of Evelina's thoughts, actions or feelings. She is as always but his wife, mother of their children, housekeeper, and a mere woman.

So much for this hypothetical 'answer of the Board of Guardians' and, on their anonymous behalf, the reply by Peter Peeper.

Thanks to Peter Peeper we now have both sides of the story. Beyond the vitriol it becomes clear that Tancred's actions, and his account of events, carry little conviction. I was left pondering: what on earth was he about? A clever, educated man perhaps and, in a later age, discerning eyes might have spotted 'something amiss here' and diagnosed the presence of a man prone to mania, paranoia, or some other mental malady. At the time, though, Tancred was seen as bad rather than mad. The year, we remember, was 1838.

Now, the gentry were out for revenge, Tancred a juicy scorpion squirming beneath a magnifying glass, the full strength of the rays of the sun trained upon him, his sting neutralised. He was about to suffer the pain of it all, with Evelina the innocent victim beside him. His foolish words and deeds would cost them dear.

Once again, things were about to get very much worse.

13

DOCTORATE? WHAT DOCTORATE?

At least Augustus still held the post of curate at Bulwell. This would provide a home for the family and sufficient income to keep them fed and clothed. If only he could settle for that.

It was not to be. The curtain was about to come down, the lights slowly dim, on what would turn out to be Augustus' final performance in Europe. Barring a few walk-on parts awaiting him, this was it, tragedy, not comedy, even if there were some who no doubt laughed hilariously at his downfall. Augustus, once a possible leading player, was now sidelined in the game of clerical life, the weapon of his own self-destruction, doomed by the traits in his personality which rendered his intelligence and education null and void, compromised by flaws buried deep in his psyche. Can he, can anyone, be so flawed as to be only partly responsible for his actions? He was a man subject to moments of irrational behaviour and, perhaps, a fondness for the demon drink. For those who see him only as evil, he gets his just deserts. To others, he is subject to moods and actions beyond his control. It is his wife and children who probably paid the highest price. Whatever the truth of it, the axe was about to fall.

WHAT DOCTORATE?

The *Nottingham Review and General Advertiser* probably sold extra copies covering the Tancred story. As the curtain rose on the final act it recounted how Mr Ashton, Clerk to the Board of Guardians of the Basford Workhouse, appeared on stage in a leading role on Friday 30 November 1838, with a headline announcing, '*Dr. Tancred again!*'

The report that followed covered a public meeting in the schoolroom at Bulwell, convened by the Venerable Archdeacon Wilkins, to inquire into the charges brought against the Reverend A. Tancred, D.D., Curate of Bulwell, by the said Mr Wm. Ashton, Tancred's old adversary from the workhouse guardians.

The charges, when read out, must have made for dispiriting listening for Tancred, as well as for Evelina if, by chance, she was present.

The allegations were that on Sunday 11 November 1838, in the church at Bulwell, Dr Tancred, before pronouncing the blessing, launched into 'a few words' he wished to say to the congregation. Tancred was seldom a man of few words. Referring to his enemies he said:

> There are a number of animals in the parish without a name; but I call them mushrooms – bubbles that will soon burst.

Having begun his tirade, he continued by explaining that the 'bubbles' were saying he must leave; this only showed how little they understood him for he would remain in the parish carrying out his duties as curate for sixty years. It may of course have occurred to the audience, if not to him, that by that time he would be ninety-four years of age and presumably beyond his prime as a servant of the Church. He then explained how he had received an anonymous letter urging him to flee the area. Then came a rhetorical question: did the locals intend to murder him? Certainly not, he thought, for he held them in higher regard than that. As for the anonymous letter, he would give £300 to anyone who revealed the name of the writer. Surprisingly, £300 would be worth many thousands of pounds in today's money, surely a sum beyond the reach of Dr Tancred.

Dr Wilkins then explained the law as it covered the allegations against Tancred, commencing with brawling in the church. If this was substantiated, the penalty was suspension from office. Wilkins then called for evidence from the Parish Clerk and six other men.

It is the cross-examination of Tancred by Dr Wilkins which is significant, not least as it finally unravels the truth behind the source of Tancred's elusive doctorate:

Dr. Wilkins – May I enquire where you obtained
      your diploma?
Dr. Tancred – From Toulouse.
Dr. Wilkins – Then our church does not recognise it?
Dr. Tancred – Oh, yes; I offered to graduate at Oxford,
      but they told me it was not necessary,
      my diploma being a proper one.
Dr. Wilkins – They could not tell you so at Oxford,
      they know so much better.

There it is, and from his own mouth: 'Dr' Tancred is but the holder, or may have been the holder, of a diploma from Toulouse in France, not a doctorate from Oxford in England or anywhere else, and certainly not from Trinity College Dublin, as claimed in the obituary.

At the time, the Church of England required its curates to hold degrees, at that time generally from Oxford. Had no one thought to check his qualifications before appointing him at Christchurch, Coggeshall, Redruth, Basford or Bulwell? It seems beyond doubt that all along the way he had been economical with the truth regarding his qualifications. He had all this while practised in the Church of England under false pretences.

Together with his alleged behaviour in church on 11 November, and now with the evidence of his lack of an appropriate qualification, there was only one possible outcome: his career in the church was finally over.

How could he hope to support his family in future? This was the only job he knew.

In that moment the rollercoaster lives of Tancred, his wife, Evelina, and their three children were beginning to accelerate downhill at an alarming speed towards financial ruin, hunger and homelessness.

LOCK, STOCK AND BARREL - THE SALE OF ALL THEIR POSSESSIONS

On 4 November 1838, Tancred had conducted his last baptism at Bulwell. He was not involved in any further marriages or burials.

How Peter Peeper and his rich friends amongst the gentility must have laughed when they saw this advertisement in the *Nottingham Review* on 14 December 1838:

SALE AT BULWELL RECTORY

Valuable Household Furniture, Glass and China, Six-and-a-Half Octave Cabinet Piano-forte, Mangle, Store Pigs, Potatoes, Garden Water Engine, Brewing Vessels, &c.

TO be SOLD BY auction, by Mr PEET, on the Premises of the Rev. Dr. Tancred, at the Rectory House, Bulwell (who is leaving this part of the Country), on Wednesday and Thursday, the 19th and 20th of December, 1838.

Comprising Goose Feather Beds, Hair Mattresses, fine Blankets, Bedsteads (with Moreen and other Drapery), Mahogany Chests of Drawers, Brussels and Venetian Carpets, Toilet Tables, Mahogany Chairs, Tables, Couch, Bookcases, handsome China Dinner, Dessert and Tea Services, Eight-days Clock, Kitchen Requisites, and a variety of other Effects.

Particulars in Catalogues, to be had of the Auctioneer.

One survivor of the items offered for sale was the silver snuff box presented to him at Christchurch. The range of possessions offered for sale indicates both an urgent need for funds as well as the degree of affluence enjoyed by the family up to that point. Here there are signs of affluence but what was the source?

For the first time we have with the sale an insight into the domestic conditions in the Tancred household, evidence of a degree of comfort beyond the lifestyle one might expect in the home of a man who only recently applied for a bag of free clothing. Had Tancred run up debts to furnish the vicarage to this standard, to feed the family, or perhaps maintain a flow of wine, spirits and beer? The question lurked throughout the story: how does a man with modest earnings from episodic employment afford this domestic lifestyle? Had a wealthy family, perhaps related to Evelina, set them up for married life? As is always the case with Augustus, there are more unknowns than equations, leaving the solution indeterminate.

Did the case he brought against the Governor and Schoolmaster before the court in Nottingham involve him in costs? Or did the subsequent charges brought against him by Mr Ashton involve costs? No evidence has been unearthed in answer to either of these questions.

*

The two-day sale ended on 20 December 1838. Can the family ever have had a less happy Christmas? Evelina, aged twenty-six, her life so dependent on the actions of her husband, looked out on a bleak Christmas and the future beyond. And there were the children, Augustus Frederick aged four and a half, Evelina barely three, and Oswald not yet two. Even Charles Dickens might have struggled to depict in words a family in these circumstances during the festive period – a bleak house indeed.

Now aged thirty-four, Tancred's career had crashed

and burned, bringing his family down with him. His humiliation was complete, his claim to be a Doctor of Divinity rubbished, the performance of his duties at the Basford Workhouse mercilessly exposed as inadequate, his work as curate at Bulwell found wanting, the contents of the family home sold lock, stock and barrel, and he himself, the master of his own misfortunes, reduced to a figure of ridicule. Peter Peeper in the newspaper article had played with him like a cat tormenting a mouse. If Tancred was a man with psychological or mental health difficulties, these symptoms were generally misunderstood at the time. His present circumstances can only have increased the stress he was under. There are no signs of any kind of support coming from friends or family.

Surely there could be no way back to respectability with every finger now pointing inexorably towards the door marked 'exit' – from a career in the Church, from the local area in which he was by now held in such low regard, perhaps even from England, from anything short of a period of penury. The influential men he had insulted in Nottingham may well have briefed against him and there seems little doubt that the reputation that would follow him from Basford would prove a hindrance. The challenge now was survival, the ultimate humiliation perhaps a place as a pauper in a workhouse.

Nothing much is known of the following eight months before he bobs up to the surface again like flotsam in a rough sea. Without the 'right' to call himself 'Dr' Tancred, applying for other positions in the Church, without a qualification required for the ministry, or a reference from his previous employer, he must have been desperate to find any future employment to enable him to support his wife and their three children.

He never did drop the title 'Doctor of Divinity' and there is no known later reference to anyone questioning his right so to do. Perhaps he did hold a diploma from Toulouse, perhaps someone at Oxford did tell him it was equivalent to a doctorate? If he relied on the falsehood that he held a doctorate from Trinity College Dublin, it was simply dishonest.

Where next? Might he have another iron waiting in the fire? It seemed unlikely. According to some sources the Pillars of Hercules displayed the words *Ne Plus Ultra* inscribed in the stone, warning seafarers that there was nothing more beyond the Straits of Gibraltar. In family history research there is always more beyond, *plus ultra*, and rarely more so than in the case of Augustus. But what was it that lay beyond what we know of the man?

14

IF THE HUSBAND WERE GONE

*… he retired to Belgium, where, after a residence of three
years, he determined, with his wife, to join the Roman
Catholic Church. Some time after this he determined to
emigrate to this colony…*
Obituary, *De Zuid-Afrikaan*

Some of the bricks missing from the obituary wall,
the gaps between the departure from Christchurch
and the unproven years spent in Belgium, have now
been cemented in place. But not all. The time spent at
Coggeshall in Essex, Redruth in Cornwall, Basford and
Bulwell in Nottinghamshire, all help to locate where he
was and what he was doing, as well as the nature of the
man and the consequences for the family. Two questions
remain: if the obituary is to be believed, how and why
did he go to Belgium, and thence to the Cape Colony?
In particular, were there any significant events between
Bulwell and Belgium?

*

One such incident that may have remained in hiding came to light thanks to the arrival of internet searches on the family history scene. This resulted in a last view of the family in England before their departure for the Cape, confirming as it did Tancred's talent as a master of surprise. It goes some way to showing what happened after the departure from Bulwell, and after the sale of what must have been all, or most of, their household possessions. It also hints at why and how they may have spent time in Belgium, and the possible source of the idea that the family might emigrate, as well as the funding to make it possible. Financially they must have been on their beam ends: family members, most likely from Evelina's side, may have come to the rescue. What is certain is that, at this point, Augustus, the disgraced Catholic priest turned Church of England curate, seems to have sought refuge back in the arms of the Church of Rome.

Although nothing is known about the eight months after leaving Bulwell in December 1838, the family came to the no doubt unwelcome attention of the Roman Catholic Vicar Apostolic of the Midland District, Bishop Thomas Walsh, in August 1839. In a letter to Walsh dated 22 August 1839, H.R. Bagshawe, a London lawyer, wrote from Lincoln's Inn, London:

> My dear Dr Walsh
>
> … I spoke to Mr Wright about Mr Tancred – Wright says Mr Tancred might go to New South Wales for about £40 and for 2/6 an acre could get land and for £100 in all he might be placed in a situation sufficient for his personal support; a short time ago he might have gone free.

Mr Wright suggested for Mrs Tancred that she and her family might go to Canada for £8 apiece and that probably £100 in all would set her up in some way – but if the husband were gone, with industry she would do very well at home.

At all events I think your Lordship would do well to require Mr Tancred and his wife to consent to their going to separate parts of the world as a sine qua non to one farthing's further assistance and that he should himself find out all about the emigration etc. and that the money to be further applied should be paid for the passage and should be paid on landing at the colony. Wright stated this to be very important. The more I think of it, the more I am clear that your Lordship ought not to interfere on any other terms than some such as I have mentioned, and I think your Lordship should acquire references as to the original history of Mr Tancred – where he lived – his bishop etc. for if he emigrates under your auspices all this may become very important…

… In haste I remain, my dear Dr Walsh, with our united wishes for your Lordship's prayer

Your obedient servant

H.R. Bagshawe[17]

Several salient points emerge. The Tancreds had fallen on hard times and disgrace was in the air; it implies that the disgrace was Mr Tancred's and not his wife's. But what was the cause of this disgrace? It was clearly a matter

---

17 Birmingham Archdiocesan Archives, document reference number B431, Hierarchical Number Z4/2/1/1/3/1. 22 August 1839.

of considerable import, the consequences dire in the extreme. If the husband (Mr Tancred) were gone, with industry she (Mrs Tancred) would do very well in England ('at home') with 'her' children; failing that both must go abroad to countries very far apart (New South Wales and Canada). It is assumed here that the children will remain with Mrs Tancred ('her family'). If there was to be 'further assistance', did this follow on some previous assistance? Mr Tancred should not be given cash in hand in England but only on arrival in New South Wales: he is not to be trusted with money so he is to be 'paid on landing at the colony'. Had they reason to believe he might misuse money paid to him while still in England? The sums discussed were not inconsiderable. The £100 each which would set them up in their new lives equates to many thousands of pounds at the present-day value of the pound. Why might the Bishop offer that sum of money to disperse Tancred and his wife and children to different corners of the world?

Throughout the letter runs a whiff of the shame of it all; the shame, however, is not identified. Bagshawe clearly has doubts about 'the original history of Mr Tancred' who is now no longer referred to as 'Dr' Tancred. Might whatever 'it' was reflect badly on the Church? Was there an unknown benefactor waiting in the wings? Was there any subsequent involvement of the Bishop? Do the Bishop and Mr Bagshawe not read *The Times*? This might have alerted them to goings-on in Christchurch and Nottingham.

Unfortunately no further involvement by or on behalf of Dr Walsh in the lives of the Tancreds has been traced. It is not surprising that Tancred's obituary makes no mention of this episode, for he would not have listed it among his achievements. Not for the first time he seems to have edited his life story. Was this forgetfulness on his part, or perhaps of others, or was it just that he, whenever possible, concentrated on those episodes in his life which showed him in a good light?

I have found neither confirmation nor rebuttal of the Belgium story.

The time between the family coming to the attention of Bishop Walsh in August 1839, and their departure for the Cape Colony in December 1841, is consistent with the possibility that Belgium accounted for this gap of about two years in the Tancred timeline. They reached the colony in 1842, and not the 1844 of the obituary.

This may have been the moment, and Belgium the place, which saw Evelina, who was baptised in the Church of Ireland at Tullamore, convert to the Catholic faith which she followed thereafter until her death. With Augustus, who was baptised a Catholic in Cork, educated, trained and subsequently practised as a Catholic priest in Ireland, the notion that he converted to Catholicism in his mid-thirties seems somewhat strange at first glance. Perhaps not, for he had left the Catholic faith in disgrace in 1831, practised as a curate in the Church of England until his second disgrace in 1838, when he must have found himself in a very awkward position. In this context, it does seem plausible that Belgium, like Ireland a predominantly Catholic country, provided him with the opportunity to return to the faith of his youth, perhaps a choice made under some kind of duress. If Bishop Walsh established the background to the Tancred case, might he have advised, perhaps required, a period of reflection and atonement out of the limelight in Belgium before Augustus could be accepted back into the Catholic Church? Beyond doubt Augustus had sinned; was a spiritual and secular penance the price he must now pay? Did Walsh or his agents make that choice and perhaps arrange and fund the venture?

The children, baptised in the Church of England, may have been received into the Catholic Church at the same time. Like their parents all three were committed to this faith for the rest of their lives. For some unknown reason, this loyalty ended with the death of Augustus Frederick, the eldest, whose descendants were perfunctory members of the Church of the Province of South Africa, part of the Anglican Communion. Neither Evelina nor Oswald married or had children.

15

TOO THICKLY POPULATED

'Emigration will bring a great and lasting benefit upon your natural country, not least because England is by now too thickly populated.'
Sir William Molesworth addressing an audience at Devonport, February 1840

In 1841 the first national census of England and Wales recorded a population of 15.9 million people. Molesworth, explaining to the audience at Devonport why he sent Francis, his twenty-one-year-old brother, as an emigrant to New Zealand, described how such men could make the colonies productive and capable of trade between colony and mother country, and hence beneficial to both. This notion that trade following the flag, benefitting people individually, and producers and consumers collectively, both at home and abroad, bestowed an overarching beneficence on the system. It did not take long to become apparent to some that the major beneficiary was the 'natural country'. An additional benefit, it seemed to some, was reducing the population in England by emigration.

When Daniel Defoe, soldier, businessman and spy,

made his *Tour thro' the Whole Island of Great Britain*, in the 1720s, England appeared to be a very settled place. Then the canal boom from the 1770s, and developments in agriculture, industry and commerce, kick-started unimagined changes. By the time of the railway mania from the 1820s, England was a very different place.

Not all the prominent intellectuals of the time who pondered the size of an optimum population agreed with the overcrowding hypothesis. Adam Smith, in his *Inquiry into the Nature and Causes of Wealth of Nations* (1776), advanced the view that population growth benefitted a country by allowing more workers to divide the available work into more units with the benefits following the specialisation and division of labour.

Molesworth, though, was not alone in thinking that England was overcrowded. Robert Malthus, in *An Essay on the Principle of Population* which appeared in 1798, had offered an analysis that appeared to be convincing. Population, he asserted, grew geometrically, hence exponentially, while the supply of food and other resources grew arithmetically, as in a linear function. Therefore, in order to maintain an adequate food supply to nourish the population, and provide them with the other necessities of life, it was essential to limit the growth of population. If, however, the indigent poor bred to excess, remedial action could include sending some of their number abroad. Not for the first or the last time, economists offered policy-makers conflicting opinions.

When William Cobbett, journalist, agriculturist and political reformer, saddled up for his *Rural Rides* in the early 1820s, England was in the throes of rapid social and economic change. When British settlers arrived at the Cape in any numbers in 1820, the 'Dark Satanic Mills' (1804), in the phrase forever associated with William Blake, were already beginning to powder the towns and adjacent rural landscapes with factory dust. By the time Blake died in 1827 agricultural workers seeking employment populated the bleak new urban areas which offered little by way of security or creature comfort. Unsurprisingly, many decided to quit the land of their birth and head overseas.

Rising political tensions at home also pointed to the value of exporting some of the British population. The end of the Napoleonic Wars at the Battle of Waterloo in 1815 resulted in the perennial post-war problem of large numbers of now unemployed men returning home from the wars. Prices were rising. 1819 saw the Peterloo massacre in Manchester in which between ten and twenty unarmed civilians died, with hundreds more injured, at the hands of the Manchester Yeomanry, a local volunteer force. The agricultural scene was also changing. New farming methods may have been more efficient but could also cause distress to farm workers dependent on the old ways, as we noticed at Christchurch. The Swing Riots were a response to this change, another cause for alarm in the households of the gentry and in the corridors of political power. The eighteenth century had closed in the shadows of the French Revolution (1789–1799), and the American Revolution (1775–1783), whose influences hung long in the air in England. With the lurking fear that revolutionary seeds might germinate, allowing the possibility of revolt to become rooted in England, the ideas of radicals like Tom Paine (1737–1809) were seen as downright dangerous.

There was much to suggest that England could benefit by venting some of the population abroad. It is estimated that between the end of the French Wars in 1815, and the outbreak of World War I in 1914, as many as ten million people emigrated from Britain. Only Ireland, Norway and Italy had higher emigration rates from Europe at this time.

A variety of circumstances led individuals to emigrate. For some, like convicts transported to lands across the seas, it was not a matter of personal choice. For others, remaining in their home country might mean starvation. The highland clearances in Scotland between 1750 and 1860 and the Irish potato famine from 1845 to 1852 saw desperate people exercising a limited choice whether intra-national or international. And for the others? Perhaps it meant joining friends or family abroad, or the prospect of imagined fame and fortune in a land of milk and honey, or the rich pickings to be found in the newly discovered gold mines. Then there were those who had offended but were fleet-footed or wealthy enough to escape the law, and those who sought shelter from some personal or public disgrace. There were the men of the cloth intent on civilising the heathen, and the younger sons of titled families who missed out on the pickings at the top of the family pecking order. There were indeed a multitude of reasons why people emigrated rather than remained in the mother country.

WHY THE TANCREDS?

Why did the Tancred family leave Europe? The answer seems simple: Augustus had run out of options after his misadventures in Ireland and England. A later account of the reason for their leaving England comes from the pen of Ralph Kilpin in Cape Town who, in 1918, recounted how Tancred's friends:

> … were shocked at the news that he had converted to Roman Catholicism and eloped with a nun and he was pained to find that their friendship was unequal to the strain imposed on it. Unbalanced before, he now became petulant; and morally broad-minded in a narrow-minded age, it was probably as much his own desire to be rid of his one-time friends as it was theirs to be rid of him that led him to seek his fortune abroad.[18]

The times when he was 'unbalanced', and 'petulant' are certainly characteristics readily recognisable in his known behaviours. 'Morally broad-minded in a narrow-minded age'? Is this phrase an apt description of his morality or that of the age? On the whole, though, the drift of the Kilpin account matches what is known about the man.

Family influences may have been behind the decision to leave Europe, but perhaps not family alone. Dr Walsh or his staff may have encouraged, and perhaps financed, their emigration. Might a government scheme have provided the money?

---

18 Ralph Kilpin, *ibid.*, *Cape Argus*.

16

DEPARTURE

Some time after this (Belgium) he determined to emigrate to this colony, which he reached in 1844.
Obituary, *De Zuid-Afrikaan*

In any event their next geographical destination was not determined by the advice of Bagshawe, the lawyer in London, to Bishop Walsh, for Mr Tancred had not gone to New South Wales, and neither had Mrs Tancred and the children gone to Canada. Had they split up and gone asunder, how might they have fared? Living a life with the children, but without her husband, might Evelina and the children have fared better? It is not difficult to construct alternative scenarios with happier endings.

Leaving Christchurch in 1834, Augustus said he had 'shaken the dust off his feet'. He had indeed shaken the dust off his feet not only in Christchurch, but also in Coggeshall, Redruth, Basford, Bulwell and, perhaps, Belgium. It had become something of a habit. Now, in December 1841, as the family assembled at Gravesend, down river from London on the banks of the Thames, preparing to depart for the Cape Colony, he was about to shake the dust of England off his feet. They were about to set off on a voyage of 8,000 sea miles to an unknown land. Up to this moment Augustus had squandered every opportunity that came his way. Surely this time it would be different?

In the past, he always seemed able to come up with plans for a successful future, and now was no exception. With the decision taken, he was up for the challenge. If he had failed five or six times as a churchman in charge of a flock of parishioners, why not transfer his skills, knowledge and experience to tending a different flock? He found the answer bleating in his face. He would go abroad and become a farmer. Admittedly, he would be new to the farming life but why should a man of his calibre give pause for thought on such matters of detail? A flock was a flock. He must purchase some sheep.

*

The autumn before their departure had been wetter than usual, the railway building boom suffering from delays when cuttings collapsed as the lines scythed through rural landscapes unchanged for generations. In the cold of winter, with its short days and insipid light, it may have seemed a good climate to leave behind. Sunnier climes awaited them.

On 30 November 1841, an advertisement appeared in the *Shipping and Mercantile Gazette* for a vessel, the *George*, 'having one-half of her cargo engaged and shipping' and due to sail on 10 December for the Cape of Good Hope. She was described as 'a fine, fast-sailing, first-class, British-built Barque of 250 tons, coppered and copper-fastened', and 'lying in the London Dock'. She was due to carry cabin and steerage-class passengers and freight to Algoa Bay. Her Commander was Captain George Donaldson, 'under engagement with Her Majesty's Commissioners', who 'being an old trader, and well acquainted with the place, will give every information to persons about emigrating to this flourishing colony'. The crew included an 'experienced surgeon'. Intending passengers were invited to apply to Captain Donaldson on board ship or to his London agents on land. The Tancred family booked their passage.

The sailing was, however, delayed. An advertisement appeared in the same newspaper on 10 December announcing a later departure for the *George* which would now 'positively sail on Saturday next', 18 December. The *Shipping and Mercantile Gazette* on 16 December had the vessel loading in the Port of London. The *Public Ledger and Daily Advertiser* on 20 December showed she had been 'cleared out with cargo' (ready to depart) on 18 December. On 21 December *Lloyd's List* showed the *George* sailing from Gravesend for the Cape of Good Hope on 20 December. The list of passengers included the Reverend Dr and Mrs Tancred among thirteen adults with five unnamed children, in all probability including the three Tancred offspring. Also unnamed were thirteen persons in steerage. Doubtless a man of the status of the Reverend Dr Tancred would not have countenanced steerage. It seems he did not need so to do.

And then they were gone. On 23 December, *Lloyd's List* shows that on 22 December the *George* arrived at Deal on the Kent Coast from the River Thames and bound for the Cape of Good Hope. The Tancreds were now finally poised en route to the southern hemisphere. Kicking the coasts of Europe behind, the *George* now headed south, sailing first down the English Channel before proceeding down the western coasts of Europe and Africa to Cape Town and thence to Algoa Bay.

Augustus, the once devoted biblical scholar, was now aged thirty-seven, and hoping to make his fortune as a farmer. Evelina, his wife, was aged twenty-nine and Augustus Frederick seven, young Evelina six, and Oswald four. With 'Dr' Tancred as husband or father they had endured much to date. Of these five Tancreds only one would never set foot in Europe again. Did a secure and settled home life now lie ahead?

High hopes are one thing; a reality check awaited. Had anyone, the family of Augustus or Evelina, or their friends in England, or Captain Donaldson, or the Colonial Office, ever mentioned the two words, 'war' and 'zone'?

Africa for its part could have had no inkling of the unusual character about to step ashore. When he died someone said, 'we shall never see his like again'. Accompanied by 'some of Lord Western's best sheep' he was now about to make his mark on Africa. He was taking the farming idea seriously.

AFRICA

17

SETTLERS AT THE CAPE

After calling at Cape Town the *George* moved on, going further east in the South Atlantic past Cape Agulhas, the southernmost point in Africa, and then into the warmer Indian Ocean and on towards Algoa Bay. Augustus later regretted not taking the opportunity to visit the Governor in Cape Town. Was this simply a manifestation of his *folie de grandeur*, a delusion of greatness, at its worst a symptom of borderline madness? Surely the then Governor, Sir George Thomas Napier, with much else on his mind, would not expect to be called upon by every passing indigent immigrant with a shady past?

The *George* reached Algoa Bay on 13 March 1842. In the absence of a pier, they were ferried ashore in small boats, likewise their luggage and Lord Western's best sheep. The men helping the passengers ashore were mostly dark-skinned and shouting to one another in strange languages.

If the Tancreds imagined they had reached their journey's end they were mistaken. Onward travel of some seventy or eighty miles inland over the rough dirt road to

Grahamstown awaited them. Leaving the salty tang of the sea air behind, travelling by cart or ox wagon, on a journey lasting several days, they would sleep overnight in tents or under a wagon. Summer was giving way to autumn, the nights already turning colder.

During the day there were unfamiliar sounds, the creaking of the ox wagons as they rumbled along unmade roads, often rutted by the passage of previous wagons or washed out by rain. Black-skinned men and boys drove the oxen forward with the threatening sound of the loud cracks of their long, curling whips. Day and night came the calls of new animals: hyenas, jackals, with wild dogs and baboons barking. Out of range of the travellers' guns, sometimes silhouetted on the horizon or hiding behind koppies (small rocky hills), were the sights of strange animals: quagga, antelope, springbuck, eland and more. Along the way there were unfamiliar plants such as euphorbias, plumbago and aloes, plants like the strelitzias that in a later age would be found in garden centres on sale waiting to grace European gardens.

Along with most of the new arrivals, Augustus, Evelina and their children can have had no more than the slightest inkling of conditions in the land in which they planned to make their new life, among its many peoples embedded in a different history.

*

From 1652 onwards waves of white people of varied European nationalities planted their seed in southern Africa. In the beginning of these things 'the Cape' was a promontory that European sailors attempted to round before heading further in search of a sea route to the East. It is not the southernmost point in Africa, although to some it must have seemed so. More often than not it amounted to no more than a distant view of a chunk of Africa seen from the sea. It is said that the Phoenicians came this way but records are scant. What is certain is that Portuguese navigators rounded the Cape in the fifteenth century, in what later became known as the Age of Discovery. They were the first Europeans to reach this far, first Bartolomeu Dias in 1488 to whom, buffeted by rough seas, it was Cabo das Tormentas, the Cape of Storms. Vasco da Gama followed in 1498 and continued on into the Indian Ocean before reaching Calicut. He was the first person to sail directly from Europe to India. The sea route to India was now open for business. These early navigators did not settle at the Cape. Bartolomeu Dias and his crew died in these waters when his ship sank in a storm near the Cape in 1500. For them it certainly was the Cape of Storms. No trace of their vessel has ever been found.

An Englishman, Sir Francis Drake, rounding the Cape in 1580, saw it in more favourable conditions, describing it as 'the fairest cape we saw in the whole circumference of the earth'.

Around the Cape to this day there may still lurk the ghost ship, *The Flying Dutchman*, the stuff of myths, legends, and Wagner's opera of that name. Less romantically perhaps, it is now a place where round-the-world yachtsmen and women call to replenish provisions or make repairs.

JAN VAN RIEBEECK AND THE ARRIVAL OF THE DUTCH

European settlers did not arrive at the Cape until the seventeenth century. Apart, arguably, from the missionaries, settler motives from the start were based almost entirely on self-interest or, more charitably, exploration for the sake of exploration, a sense of adventure, or the quest to prove there was more beyond the shores of Europe. Or was it simply 'because it is there', the four little words about climbing Everest famously ascribed to George Mallory who died on the mountain in 1924.

In 1652 Jan van Riebeeck, acting for the Dutch East India Company, established 'the tavern of the seas', a fort for security and a market garden to improve the diets of ships' companies by providing fresh produce for vessels sailing around the Cape trading between Europe and the East. The settlement at the foot of the great southern mountain would later grow up to become Kaapstad, or Cape Town. For the moment it was a way station for those trading between the Netherlands and Batavia. Fresh produce reduced the incidence of scurvy, the vitamin C deficiency which caused serious health conditions for sailors on dry rations. The motive for reducing scurvy was to an extent economic rather than humane: fit, living sailors cost less.

The market garden produced not only vegetables and fruit, for in 1659 van Riebeeck noted in his journal, 'Today, glory be to God, wine was pressed for the first time and the new *must* fresh from the tub was tasted'. 'Must' is freshly crushed grape juice including the skins, seeds and stems of the grapes which mostly made muscadel. If the wine was inferior, nonetheless the Cape's oldest industry had been born.

In this understated way a white tribe of Dutch Europeans began to settle in the area. Gradually they spread out, establishing fine estates and houses in the Dutch colonial style. Later, English-speaking and other European settlers would follow, bringing in their midst missionaries, traders, farmers and soldiers, rogues and vagabonds, many of whom may have meant well, although 'well for whom?' was always the unspoken question.

It did not begin as a serious land grab by Europeans wanting a large slice of the continent. In time things would turn out rather differently. For now, the nineteenth-century 'scramble for Africa' and the discovery of diamonds and gold were not due for another two centuries. Inevitably, a proportion of these early settlers, mainly but not exclusively from the Netherlands, whether administrators, soldiers, or those who farmed the vegetables and fruit, stayed on, married and had children. They spoke Dutch and their descendants became the Afrikaners, their language a colonial derivative of Dutch. They would later become the bedrock of the majority members of the white tribe of South Africa, proud of their heritage.

In this beginning the Cape became a Dutch colony.

HUGUENOTS

Another significant, though smaller, group of Europeans arrived in 1688 and 1689. These were the Huguenot refugees fleeing from religious persecution, of whom 180 were from Catholic France, as well as eighteen Walloons from what is now Belgium. In time there were more. The Huguenots are remembered not least for the skills they brought with them wherever they went, and at the Cape this was notably wine-making as in the aptly named area around Franschhoek, 'French Corner'.

LET BATTLES COMMENCE, THE EARLY WARS WITH THE XHOSA

It might have all turned out so very differently if only the European settlers had entered an empty continent devoid of other people. There was every possibility that, in the event, they could have felt at ease and lived at peace amongst other white-skinned people. The Tancreds, their predecessors and successors, would have found it easy enough to rub shoulders with those such people from the Netherlands or France or other European nations. But no, they would, from the moment of their arrival, have become aware of people who were not white-skinned, did not speak a European language, and therein lay the time bomb waiting to explode – the ire of the indigenous people who regarded the land as their land. If the incomers saw their presence as a civilising influence, it was not a dish served to everyone's taste.

Crucial amongst the disaffected were the Xhosa to the east, and the notion of land theft is how the Xhosa came to see matters. There were others in the Cape, the Khoikhoi, the traditionally nomadic pastoralist indigenous population, once known as Hottentots, and the San people. If one selling point justifying white settlement was bringing civilisation to Africa, it was not appreciated by the intended recipients. Augustus and family would soon become a part of the maelstrom of distress affecting both black and white people. The early Europeans had not entered a paradise of milk, honey and easy livings and on discovering this simple fact raged at 'man's ingratitude' to man. The settlers came to see the Xhosa as cattle thieves prone to damaging farms, murdering settlers, and little more than land thieves by another name.

In the first war against the Xhosa, or from a Xhosa viewpoint the first war against the settlers (1779–1781), Dutch settler grievances over the alleged theft of cattle by the Xhosa led to an armed response, resulting in the recapture of at least some of the cattle. This was followed by a period of relative calm with the Dutch confident that they had driven the Xhosa back from an area known as the Zuurveld (sour land, an area between the Sundays and Great Fish rivers). If this was seen by the Dutch as a victory, the ensuing peace proved illusory.

The Dutch viewed the second war (1789–1793) as unfinished business. This time a Xhosa clan moved back into the Zuurveld, leading to Dutch settlers joining forces with a branch of the Xhosas to repel the invaders. This kerfuffle was enough to cause Dutch farms to be temporarily abandoned. The frontier was now confirmed to be an unsafe, inhospitable place.

The third war (1799–1803) was an altogether more serious affair covering a wider area. This time the Khoikhoi and the San joined with the Xhosas and attacked white farms to regain land they still saw as belonging to them. The Dutch government in Cape Town, anticipating a wider Khoi rebellion, did a deal with the Xhosa which allowed them to remain in the Zuurveld. If this resulted in peace, it once again proved short-lived. It must by now have seemed self-evident to the white Dutch settlers that they might never be welcomed by the non-white people in this newfound land. History would roll on to prove it was a collision of worlds that might never conclude in a satisfactory resolution. The blueprint of the future of southern Africa was already on the drawing board.

DUTCH TO BRITISH

The political map of southern Africa changed again. The Cape had been a Dutch possession from 1652 to 1795, then briefly British in 1795 when Britain was at war with France and determined to secure communications with India. The Cape was Dutch again from 1803 to 1806 when, after the Battle of Blaauwberg (or Battle of Cape Town), the British ruled once again. The Anglo-Dutch Treaty in 1814 finalised this settlement. The Cape was now a British colony, administered by a Governor in Cape Town following policies laid down by the Colonial Secretary in Downing Street, London, and ultimately the British Parliament.

At the time of the Tancreds' arrival at the Cape this meant the security of the frontier was now a British responsibility with a naval base at Cape Town on the sea route to India and an army presence on the land. If the security of the trade with India was a benefit, the cost in terms of the civil administration and resources for the British Army would, from now on, weigh heavily on London.

Because of the large number of Dutch inhabitants, a new element in British colonial policy was added to the mix. It became seen as desirable to increase the proportion of English-speaking settlers. This coincided with the simultaneous perceived need to vent some of the surplus population in Britain.

Tensions became a long-running feature of relations between those in the established area in and around Cape Town, and those in the settler territory, especially the Albany district in the Eastern Cape, the frontier between the settlers and the Xhosa. Successive governors, aided by the British Army, endeavoured to manage this tension, seldom to the satisfaction of one and all. Continuing unrest persisted on the frontier with settler versus Xhosa, English-speaker versus Afrikaner, and the ever-present feeling that relative to Cape Town and the surrounding area, the Eastern Cape was always short-changed. This eventually led to a campaign for greater autonomy.

By the time of the fourth war (1811–1812) the British were aware of the costs incurred by their possession of the Cape which was now seen as something of a poisoned chalice, sucking in the resources of the British Army and making financial demands on the British Exchequer. The fourth settler war, the first involving the British, was a dress rehearsal for much that followed between the white settlers and black indigenous peoples. The Zuurveld, established as a buffer zone between the white settlers to the west and the Xhosa to the east, was defined by porous boundaries. When the Xhosa entered what was supposed to be an empty area there were incidents at the interface with the white settlers. The British under Colonel John

Graham responded with a mixed military force and drove the Xhosa out of the Zuurveld and beyond the Fish River. The then Governor of the Cape Colony (Cradock) explained in chilling words that the bloodshed suffered by the Xhosa was 'necessary to impress on the minds of these savages a proper degree of terror and respect'.[19] Race relations in southern Africa were not off to a promising start.

SLACHTER'S NEK, 1815

Relationships between the Dutch settlers and the colonial British power would also soon deteriorate. Significant numbers of Dutch settlers moved inland from the Cape Town area as farmers, hence the origin of the description 'Boer' or 'Boere', or 'Boers' to the English – the word 'boer' meaning a farmer, often carrying a dismissive tone. Tensions, arising from the perceived preferential treatment afforded to those living in or near Cape Town, the hub of the colony, were about to get a whole lot worse.

Slachter's Nek, literally Butcher's Mountain Pass, was the site of a Dutch settler rebellion on the Eastern Cape Frontier. It also saw a prime example of the ability of the British to make crass and inhumane decisions, the consequences of which would echo down the years.

In 1815, Frederik Bezuidenhout, a settler of Dutch extraction, farmed on the eastern border of the colony. Accused of the ill-treatment of one of his Khoi labourers he was summoned to appear at the local magistrates'

19 L.M. Thompson, *A History of South Africa*, 3rd edition, 2001. Yale University Press, quoted in Wikipedia 'Xhosa Wars'.

court. After resisting arrest, he fled to a cave where he was shot dead when 'coloured' (mixed race) soldiers were sent to capture him. To white Dutch settlers a white man being shot by a non-white man for mistreating a non-white employee marked an incendiary moment in the history of the Cape. To many Dutch settlers it was a grievance amplified by the fact that it occurred under, and was a direct result of, the authority of the British who, to make matters worse, were seen as making no effort to ensure their safety or to redress the numbers of cattle stolen by Xhosa tribesmen. Seen as favouring non-white people over white people, this made for a flash point among the Dutch farmers, a group of whom set about preparing an uprising against the British.

In November, a rebel commando met the local British military commander on the frontier at a place called Slachter's Nek. Unfortunately, perhaps, if coincidentally, the Dutch '*slachter*' means 'butcher'. When negotiations failed, the rebel party departed peacefully. Cuyler, the Military Commander ('Landdrost'), was not content to let the matter rest there and set out to arrest the rebels. Some surrendered and others, when they refused, were pursued by the colonial forces. In the end only Hans Bezuidenhout, brother of Frederik, did not surrender and died resisting arrest.

Wise heads atop the British military and associated body politic might have seen the wisdom of letting matters rest there. It was not to be. Twenty rebels were brought for trial before the court in Uitenhage. Although most were acquitted, six were sentenced to death. Although one was pardoned by the Governor, Lord Charles Somerset, five were hanged in public at a place called Van Aardt Pos in 1816. If that was not bad enough as a public relations disaster, four of the nooses broke during the hanging, only for the executioner to order the living men to be hanged a second time, in spite of the victims and their families pleading for their lives.

The Dutch struggle against British rule, and for many a hatred of the English, had gained a new momentum. They now had a notion of themselves as freedom fighters, and their resistance certainly did not end there. Nor did the British capacity for calamitous political judgements. By the end of the century, when diamonds and gold were the prizes, the Boers would come close to toppling the armed might of the British Empire.

Meanwhile, the fifth war (1818–1819) was waiting in the wings. In 1817 officials of the government of the colony in Cape Town decided that the Xhosa must return cattle stolen in the disputed area in the Eastern Cape. Stolen cattle, land seizure and overcrowding in the Xhosa territory would continue to be a source of friction between the British forces, together with the white settlers, and the Xhosa. A Xhosa, both Chief and prophet, promised to overrun the white settlers and drive them into the sea. His name was Maqana Nxele, otherwise known as Makana, and he made the bold, if unrealistic, claim that he had the power to turn bullets into water. It did not work.

In 1819 Makana, now armed with a superior force of an estimated 10,000 men, attacked Grahamstown, the military headquarters of Lieutenant-Colonel Graham, defended by 350 British troops. A ferocious battle ensued. Captain W.W. Harding, one of the British officers present at the engagement, later said that he 'absolutely thought the savages would have gained the day'.[20] It was in fact a close-run thing but superior firepower won the day. The British garrison and the white settlers were saved. Defeat for the British might have seen the settlers swept from the frontier in full retreat towards Algoa Bay at the coast or even as far as Cape Town. In one form or another it was an ambition of indigenous black people against what they identified as invading white settlers that would linger down the years. For the moment it was another war ending in defeat for the Xhosa. It is somewhat misleading to see the conflict as one between the British Army and the settlers against a united Xhosa population. There were some divisions within the Xhosa ranks which were at times exploited by the British.

The Xhosa losses were estimated at 1,000 killed in the battle. Makana was captured and became the first member of a distinguished group of freedom fighters (or terrorists depending on the point of view) imprisoned on Robben Island. Attempting to escape, he drowned. In June 2018 Grahamstown was renamed Makhanda. To some it seemed that the losers were now the victors.

Cattle raids on the settler farms continued to provoke a drastic response from the British in the sixth war (1834–1836). This time it was the killing of a chief that enraged the Xhosa who assembled an army of as many as 10,000 men who advanced across the frontier seizing cattle, burning farmhouses and killing settlers. A flood of refugees poured into Grahamstown and found shelter in the church. By

---

20 Noël Mostert, *Frontiers*, 478.

the late 1830s the British Army was replacing the .75 calibre Brown Bess musket with the vastly more effective muzzle-loading rifles with smaller calibres. The British Army, together with Boer commandos, launched a fierce counter-attack which proved decisive. Many were killed in these actions, black and white, and the survivors were often hungry and homeless. The frontier now seemed a dangerous, inhospitable place to live the farming life.

THE GREAT TREK, 1836

If the Xhosa were not best suited to life under the British, then neither were the Boers. The Dutch settlers had never rested easily under the yoke of British colonial policy.

Very often present circumstances contain roots that reach far down into the past. The antipathy between Dutch and English-speaking colonists illustrates this point. In the immediate aftermath of the ending of the sixth war in 1836, Piet Retief, a Boer (whose family were of French Huguenot ancestry), who had grown up on the family wine farm near Wellington in the Western Cape, came to the fore as an unsuccessful entrepreneur who became a land speculator and, in short order, a highly successful Boer leader. There were many occasions when, faced with a common danger, Boer and Briton closed ranks. In addition to the British Army presence in the Eastern Cape, there were a number of settler militias of whom the Boers were often the most effective. Piet Retief had himself been active in the bloody sixth war. Like many Boers and British settlers he was disillusioned with conditions on the frontier.

Increasingly disaffected by British rather than their

preferred Dutch rule, Boer grievances began to multiply. the British Army was seen as ineffective in protecting the frontier; the abolition of slavery, crucial to the financial viability of their farms; and the increasing number of British, hence English-speaking rather than Dutch-speaking settlers.

The abolition of slavery was a particular bone of contention with the feeling among the owners that the compensation they received for freed slaves was inadequate and that, with abolition introduced at the start of the harvest season, slave labour became unavailable at the worst possible time. Retief drew up a manifesto outlining the Boer grievances. His manifesto fell on deaf British ears. Totally disenchanted with colonial rule by 'the English' officials in Cape Town, and ultimately London, he decided to leave the frontier and find a territory beyond the Cape Colony that could become a Boer republic. Retief and others were part of a Dutch exodus from the Eastern Cape, known as the Great Trek, an exodus of almost biblical proportions that later attained mythical status in the annals of the Afrikaner people. The gap they left behind meant more farms becoming available for British settlers. It also meant the loss of the highly effective fighting force formerly seen in the Boer commandos. All this added to the fault line that would run through South African society for over 300 years with layers of mistrust, as unyielding as granite, forming between Boer and Briton, side by side with that between black and white. It was a country getting used to people speaking different languages disliking one another, side by side with people forging barriers of prejudice based on skin colour.

Settling in at Basford and Bulwell in Nottinghamshire in England in 1836, Augustus would no doubt have been oblivious to events in Africa. The Tancreds reached the Cape in 1842 during a ten-year lull in the frontier wars. Although technically a period of peace, the underlying problems remained unresolved, the accompanying tensions never far below the surface.

For a while there seemed to be some grounds for optimism. Thanks in no small part due to the enlightened views and policies of Andries Stockenström, then Lieutenant-Governor of the Eastern Province and veteran of earlier Xhosa wars, a more harmonious relationship between Xhosa and settler might have been achieved. He introduced a new policy with treaties based on respect for the Xhosa, and this trust proved mutual. For a while there was a brief opportunity to forge something different. But his ideas fell on unsympathetic white ears and before long, following an energetic campaign by Robert Godlonton, the Stockenström approach was consigned to the dustbin of history.

Godlonton was an 1820 settler who in 1838 became a partner in the *Grahamstown Journal* and then in 1839 the owner. As editor of the *Grahamstown Journal*, he was well placed to campaign against Stockenström's ideas. Godlonton believed among other things that 'the British race was selected by God himself to colonize Kaffraria'. In this he anticipated the later racial arrogance of Cecil John Rhodes. Godlonton's book, *A Narrative of the Irruption of the Kaffir Hordes into the Eastern Province of the Cape of Good Hope, 1834–1835*, indicated – both by the language of the title and the detail in the content – the predominantly racist outlook of the white settler community which hastened the abandonment by the Governor in Cape Town of the treaties negotiated with the Xhosa and the dismissal of Stockenström as Lieutenant-Governor of the Eastern Province. What may have been the last opportunity to deflect a false step in the direction of Cape history was lost.

Neither Captain Donaldson of the *George*, the 'old trader' who had advertised that he was 'well acquainted with the place' and willing to 'give every information to persons about emigrating to this flourishing colony', nor the Colonial Office in London, had warned intending settlers of these dangers or of other difficulties that they might encounter.

As Augustus and Evelina would soon discover, the Cape was not a place where he might make his fortune, but rather a place where the tensions between Boer and Briton, black and white, were firmly in place. They were now in ringside seats for the outbreak of the seventh settler war which came four years later in 1846, ending in 1847.

18

THIS FLOURISHING COLONY

'Dr' Tancred, his wife and their three children arrived from England with no known visible means of financial support. Discounting the remote possibility that he was a man possessing private means, the family breadwinner faced an urgent need to earn an income.

As with each new beginning for the family, it was reasonable to assume that from such a low base, things could only get better. Looking back in 1846 to his arrival in 1842, Augustus had begun with just such a belief:

> In 1842 I left England with a view to acquire an independence in this Colony of whose flourishing condition I heard so much. I arrived at Algoa Bay with a number of Lord Western's best sheep, and proceeded to Graham's Town, where I thought nothing could exist to prevent me immediately commencing sheep farming. A.J. Tancred, *Letters to Sir Peregrine Maitland*, 1846

When it turned out very differently it was of course not his fault, and for once there was some truth in this. The frontier had been relatively peaceful since the end of the sixth war in 1836. He did not immediately commence sheep farming but instead, for reasons unknown, applied his talents in other directions.

After many false starts and deviations, now was surely not the moment to choose another path, yet one more of the sensible roads not taken. But he was alive with ideas. Surely, he may have thought, having set forth from England intending to become a farmer, a temporary change of plan could do no harm? He was, after and above all, a man of intellect rather than a practical man. It would be a while before his thoughts returned to tilling the soil. For the best part of four years that would remain the road not taken, a route barred.

THE AUTHOR

Saturday 12 June 1842 marked the memorable moment when he would enlighten his fellow settlers with his thoughts on polite philosophy. If they did not see the need, he certainly did. But what are the primary needs of settlers in the remote corner of a turbulent land? First of all, physical survival, shelter, food, water, clothing suited to all weathers and, above all, safety. Given the frictions inherent in settler life, did he foresee a need for a calming balm when tempers frayed? Could he not fulfil his economic potential as a husband and father while at the same time making a contribution to the amelioration of frictions in the community he had so recently joined? The answer was at hand: he would offer his fellow settlers his thoughts on polite philosophy thus enabling them to resolve any differences between them.

To accomplish this goal, he would become an author, an occupation that would match his many talents while providing a steady income. Alas, a moment's reflection might have persuaded him that philosophy, polite or otherwise, was neither of primary concern nor marketable to the settler community.

But no, he was a man in need of an income. After all, his earlier volume, *Sermons,* published in England in 1834, had come with a gold-plated endorsement when it appeared 'under the special patronage of Her Majesty's Royal Parent, I ventured and succeeded'. Her Majesty was of course Queen Victoria. Victoria's father, the Duke of Kent, died shortly after her birth so he cannot be the royal parent in question. This must therefore have been her mother, Princess Victoria of Saxe-Coburg-Saalfeld. How, or if, Augustus obtained this good lady's blessing on his book remains a mystery. How might someone from his station in life, at that time a workhouse chaplain at Basford and curate of the nearby church at Bulwell, both in Nottinghamshire, have obtained such an endorsement? Veracity was never his strongest card. Was it possible to advance such a claim unchallenged? He did so claim and yet it never seems to have been subjected to scrutiny.

When publishing his treatise on polite philosophy in Grahamstown in 1842, he also boastfully proclaimed that he did 'venture and trust that I shall not be less successful in Africa than in Europe'. Had he momentarily forgotten that his book, *Sermons,* was not a resounding commercial success in Europe? Might Africa prove any different? Would it sell well and bring him a tidy profit? The idea he had in mind may have preoccupied him before he left England, or as he whiled away the hours on the long sea voyage to the Cape. He was now set on earning his living as an author. The most junior market researcher would have advised him against this direction.

There is another possible explanation. Was his book ready for publication when he landed at the Cape? It seems unlikely that he could have completed it after his arrival in time to publish it a mere three months later. Much more likely is that it simply adds credence to the unsubstantiated claim by a later detractor (William Porter) that he was not the author, but someone who brought with him another man's book which he published under his own name. The scoundrel, a plagiarist without equal! Or was he?

Whatever the truth of the book's provenance, Augustus approached Robert Godlonton, the Grahamstown printer, publisher and newspaper editor, and ordered a print run of copies of *A Treatise on Polite Philosophy, or an Easy Manner of Settling Differences Among Men*, by the Reverend Augustus J. Tancred, D.D., M.L.S.N. No records of the cost of this venture, nor the size of the print run, nor sales of this slim volume survive.[21] Had it sold well, he may have hoped to sit back in the sun and pen a further volume. It was not to be. Differences among women, or women and men, do not seem to have required his advice, nor, for that matter, differences between people with different skin colours.

It no doubt quickly became evident even to Augustus

---

21 It can be purchased in a facsimile edition.

that his advice on interpersonal conduct, however necessary, was not welcomed. Facts now had to be faced: he was not about to earn a living from his writings. The likely balance sheet at the end of the day must have read: expenditure, significant; sales, disappointing; resulting income, negligible.

Then all of a sudden, and for unknown reasons, things once again took a turn for the worse.

TANCRED UP FOR SALE

In Nottingham he had sold up lock, stock and barrel when financial disaster struck. He was now about to repeat the performance. This indicated a new dire financial calamity which intervened before Augustus took his next step along his career at the Cape.

On 28 July 1842 the *Grahamstown Journal* announced that 'The Rev Dr Tancred, about to leave Grahams Town, will offer for sale ON SATURDAY WEEK several very valuable conveniences which have been brought out for his own appointment.' Why was he leaving Grahamstown some four months after his arrival? Was he planning to leave not only Grahamstown but the Eastern Cape, or even the Cape Colony, as well? Was Evelina homesick and pressing for a return to Europe? Her life at the Cape was so very different from the world in Ireland where she grew up.

Had Augustus sniffed the local air and found it wanting, concluding that the settler life in this place was not for him and his family? Was it time once again to shake the dust off his feet? Or was he simply drained dry of available funds sufficient to meet his day-to-day living expenses and, perhaps, the cost of publishing his *Pocket Companion*?

*

This was the extraordinary list of items he offered for sale: a self-cooking, wood-consuming apparatus which could prepare a dinner for twenty in about one hour and a half; some iron-mounted French bedsteads, bedding and a sofa; very valuable and rare works in the German, Italian, French, Hebrew, Greek, Latin and English languages; Catholic and Protestant works of Divinity in Latin, French and English; a very highly finished rifle, percussion lock, hair trigger, case, all complete; cast-iron chess table, enamelled top; several masons', carpenters', farmers' and gardening tools; ploughs, saddles, bridles; travelling trunks and patent straps.

These items were ALL WITHOUT RESERVE and also included were SIX PURE MERINO RAMS, these being a 'special selection from Lord Western's flock'.

The sale was in the hands of J.D. Norden and Co., Auctioneers.

Another advertisement on the same day showed 'French Merino Rams' at sale for £12 each. Were these the same as the 'special selection from Lord Western's flock' with the additional cachet of a French connection?

On 4 August the newspaper advised that the sale had been postponed to Tuesday 16th. The sale appears to have attracted little interest.

A further advertisement appeared on 11 August, now on the front page at the top of the column. Did Augustus purchase most of this rather strange mix of 'conveniences' in England, rather than on arrival at the Cape? The sheep certainly seemed to come with him from England. If the other items were brought from England the cost of transport as cargo aboard the *George* would have been enormous. Wherever these goods were purchased the vendors seem to have seen him coming and leapt at the opportunity to fill their own purses.

The list still consisted of many of the items in the original advertisement, with some rebranded: the large iron-mounted bedstead was now 'with casters etc.', as well as linen tickes (sic), and horse hair mattresses. The rare and valuable books in English were now without a reserve price. Some extra items were added: a patent weighing machine, a large coffee mill, shot, powder, lead etc., a very excellent horse and, somewhat obscurely, a share in the Albany Library. Also to be sold was a complete set of 'the Waverley novels' (Walter Scott) in forty-eight volumes. The other items on the original list appear to have been sold. Some of these items – the horse, the share in the library, and most probably the shot, powder and lead – had been procured locally.

Then on 25 August the paper announced yet another extension of the date of the sale, now due on Wednesday 31 August.

But why, having reached their destination, was he now selling up and leaving Grahamstown? And leaving for where, and to do what?

It is impossible not to feel for Evelina, seemingly no more than a bystander faced with her husband's erratic actions. What were her feelings, thoughts and actions? Once before, in Nottinghamshire, she had seen the entire

176

contents of their household put up for sale. And now this. Did her husband's latest debacle bring her to a new low ebb, in a foreign land, away from family and friends, penniless once again? Had it been her family that put up the money? That would have added additional salt to the wound.

At this point the line of enquiry peters out like waves sinking into the sand on a beach: there is no indication that the sale actually took place or, if it did, which of the items found new homes.

It was time now for another fresh start. Having apparently sold the six of Lord Western's best sheep that accompanied him from England he had clearly abandoned the idea of farming in Africa. Instead, why not try something completely new, another occupation that would come easily to a man lacking neither skill, knowledge nor experience? There was before him the example of what such a man might achieve.

AVELINE, AN ASIDE, A REGRETTABLY SHORT STORY

On 10 January 1839, the *Grahamstown Journal* informed its readers that 'the Rev. Mr. Aveline, who has been appointed Pastor of the Baptist Church, Grahamstown, has reached his destination in safety, and that he has entered upon his pastoral labours with a very pleasing and encouraging prospect of future usefulness'.

As evidence of his pastoral labours *The History of the Baptist Church in South Africa* recounts how Aveline, a bachelor, 'within a month of his settlement as pastor, advertised for a certain number of young gentlemen as boarders and day pupils, and established an academy, restricting the number in the first instance to eight – four resident and four non-resident'. By the time of the report of the Sunday School anniversary on 25 April 1839, it was 'stated that there were 90 English children and 40 Coloured, also that a school had been commenced at Bush Hoek, on the borders of Uitenhage, where there were 40 children in attendance'. This must indeed have seemed 'a very pleasing and encouraging prospect of future usefulness'.

By the time of Tancred's arrival in Grahamstown in 1842, Aveline's reputation seems to have continued to flourish as when, on the 12 March 1843, the Bathurst Street Chapel was opened, it was said that Mr Aveline delivered an 'eloquent and animated speech'. Then, in May, he 'delivered an address at the annual meeting of the Public Library, which was printed in the *Grahamstown Journal*'.

This was his high point on the frontier, for his success was not to last. *The History of the Baptist Church in South Africa* rounds off the story:

> Soon after this the career of Mr. Aveline ended in disaster. He committed a grievous offence, to which he pleaded guilty, and was sentenced to two years' imprisonment on Robben Island, and afterwards banishment for life. This is a sad page in the history of the Church, which no doubt caused much grief and injury to the cause, the influence of which was not wholly gone as late as 1877.

But to an alert observer of the scene it did at least prove that education could thrive in the colony.

A tantalising year elapsed after the Tancred sale during which nothing is known of Augustus. In 1843 he was still in Grahamstown and hatching his new plan for making money.

This was the moment when the inhabitants witnessed the entry, stage left, of Augustus the would-be colonial educationalist. The settler parents in the area, and he was after all one himself, would surely welcome a school for their children? What other activity could better engage their support and bring an income for a man of his high education and intellect? Surely Aveline had shown by example what might be possible?

Starting a school was the obvious answer. Notwithstanding his lack of any experience establishing, running or teaching in a school, he could surely plug the hole in the market. As it would be a commercial venture, he would of course charge fees. It would not be any old school, but rather a Tancred school modelled on Oxford University.

The necessary qualities for a school at that time and place seem fairly clear. Bearing in mind the nature of frontier settlements there was a need for boys to acquire a wide range of practical skills to equip them to make and mend equipment, build houses, work with wood and metal, shoot, and become hard-working, skilful farmers in a strange and at times hostile environment. Girls would marry, bear children, benefit from some training in domestic skills, learn how to manage the servants. Married women, with husbands and children to care for, must at least be trained to cook, sew and manage the household so that their children would grow into stalwart citizens, their husbands the beneficiaries of a comfortable home life when they came in from their farms or other workplaces. By such means domestic and economic harmony would reign across the region! Such was the caricature of that world long gone in a lot of places, if not all.

The Bible was important, for surely the settlers were in Africa not solely to enhance their own pockets, but simultaneously to advance the spiritual state of the heathen population fortunate enough to bear witness to their arrival in this previously godforsaken place. Religion and commerce were always uncomfortable bedfellows in the colonial mindset.

*

Although there is no record of the local response, readers of the *Grahamstown Journal,* on 15 June 1843, may have been a little perplexed to read an advertisement with details of the educational provision that Tancred had in mind for the education of their children.

Dr Augustus J. Tancred, L.L.D., D.D., was to be the founder and self-appointed principal of a new school in the town, the 'Albany College', into which he would be willing to enrol ten to twelve pupils, either as day boys or boarders. It would be an establishment for boys only and would certainly not include the 'coloured' children in the Reverend Aveline's scheme of things. In time, as the college expanded, he would be happy to unite with three or more men of classical and scientific education to enable the establishment to expand. Should the college meet with success, professors of ability would be sought to fill the different chairs of literature.

Students would be required to attend in the college-dress of Oxford: black cloth caps and silk tassels, with long camlet coats. There was no mention of a school clothing supplier in Grahamstown able to supply such apparel. Might clothing suited to Oxford prove rather warm in the climate of Grahamstown in summer? These questions seemed not to trouble the lofty mind of Augustus.

He continued, pointing out that the aim of the education he provided would be to equip those destined for careers in any of the learned professions or mercantile pursuits. Would young men so equipped be much in demand? He seems not to have studied the labour market nor considered the education of girls.

The curriculum included an impressive array of subjects. Dr Tancred would himself be in charge of instruction in Latin, Greek, Hebrew, English, French, Elocution, Rhetoric, Logic and Metaphysics (the latter if required), with yet-to-be-recruited staff to take care of Italian, Reading, Writing, Geography, Arithmetic, Algebra, Mathematics, History (both sacred and profane). It was beginning to sound like a lengthy and expensive list of staff for a college starting out with ten or twelve pupils. When, in time, he came to enlarge the school, boarders would be admitted. Nothing is said about premises to house this ambitious project.

Examinations would be half-yearly and public. As a bonus, 'Dr. Tancred will occasionally deliver lectures to the students, at which the public may attend gratis.'

In view of the importance of elocution, strict attention would be paid to this, as in the public lectures lately delivered in England by Dr Tancred, regulated by the principles contained and approved by men eminent for learning. Mrs Kirkpatrick in Cork had remarked on his 'sonorous' voice. How well did that on top of an Irish accent go down in Grahamstown?

In addition to literature, the arts and sciences, students would be familiarised with the passing occurrences of the day, perhaps in modern parlance 'current affairs'.

Needless to say, none of this came free and parents would have to agree to pay a two-guinea entrance fee as well as fees of £20 per annum, payable quarterly, in advance. There would be extra charges for music, drawing, painting, dancing, fencing, medical attendance, the postage of letters, and the purchase of schoolbooks.

As was to be expected at the time there are one or two notable omissions from the languages on offer: the curriculum included no local languages, Dutch or Xhosa.

What did the townspeople make of Tancred's Albany College? What indeed. Alas, history is silent on the matter. Probably not very much. The settler parents in the area may not have taken long to decide that this menu of learning on offer either fell short of, or exceeded some of, the educational needs of their children. In devising the advertisement, a prospectus really, he no doubt expended a good deal of time and effort. Or was it a copy of a similar advertisement brought with him in his luggage from England? Perhaps Godlonton, the newspaper editor, welcomed the fee attached to such a large advertisement.

No more was heard of the Albany College and little more of his own children's education in Africa. His attempts to become an author or educationalist seem to account for most of his two seemingly 'inactive' years in Grahamstown.

The Reverend Aveline lived on Settlers Hill and, although I am unable to confirm that this was contemporaneous, Tancred lived two doors away on the same street. Both men were certainly resident in Grahamstown at this time. Was it no more than coincidence that at about this time Tancred advertised his Albany College? Did Aveline's school provide him with the idea, its failure pointing to a sudden gap in the market? And did Aveline's reputation as an educationalist leave settler parents wary of anyone advertising a school? Could this in part explain the apparent lack of interest in Tancred's Albany College or was it just too whacky for Grahamstown?

Once again it was onward and possibly upward, or perhaps not, and to what? Success in the colony had so far eluded him; might success lie ahead around the next corner? Farming perhaps? Hadn't farming been his first thought?

A typical early settler view was that the country was well suited to sheep farming. And who had sold his sheep, not any old sheep but some of Lord Western's best sheep? Had he not once owned a horse, only to sell it? It meant starting from scratch. Suddenly he was in need of livestock, farming equipment of various kinds and, not least, a farm. It was not long before the seventh war broke out in 1846.

With two failures since arriving at the Cape behind him Augustus must have pondered 'what next?' If he was ever to become a successful farmer this was the worst possible moment to put it to the test. So he put it to the test.

19

LIFE AND DEATH ON THE FRONTIER

Such few details as can be found about his new career, as he entered into a farming life in the colony, begin to crop up from time to time either in his own writings or recorded in the *Grahamstown Journal.* In March 1845, three years after his arrival at the Cape, it was reported that the Reverend Augustus Tancred had acquired James Wilmot's allotment in Beaufort Vale near Bathurst. The timing was inauspicious with the next war awaiting around the corner in March 1846.

The farm meant the family moving out of town to a rural area some twenty-six miles beyond the comparative safety of Grahamstown. Here Augustus embraced the farming life by combining his undoubted vigour with his limited skill and knowledge. He soon immersed himself in the concerns he now shared with the local settler community, concerns almost exclusively related to safety on the frontier and the ongoing grievances about the standard of governance in the Eastern Cape.

Baines' picture of Bathurst in 1849 shows a town not very different from the way it was when the Tancreds arrived. A scattered collection of settler houses, ranging from the simplest to the more sophisticated, are all overlooked by a simple church on the distant hillside. An ox wagon lurches, creaking, through a dip in the road, the oxen led by a black man, the driver seated with a long, curving leather whip snaking ahead of the lead oxen. Waiting before the road curves around to the left is a white woman in a white skirt and red blouse. Is she expecting a delivery from the heavily loaded wagon? A black man walks ahead of her, perhaps a working member of the reception party. A couple are working in a field in front of one of the cottages. It is not difficult to imagine the sounds of the wagon, the shuddering, jolting of the well-used timber of its construction, the creaking of the axles, the crack from the whip, the shouts from the driver. Supplies are reaching Bathurst. It is a town engaging in commerce in which black and white people are involved; black people already appear in the minor roles. It all looks very peaceful. On the frontier at this time peace was a relative term, and always short-lived.

James Wilmot was one of a number of the early settlers who gradually dispersed away from the frontier. Originally a lawyer, James and his wife, Ann, of Little Ormond Street, Queen Square, London, were 1820 settler members of Willson's Party. Wilmot employed four servants, one of whom had the misfortune to die on the voyage. The presence of servants indicated a degree of affluence and social class. Willson was only chosen to lead the party because an official in the Colonial Office confused two names, Willson and Wilson. Unfortunately, Willson proved to be a disreputable character who abandoned the settlers and returned to Algoa Bay as soon as they reached their destination in Beaufort Vale. Later, James Wilmot must have decided that after twenty-five years as a farmer in the area it was time to move on, a fairly typical experience as settlers moved from insecure rural settings to urban areas where they might hope for employment using the skills they had acquired at home.

As he was able to buy a farm, Augustus was clearly not penniless at this time. He was now a landowner dependent on farming for the family income but with conditions on the frontier deteriorating all the while. It was not long before the Tancreds would reach yet another turning point in their lives.

The complaints by the settlers focused on thefts of cattle or attacks on property. On 6 March 1845, Augustus noted that 'a plunder was committed on myself'. By 30 March he was describing how the deteriorating situation affected the family:

> … cattle stolen. My servants and myself went in pursuit… I was informed that 8 kaffirs had again been on my farm, were about to carry off the most valuable lot when the cattle were rescued from them. I was told that a large puff adder got in amongst my family at dinner and would have terminated their lives had not the hand of God been stretched to save them by means of a faithful dog who lost its life in their defence.

It was not uncommon for Cape newspapers at the time to carry reports of white people of all ages dying from snake bites. Not everyone was saved by the hand of God – or an inquisitive dog. For Augustus the main threat was from the Xhosa. With cattle theft a recurrent problem, tempers were rising along the frontier. There was another perspective in all of this: to the Xhosa, land dispossession and their loss of life in the wars showed a mirror image of the settler sense of grievance. It should have come as no surprise that the perceived theft of their land would rankle down the years beyond the immediate crises.

Early in 1846 the situation deteriorated rapidly as reports in the *Grahamstown Journal* indicate. On 27 February, a public meeting was held at Bathurst to consider the state of the frontier and to take steps to meet the coming danger. At this meeting 'the Reverend August (sic) Tancred, who had built a house at Beaufort Vale seconded, that the local field-commandants be nominated in their several neighbourhoods'. Content to second nominations for military duties Augustus, unlike John Molteno and others, showed no appetite for putting himself forward in a physically active part in subduing the unrest.

In March 1846, the seventh settler war broke out. It was described at the time as the War of the Axe or the Amatola War.

For a while civilian life went on in an approximation to normal. On 11 April, the *Grahamstown Journal* reported that Tancred had built a house on his 560 morgen (about 1,185 acres) in Beaufort Vale. The man born in modest circumstances in Hanover Street in Cork was now a property owner. The timing, though, marked the high point of the family's life on the frontier. The ever-present danger, simmering up to this point, was coming to the boil. Their lives were about to change forever. Anything Augustus could do now would prove to be too little, too late.

April saw the effective end of Tancred's hopes of a successful farming life in the Eastern Cape. Later, in his address to Earl Grey in 1847, he recalls:

> I shall forever recollect the 12th April 1846, that cold and dreary night I fled into Graham's Town, South Africa, where I had not one friend that I could ask for my family a temporary shelter, or the least hospitality. I procured a cold damp store, occupied for years by salt hides (the only place to be had) belonging to a Kaffir trader who demanded an exorbitant and usurious rent when he found I could procure no other shelter. There, in the depth of winter, without even a fire place, amid stench and annoyance of every kind, I was compelled to remain during three months unassisted by any one, and cared for by few, until I was able to procure the small contracted place from where I write to your Excellency amid the noise, hubbub and uproar of children.

The family were back in Grahamstown where they had begun their life in Africa. This extract contains vintage Augustus, a man with no apparent thought or feelings for what it was like for Evelina and the children. It was all 'poor me'. There was certainly no awareness of, or concern for, black perspectives; the wishy-washy, liberal, less racist views of missionaries, and other men of the cloth, were something he came to heartily despise.

Then a seemingly insignificant event occurred on 9 May 1846 when, unknown to Augustus at the time, John Crawford Smith, a civilian wagon driver, was flogged at Fort Peddie on the orders of Lieutenant-Colonel Martin George Thomas Lindsay, the commanding officer of Her Majesty's 91st (Argyllshire) Regiment of Foot. The army had need of civilian labour and expected such men to work under martial law. It proved an expectation too far for the settler community. This incident and the events that flowed from it would figure prominently in what was said about Tancred long after he was gone from the frontier. His popular reputation as a champion of civil rights outlived any memories of his earlier attempts to launch his career as author, educator or farmer.

EVELINA

Further dark clouds now hung low over the family horizon when 'disease, brought on by damp, attacked my family during several weeks' and he found himself 'attending on the partner of my existence in her helpless, dangerous, and rheumatic state'. The conditions they were living under affected Evelina most of all.

Meanwhile, 'continual reports of losses were brought to me, of my cattle carried off by the enemy, of my crops burnt, my house shattered and other things destroyed too tedious to mention'.

Evelina's health continued to deteriorate until 'the next loss I apprehended was of one, whom I valued more than all I lost; and which Heaven was pleased not to inflict'. On this occasion, to his great relief, she pulled back from the brink. This is a unique expression of the strength of his feelings for his wife, the mother of their children. It is the only time he speaks of his feelings for anyone other than himself. Evelina and the children are absent from anywhere else in his writings.

With the frontier in a state of turmoil and Evelina in poor health, things could hardly deteriorate further. Then they did. The war would continue till the end of December 1847 but before that something more personal befell the family. The *Grahamstown Journal* announced that Evelina died in Grahamstown on 20 March 1847. Later, when Augustus died in 1867, his obituary included this pitifully bleak statement in remarking on her death in Grahamstown:

> Here it was that Mrs. Tancred, naturally of a delicate constitution, contracted a disease which resulted in her early death.

Her death notice, signed by 'A.J. Tancred', shows that she died aged only thirty-five years, ten days after her birthday, in the 'Residence of the Rev. Dr Tancred, Settlers Hill, Grahamstown'. She was twenty when she married, Augustus twenty-eight. The funeral service was held in St Patrick's Catholic Church whose foundation stone had only recently been laid (1839) and dedicated (1844). In these early days the church became an occasional refuge in times of war. Perhaps this explains its military appearance, reminding some of Battle Abbey, commemorating the arrival in England and subsequent victory of William the Conqueror near Hastings in 1066.

The burial register shows Evelina's burial in the Catholic section of the cemetery on 22 March 1847. Unusually, no comment is entered after her name unlike those above or below her on the list who merit an entry, however brief. Examples include 'accidental death' or 'Irish' or 'age' or 'large funeral' or 'drink' or 'pupil of St Aidan's – drowned'. Attempts to locate her grave drew a blank. In any event, if there ever was a memorial stone, any inscription is unlikely to have survived the harsh winter and baking summer weather on this exposed hillside. If there was once a wooden cross it was certainly long gone. I spent an afternoon scouring the Catholic section of the cemetery in 1995 but gave up the search when a raucous hullaballoo started turning up the volume in the nearby 'township' – the then non-white part of town – while on the road below SAP (South African Police) cars screeched down the road to erect roadblocks intended to prevent demonstrators entering the mainly white part of town. Did this experience hark back in time to white fears in 1846? No matter, Evelina was forever safer in her grave than she ever had been since she first fell in with Augustus. Now there was no real danger, what I saw and heard from the angry demonstrators was no more than a faint echo of the 'irruption of the kaffir hordes'. They were still angry and, I thought, why not?

Was Evelina's life with Augustus ever anything but stressful and insecure? Happiness? Who can know what other people long gone felt at the time, their voices unrecorded, their feelings unknown? Her one consolation may have been the three children. Unknown to her, they went on to lead easier and more successful lives than their parents. From now on their future welfare lay in the sole, unreliable hands of Dr Tancred.

*

Evelina's passing generated a succession of myths. According to Tancred's obituary in the *Cradock Register* in 1867, 'having allied himself to a lady of some fortune, he left England for this colony'. This may of course answer a question long hanging in the air: how did the family afford the journey from England and various expenditures before and after their arrival in the colony? Did assistance come from her father's family, the Latteys, or perhaps the Pittars, her mother's family, who were noted Huguenot silversmiths in Dublin and later Calcutta.

After Evelina's death there were conflicting accounts as to what happened next. The most easily refuted version is carried in the *Cradock Register* on 11 January 1867, which tells how, in consequence of the failure of his wife's health, Tancred removed with her to Cape Town before her death, where she died and, soon after her death, he left for Europe with her remains, which were interred in Devonshire, from which county she came. It is a romantic story but almost certainly a complete fabrication.

If not, would some memorial survive? It seems not. No trace of her has been found among the graves in the church and churchyards connected with the Molesworths, either in Cornwall or their Devonshire seat at Tetcott. To be sure, I did look but did not find anything. The body back to Devon story does rather seem like another romantic invention probably emanating from Augustus.

There are in any event a number of objections to this account: every record of her death places it in Grahamstown and not in Cape Town; she came from Tullamore in Ireland not Devonshire in England; and whatever form her remains took, there would have been practical difficulties in taking them to Europe, which Tancred did not visit again until some eighteen months later. Being buried in England or Ireland might perhaps have been her wish, but the burial register of St Patrick's Catholic Church in Grahamstown provides clear evidence that she was buried there. It is just possible that her body was exhumed and her remains taken elsewhere, though this seems highly unlikely.

Most of the fishy stories which wash up on the Tancred shoreline arise from things he told other people about his life, not all of which turn out to be the truth, the whole truth, and nothing but the truth. There are sound reasons for believing that Evelina lies somewhere in the Catholic section of the cemetery in Grahamstown, her body beneath the soil on that lonely, desolate, windswept hill on the outskirts of town.

December 1847 witnessed the end of the seventh war.

A MAN OF DISCONTENT

With the death of Evelina behind him, Augustus barely mentioned her in print again. As his life on the frontier fell apart, he took to writing lengthy letters to Maitland, the Governor in Cape Town, or Earl Grey, the Secretary to the Colonies, in London. These were shared amongst readers of *De Zuid-Afrikaan,* and then published in two books in 1846 and 1847. These verbose, bombastic letters covered only two topics: his losses as a landowning farmer on the frontier, which amounted to more 'poor me', and his contempt for those responsible for the government of the Eastern Cape where people were 'overwhelmed by a tide of savages' as when he himself 'was forced to desert my comfortable home in the country where I remained to protect my property, even when every place around me was forsaken and abandoned'. He had very little to say about policy alternatives.

Seemingly unaware of his lowly status in the colonial hierarchy, his other tack was a vituperative series of rants about the personalities of those in charge of colonial matters, with these outpourings of bile no better than personal abuse as in this letter to Rt. Hon. Earl Grey, Secretary to the Colonies, in which he reveals:

> I once respected you on account of your noble father, and I thought you would follow in his footsteps, though there is not a feature in your face resembling him. For that deficiency your mother I dare say can satisfactorily account.

On one occasion when his letters were received in London, an official wrote: 'the enclosed are a continuation of Dr Tancred's ravings'. His 'ravings', predictably, were not effective. Once again, it is abundantly clear that he had learned nothing from his experience in Nottingham and his abuse of the great and the good connected with the Basford Union Workhouse in the London *Times*. Yet this, after all, was still the same person who had published a book offering 'A treatise on polite philosophy, or an easy manner of settling differences among men'. Augustus was, if nothing else, a man of many contradictions.

And in these letters, there is also his one consolation for, no matter how difficult his present circumstances may be, there is always a shaft of light at the end of the tunnel, as here when his 1866 address to Earl Grey in London was reported in *De Zuid-Afrikaan*:

> ... I have had cause to complain of how this part of the Colony has been governed, as your excellency would have complained were you placed in my position. For, Sir, I complain as a person your equal in every respect, with the exception of your accidental office. I certainly cannot pronounce in whose favour the scale would incline were our respective information put in the balance, and I am not as yet a Knight, but as the wheel is always going round that may also come with a Baronetcy attached to it, if the present heir of Boroughbudge (sic) should die without issue...

Why worry about the present if better times lie ahead? If this dream of future ennoblement gave him comfort no harm may have been done. He may not have known that the Baronet, 'the present heir of Boroughbudge', was not wanting in issue. Or, put most generously, news may not have reached him at the Cape. But then, why should it if he had no link to the Boroughbridge family in distant Yorkshire? No such link has ever been confirmed. Was it wishful thinking, had he merely noticed a family of distinction on whom he might piggy-back in the hope of enhancing his social status, or was there a hidden link through his father that he knew of but never revealed? Believing he would one day become a baronet, or just stating it as fact, seems to have eased his sufferings in the Eastern Cape.

His farming days were now over almost as soon as they had begun. His life in Africa, as author, educationalist and farmer, had been no more successful than his life as a cleric in Europe. The location had changed, the man had not. The death of Evelina, his new responsibilities as the sole carer of their children, the need to earn an income, and the uncertain times on the frontier, would all stretch his abilities to the utmost.

By the close of 1847 the Tancreds would be gone from the frontier but before that, as so often happened in the life of Augustus, events were about to take an unexpected turn.

20

THE NOTORIOUS CASE OF SMITH V LINDSAY

*… he always ranked with those who are foremost here in
asserting civil and religious liberty.*
Obituary, *The Great Eastern*

Long after he was gone from the Eastern Cape, and for a
while after his death, Tancred's role in the case of *Smith
versus Lindsay* would, alongside his later antics, become
his legacy, the things people remembered about him. The
mirror image of the earlier episode in Nottingham, when
he put all at risk prosecuting the alleged perpetrators of
the ill-treatment of some of the workhouse inmates, is
uncanny. In Nottingham he had challenged the power and
authority of the local gentry and lost. Now at the Cape
he would challenge the power and authority of the British
Army, the Attorney-General, the colonial government
in Cape Town and the wishes of the Colonial Office in
London. Now, like Don Quixote, he rode once more into
battle, jousting at what? Surely, humiliation and ruin
awaited him once again? What was it about the corporal
punishment of boys and young men that so inflamed him
that he was prepared to put his reputation and the financial

security of the family at risk defending those previously unknown to him?

Soon after the outbreak of the seventh war in March 1846, a civilian wagon driver was flogged at Fort Peddie on the instruction of a British Army officer. The wagon driver was unknown to Augustus who was unaware of the incident when it occurred. He did, however, play a leading role in the subsequent trial of the officer responsible for the flogging. In the trial, held in Uitenhage in 1847, the limits of the military law over the civil law were at issue and, in particular, the British Army's right to flog civilians in times of war. To any intelligent observer Tancred must have seemed bound to lose. Surely, it was Nottingham all over again when he would make it his business to intervene disastrously?

Fort Peddie, a frontier post situated some forty miles from Grahamstown, was the largest of a line of fortified posts running from Peddie to Fort Beaufort. Established on the frontier in 1835, it took its name from a British Army officer, Lieutenant-Colonel John Peddie, who was in charge of the 72nd Highlanders in the sixth Xhosa War. In 1846 in the seventh Xhosa War, it was the base for Her Majesty's 91st (Argyllshire) Regiment of Foot under the command of Lieutenant-Colonel Martin George Thomas Lindsay.

The line of posts stretching across the frontier was intended to ensure the safety of Fort Peddie, the focal point in the war. The British believed the fort to be a secure base. The fortified posts were, however, of little or no value as the signalling equipment they contained was inadequate for the purpose. The linked posts were soon abandoned and then destroyed by the Xhosa in the first month of the war.

If the British were confident about the role of Fort Peddie, the Xhosa for their part harboured ambitions to attack the fort, kill all the defending soldiers and then drive the settlers from Grahamstown, after which 'they would never stop till they have driven out the last Englishman at the point of the Cape'.

The army learned of the Xhosa plan of attack from a Xhosa collaborator. This placed them in a position of advantage. Their disadvantages were to be found in the men occupying the key posts in the local army structure, and none more so than the officer commanding at Fort Peddie, Lindsay, 'one of the most unpopular officers ever to serve in South Africa'. As well as being unpopular, Lindsay was also regarded as incompetent. In the flogging of Smith he succeeded in alienating support for the army from the settlers who saw it as an attempt to focus on the cowardice of a young colonial man rather than one of his own officers, Captain Colin Campbell, who received lenient treatment in an earlier incident in which he abandoned his wagons and ammunition intended for Fort Peddie, and retreated on hearing that a large party of Xhosas was in the area.[22]

*

The trial exposed many of the contradictory elements of colonial life: the settlers, none louder than Tancred, demanded that their safety be ensured by the closed fist

22 Noël Mostert, *ibid.*

of the British Army. The army for their part saw high amongst their needs the importance of strict discipline in the troops. Indiscipline would weaken the fighting force. Without discipline, and the unquestioning acceptance of orders by the officers, the effectiveness and safety of the fighting force would be compromised. But if this applied to the men under army command, did it also apply to civilians employed in support of the army? What were the limits to the military authority as against the civil authority?

Whereas the army claimed the legal right to flog civilians to impose discipline, Tancred took the opposing view. This issue is at the core of the case *Smith v Lindsay*. The army, the colonial administration and the ultimate authority of the British government were steadfastly in support of flogging civilians when such punishment was deemed necessary by the army who could rely on unconditional legal and financial support if their authority was challenged. Tancred, disregarding the way in which he had brought the family to near ruin in Nottinghamshire, now put all at risk once again, as before without the financial backing and the legal resources in reserve.

The trial illustrated the issues as they affected the settlers, the colonial authority and the British Army. Although the rights of the Xhosa, the enemy, were not considered, the underlying racism of the white participants flares briefly to light in the trial.

THE FLOGGING

The British Army employed local civilians, white as well as black men, in a supportive, non-military role. One of their tasks was to go out with wagons into the surrounding countryside and bring back firewood. This was not without danger; a party of wagon drivers on just such a mission had only recently been attacked by 'Caffers'. It is therefore not surprising that on 9 May 1846, the wagon drivers, including a young man called Smith, argued that the area beyond the fort was unsafe and, moreover, it was not part of their contract to cut wood. Ordered to obey, go out into the countryside and bring back wood, they refused.

John Crawford Smith was a 'proprietor of wagons'. In spite of the plural he seems to have had but one wagon, plus oxen, which he hired out together with his labour to the government in exchange for ten shillings and sixpence a day. When the wagon drivers refused the order to go out in search of firewood Smith was singled out as an example and ordered by Lindsay to be flogged. It is not entirely clear from the evidence given at the trial whether John Crawford Smith was the ringleader or merely the scapegoat in this minor insurrection. Clearly his punishment was intended as an example to the others.

Somewhat bathetically, before the flogging, Smith begged to be spared the inevitable but when his entreaties failed, he pleaded that his shirt should not be torn from his back: 'Don't tear it, I have not any other here, the Caffers have burnt my clothes.' He was then tied with leather thongs by his hands and legs to the front wheel of a wagon. He continued to demand to know why he was to be flogged but answer came there none before the order 'Commence' was given by Lindsay. Smith was duly flogged by the drummer on his bare back with a cat o' nine tails. On breaking loose at one point he was tied up and lashed again. Lindsay, according to Smith's testimony, then said it was to show the wagon drivers 'that it was in his power to do so, and that he would make them remember it was Martial law'. Smith was then ordered to go to the 'hospital' where his bleeding back was washed with salt water.

An event which may not have been uncommon, and soon forgotten in the area, was destined to remain etched in the annals of the Eastern Cape.

THE TRIAL

Sixteen months later the flogging was the subject of proceedings in the Court of Uitenhage (renamed Kariega in 2021) on 28 and 29 September 1847, in the case of *Smith v Lindsay*.[23] Tancred, who had not been involved at the time or in the place of the flogging, now entered centre stage at the trial.

But why? Tancred might at this stage have been preoccupied with other matters, such as the care and education of his children after the death of Evelina, or a search for gainful employment. But no, he had decided to involve himself in what was seen by many on the frontier as an illegal act: the army applying martial law to civilians. Needless to say, the settlers also expected soldiers to

---

23 W.G. Schulze and B.T. Hall, '*Smith v Lindsay* – A legal *cause célèbre* from the Eastern Cape in 1847', in *Fundamina*, published by the South African Society of Legal Historians, Pretoria, Vol. 4, 1998 (appeared in 1999); Notes of the Proceedings in the Circuit Court of Uitenhage, on the 28th and 29th September, 1847, in the cases of Smith versus Lindsay, and Mitchley versus Bethune, for Assault. 1847.

endure the hazards of defending the frontier and ensuring their own protection.

Smith v Lindsay is what people remembered of Tancred's brief time in the Eastern Cape. He came to be remembered as someone who had fought for the civil rights of the settlers. Throughout his time at the Cape he was oblivious, perhaps hostile, to the rights of those who did not have white skins.

It is not known how, when or why he became aware of the incident and, not least, why he decided to devote so much energy to the cause of young Smith. Flogging in the army may have been unremarkable, the flogging of this civilian in the Eastern Cape was not. Did word get around that Tancred was a man who knew about such things, how to bring a case to court, raise funds, hire an attorney? This was, after all, the Cape, the legal system different from the one he had experience of in England.

It is inconceivable that Smith, an eighteen-year-old wagon driver with no influential family behind him would have had the clout, let alone the knowledge or administrative skill, to bring a case against a senior officer in the British Army before the court. There was also the necessity of raising the funds to hire a top-flight lawyer to prosecute the case. Yet that was what happened and it was all down to Tancred, ironically the same man who complained bitterly to the Governor about the inadequate security by the army for people and property on the frontier.

The army view was that the civilian population should be grateful for the protection they provided. Furthermore, they argued, they must be free to impose their discipline on those under their command. Undisciplined troops in battle could endanger other members of the regiment as well as themselves. But Smith and the other wagon drivers were not members of the regiment, they were mere hired hands. The legal issue turned on the legality of the military law over the civil law at the interface between soldiers and civilians employed by the army in time of war. Were they, or were they not, under the command of the army and subject to its disciplinary code?

The case was highly exceptional in that it was technically Smith, insignificant in the scheme of things, who brought the private prosecution against Lindsay, alleging the crime of assault. The British Army was not used to civilians bringing its officers before the court, and certainly not a civilian whippersnapper like Smith charging a respected senior officer like Lindsay.

Surely Smith was bound to lose and hence Tancred as well, reprising his disastrous court action against the workhouse Governor and Schoolmaster back in Nottingham in 1838?

PORTER, THE DEFENCE ATTORNEY

The case represented a challenge to the authority of the army, the colonial government in Cape Town and their paymasters in London. Questioning the right of the army to deal with civilians employed by the army under the martial rather than the civil law in times of war was bound to cause consternation. To counter this threat to the authority of these interested parties, William Porter, the Attorney-General, was, in the words spoken at the trial, 'hurried from Cape Town, with pressed horses... to throw his mantle over the gallant colonel now before you at the bar'. The distance from Cape Town to the court at Uitenhage is 450 miles, the journey undertaken by Porter an indicator of its importance to the Crown. Although Porter did, on occasion, as part of his duties as Attorney-General, prosecute in circuit courts around the Cape, this was an exceptional case where he travelled from Cape Town and defended, contrary to his regular role as prosecutor.

SMITH, THE AGGRIEVED PARTY

John Crawford Smith, prosecuting Lindsay for the crime of assault, was born in Grahamstown in 1828. He came from an army family, his father having served in the British Army, notably in the 95th Regiment (Rifle Brigade) during the Peninsular War, in which he was wounded and became a prisoner in 1809. In 1814 he rejoined the army and served in the escort party accompanying Napoleon to Elba before fighting at the Battle of Waterloo in 1815 where he was wounded once again. Perhaps it came as some relief to arrive at the Cape in 1820 as head of a party of British settlers.

Smith's father had died by the time of his flogging. At the time young Smith, aged about nineteen, was living with his widowed mother who he claimed was 'entirely dependent on him for support'. However, she seems to have remarried, between the flogging and the trial, to a man by the name of Wild who once 'kept a canteen'.

Coincidentally, Lindsay arrived at the Cape at about the same time as Tancred when, in August 1842, a Reserve Battalion of the 91st arrived in Table Bay under his command. By the following June, Lindsay, plus one captain, three subalterns and 120 non-commissioned officers and men, were on active service at Fort Peddie in the Eastern Cape. They were there to guard the frontier against the Xhosas or, as they saw it in the colonial language of the day, the 'Kaffir Chief Tola'.

Lieutenant-Colonel Martin George Thomas Lindsay faced an immense and dangerous task preventing desertions and generally maintaining the discipline of the men under his command. He had served widely in the Empire and there are examples of acts of his kindness along the way. In the Eastern Cape he no doubt believed the local populace should be grateful for the protection afforded by the army and hence be willing to accept in return the rigours of military discipline.

Though born in England, Lindsay had married a Miss Bull in Ireland where one daughter was born in Dublin. Stationed in Limerick between 1838 and 1842, Lindsay can have been in no doubt that the presence of the British Army at the Cape was at times applauded for what they did do, castigated for what they failed to do and, as in this case, vigorously resented for trampling on civil rights. Against this background he pleaded not guilty of the alleged crime, the assault of Smith.

Was it the political significance of the case, or merely coincidence, that the trial brought together in the courtroom 'three of the most brilliant legal minds of the mid-nineteenth century Cape Colony, Menzies, Ebden and Porter'?

William Menzies, the presiding judge in the case, was already the senior puisne judge in the Cape Colony. Son of a solicitor in Leith, he graduated with a law degree from the University of Edinburgh. Having accepted the post of Senior Puisne Judge at the Cape he arrived in Cape Town in 1827 aged thirty-two. In 1828 he became one of the first judges of the newly constituted Cape Supreme Court. With a robust loyalty to the Crown, he was, from the point of view of the authorities, an ideal person to hear the case *Smith v Lindsay*.

John Watts Ebden, prosecuting on behalf of Smith, was born at the Cape. With an outstanding legal mind, he would not have come cheaply to the brief.

William Porter, the defence counsel for Lindsay, was Attorney-General of the Cape Colony, having been appointed in 1829. Like Menzies he was an incomer to the Cape scene having, like Tancred, been born in Ireland. He studied law in London and was admitted to Gray's Inn in 1827, then King's Inn in Dublin where he was called to the Irish Bar.

Arriving in Cape Town and becoming Attorney-General in 1839 he was accompanied by his lifelong companion Hugh Lynar who became his Chief Clerk. He would later be described as 'the father of Cape liberalism', justifiably on account of his views, advanced for the time, on justice for all, black or white, a parliament of blacks and whites, the abolition of capital punishment, and higher education for women.[24]

Having grown up in the north of Ireland, but also knowing Dublin in the 1820s, he would have been aware of the rising tide of discontent voiced by Daniel O'Connell and others in a land where one group of the inhabitants resented the dispossession of their lands by another. Like Tancred, his Irish background seems not to have influenced his imperialist outlook. Ostensibly, in any event, the trial was about law, not politics.

So it was that in 1846 the trial brought together these future luminaries of the Cape legal establishment.

Added to whom was Tancred, a barrack room lawyer with a bee in his bonnet about corporal punishment – or an early civil rights activist at the Cape?

THE TRIAL

If some of the circumstances surrounding the case are shrouded in the fog of the 'who said what?' variety, or obfuscations deliberate or otherwise, much is known thanks to the seventy-eight pages of 'Notes on the Proceedings in the circuit court of Uitenhage on the 28th and 29th September, 1847'.[25] It is primarily from this source that Tancred's role in the affair, the *what* if not the *why*, can be carefully unravelled.

---

24 J.L. McCracken, *New Light at the Cape of Good Hope; William Porter, the Father of Cape Liberalism*, 1993.

25 South African Parliamentary Library ID 27214614331.

Smith v Lindsay was what it says on the proverbial tin. But was it? Was it actually Tancred *versus* Lindsay? Or Porter *versus* Tancred?

Statements by Porter, together with information emerging from his cross-examination of Smith and others, gradually answer a number of questions about Tancred's role in the case, beginning with 'who put Smith up to it?'

Ill at ease and nervous in the courtroom, Smith was no match for Porter under cross-examination. It was David versus Goliath in which Goliath was bound to win. Cross-examining Smith, Porter demonstrated that he saw Tancred as the moving force behind the prosecution:

Porter:	When did you first become acquainted with him (Tancred)?
Smith:	I did not know him until he sent for me.
Porter:	Where was he then?
Smith:	At Mr Charles Fuller's, at Graham's Town.
Porter:	You have been a good deal with him since?
Smith:	Yes, for a fortnight.

To mount the case involved significant costs. What was the source of these funds and who set about raising them? Porter continues to press Smith on this point, fishing for evidence of the involvement of Tancred:

Porter:	Do you know that he has been going through the country to collect subscriptions?

Smith:	I knew he was going through the area.
Porter:	Have you ever got any money from him?
Smith:	No, I never did.
Porter:	Did you ever give him authority to collect money on your account?
Smith:	I do not understand you.
Porter:	Did you ever give your consent for him to collect money to defray the expenses of your trial?
Smith:	Yes, I had no objection to it.

Next Porter twists the knife in the wound as he seeks to identify Tancred as an unreliable person for Smith to have consorted with, thus attempting to weaken the case against Lindsay:

> A man who writes – God save the mark, – "D.D."
> behind his name, has been collecting subscriptions
> from the charitable and humane, – a man who is his
> own collector, treasurer, and auditor of accounts,
> – a man – it is not in evidence, but I state the fact
> on my own responsibility, – who commenced his
> career in this colony by fraudulently putting his
> name to the literary work of another man, and
> who is now going to put another man's name to a
> work of his own, – not literary but more lucrative.

Here Porter is referring to Tancred's *A Treatise on Polite Philosophy*, published in Grahamstown in 1842. The intended implications are clear: who could trust a man who published a book by another author under his own name, a man seeing in Smith a way of making money? And could Tancred be trusted with the money he had collected? There was no arrangement for any income or expenditure to be properly audited. Perhaps Tancred is trousering a proportion of the income for his own use. The costs of the trial, the fees to Ebden prosecuting for Smith, would have been significant; perhaps there was some left over, nudge-nudge, wink-wink, an amount which may have slipped into Tancred's pocket. At this distance of time, it is impossible to know if there was any basis for this insinuation. As happened many times during the course of the trial Porter is challenged by Ebden for slipping in allegations not given in evidence. Menzies, sitting in judgement, comes over as far from even-handed, frequently turning a blind eye to blatant examples of bias by the defence. At this stage the trial was not going well for Smith – or Tancred.

What Porter seems not to have recognised is the local support for Tancred and Smith, the resentment at Lindsay's decision to have Smith flogged: the nine good men and true on the jury would have shared these sentiments and also been inclined to bias. The case engaged tremendous public support for Smith and against the army. Who was the publicist behind the successful campaign before the court? Porter now asks Smith if he was present when Tancred was 'carrying a cat o' nine tails about the streets'.

| Smith: | I never carried a cat o' nine tails. |
| Porter: | Were you with him when he carried a cat o' nine tails? |

Smith:	(Silent)
Porter:	Were you with him carrying a cat o' nine tails about the streets?
Smith:	Never.

Later Porter rails against what he sees as Tancred's coaching of the witnesses against Lindsay:

> That this gentleman (Lindsay), who never had an opportunity of hearing what the well drilled witnesses against him were prepared to depose, ... is here summoned to listen for the first time to the venomous misrepresentations of John Crawford Smith – or Augustus Joseph Tancred.

He does not of course mention that the army men giving evidence in support of Lindsay also appear exceptionally well coached for the task.

There is a good deal to be learnt from these exchanges. Tancred made the initial contact with Smith, and it was Tancred who made a flamboyant publicity drive walking around the streets carrying a cat o' nine tails, collecting subscriptions. As the trial progressed, it was Tancred not Smith who was Porter's primary target. By implication, Smith had been in bad company and easily led by associating with Tancred. In discrediting Tancred, Porter seeks to exonerate Lindsay. Smith, not surprisingly, struggles at times to explain himself in the face of the expert, clinical cross-examination by Porter.

Of necessity the proceedings are largely concerned with legal matters, which statutes apply, the geographical limits of the Crown's authority, and the boundaries between the civil and military law. Porter is keen to argue that Smith, a civilian, is actually serving in the army where discipline is vital to the safety of the regiment and its success in battle. Corporal punishment is necessary to maintain discipline; it is within army law, and any number of authorities, including the Duke of Wellington, are quoted in support of it. As if attempting to reassure the court, Porter was quick to add his personal view of the matter: they were listening to 'not an advocate of flogging but an advocate who has been pretty well flogged in his time'. So that, then, is apparently all right? A classic *non sequitur*?

Although the prosecution case did not rely on the severity or otherwise of the flogging, the defence made much of its lightness of touch. The army witnesses are wholly supportive of Lindsay, and their evidence all suggests to them that Smith got off very lightly. Jennings, the adjutant, is in no doubt that twenty-five lashes were 'not severe for corporal punishment', while he saw Lindsay as a popular and humane officer who had only ordered four floggings since December 1842. Haddaway, the surgeon, present at the flogging, said that after twenty years in the army 'it was the slightest I ever saw carried into effect'. He had never seen fewer than fifty lashes whereas the most he had seen was 500 lashes when, even with this punishment, he 'never knew a man suffer in bodily health'. Haddaway, paradoxically, claimed he was personally 'very much against' flogging in the army before adding, inconsequentially, that Lindsay was 'the reverse of cruel'. Minto, the staff surgeon, 'considered the punishment a very slight one' with no appearance of injury apart from the mere marks of the stripes. None of this was strictly relevant given that the argument was about the right of the army to flog civilians, not the severity of this particular flogging.

Smith, and his friends, paint a very different picture of events with a less sanguine account of Smith's condition after the flogging. Once again this was beside the point, for whether the punishment was or was not severe was not central to the prosecution case. If, as Porter argued, commanding officers were duty-bound to maintain discipline, Lindsay was simply doing his job efficiently.

Of interest to modern eyes are not only the arguments for and against corporal punishment, but the insights into the racism embedded in that society at the time. Smith was regarded as socially superior to the nameless 'Caffers', 'coloureds', 'black men', 'dark men' who were in a majority among the wagon drivers and were amongst those who refused to obey the order. Porter is in no doubt that in instances of disobedience 'an example should be made of an Englishman, who ought to have known better, rather than a miserable Hottentot… It is not upon him but upon the Englishman, that, when punishment falls, punishment ought to alight.'

THE VERDICT

Porter's closing speech lasted two and a half hours, heavily laced with flattery for the good sense of the fair-minded members of the jury, caustic jibes at Tancred and Smith, and paeons of praise for Lindsay, a good man, a respected officer just doing his job in difficult circumstances.

With a flourish to show his own magnanimity and the breadth of his education Porter explains, 'not that I would greatly blame the reverend gentleman' before quoting Dryden:

For 'tis their duty, all the learned think,
To espouse the cause by which they eat and drink.[26]

Once again, an attempt to discredit Tancred's motives for he is 'the reverend gentleman'. Surely the jury can see he is just in it for the money. What Porter may not have realised was that quoting an unnamed Dryden to the men on the jury was unlikely to have the effect he desired. Perhaps he was closer to their sympathy for Lindsay with these words:

… I ask you gentlemen, are you trying a crime, or are you brought here to triumph and exult over the military who are defending you? … an officer engaged in the protection of the frontier, and against whom a civil action has been brought for £1000? Good God! Is not that enough? Humble the army! Bring down the army! … I expect better things from the jury I address.

The army are there to defend them, losses in the regiment were high. This was certainly true, for their graves are scattered across the veld; modern eyes might note there are no equivalent surviving memorials for the Xhosa dead.

---

26 John Dryden, *Absalom and Achitophel*, 1681. Excoriating, satirical attack on corrupt clergy.

Finally, it was the turn of Menzies, the judge, to summarise the case, of which he clearly disapproves, against Lindsay. At one point he observes that had a Hottentot been flogged for disobeying an order there would have been no case for the person issuing the order to answer. Smith, however, being a white man, had the right to have his case heard before the court.

After reviewing a selection of the evidence Menzies advised the jury that, bearing in mind all the relevant points of law and the evidence of the witnesses, 'I have laid down to you, as law, that Col. Lindsay was entitled to administer that punishment.' Confident that the jury would follow his advice on all the points of law he complimented them: having 'seen juries in this colony, for the last twenty years, I have no fear that you will act otherwise than according to your consciences, on your oaths'. Wrong.

Just in case the jury might find the need to engage in a lengthy discussion of the points of law raised during the day, Menzies told them that he could make arrangements for their accommodation that night.

The jury retired to consider their verdict. As it happened, they had no need of overnight accommodation for after a quarter of an hour they returned with their verdict:

> Martin George Thomas Lindsay, Lieutenant-Colonel of Her Majesty's 91st Regiment: GUILTY adding a recommendation that Lindsay be 'recommended to mercy on account of his position at the time'.

Had Menzies forgotten that, as given in evidence, five out of the nine jurymen had subscribed to the fund collected to cover the costs of an expensive lawyer to facilitate the prosecution of Lindsay by Smith? Tancred's influence once more.

Menzies showed no sympathy with the verdict. After propounding further legal arguments he announced that the defendant (Lindsay) 'is entitled to have judgement in his favour in the present action'.

Porter then sprang to his feet. 'With costs, my lord? – though we are not likely to get any!' This must have rattled Tancred. He had been ruined once before, in consequence of his Nottingham court action.

When Menzies decided the defendant (Lindsay) was entitled to a proportion of his costs, Mr Ebden for Smith announced that the prosecution intended to appeal to the Supreme Court. Menzies, clearly tiring of the whole farrago, instructed a commissioner to take security for the costs of the appeal. I have not discovered what this security involved or what, if any, further legal action followed.

THE AFTERMATH

There were winners and losers in all of this. For Tancred's obituarist in *De Zuid-Afrikaan* the colonists are chiefly indebted to him for the triumph of the civil over the martial law and the old commando law.

Lindsay, the army and the colonial authorities had both lost and won on the day. Were Smith, Tancred and Ebden the real losers, able to claim no more than a Pyrrhic victory? Porter's talk of a claim for financial recompense for his client seems to have fizzled out, though it might have alarmed Tancred. In the eyes of the citizens Tancred had made a name for himself as a champion of the common man, someone who took on authorities when he perceived an abuse of power. He had become a local hero in the Eastern Cape. Yes, but the populace still expected the protection of the army.

It was the local hero image that was how he would be remembered by many long after he had left the area. Did he do it just for the money? If this was his motive, he does not seem sufficiently well organised to make it as a sharp money conman. Nor does it seem likely that he did it for the possibility of fame and renown. The likelihood is that he had a burning if eccentric hatred of injustice, in some way related to corporal punishment, but why remains a mystery. Inevitably suspicion points to something in his childhood.

AFTER THE TRIAL WAS OVER

John Crawford Smith, a sorry figure in this minor colonial drama, never married, fell ill in 1853, and died in 1855 aged twenty-six.

In 1848, barely two years after the trial at Uitenhage, Martin George Thomas Lindsay retired by selling his commission (officers bought their commission) worth about £7,250, a not insignificant sum. He was fifty-three years of age. He landed back in England on 20 April 1848 at Haslar (Portsmouth) aboard the *Acosta*, with the headquarters staff and Numbers 2, 3 and 4 Companies of the 91st Highlanders. His wife, Harriet Anne, born Bull, was drowned off St Helena on 2 March during the voyage. His career was at an end, *Smith v Lindsay* its epitaph.

What memories of the Eastern Cape, and of Tancred, accompanied him? Lindsay was still on the retired list when he died in London aged sixty-five in September 1860. Back in the Eastern Cape he would long be remembered by some as one of the most hated British Army officers to serve on that front. His brutal, ill-tempered punishment of Smith had done little to advance his cause.

Mr Justice William Menzies continued his distinguished legal career in which he was regarded as 'the first great interpreter and expounder of Roman-Dutch jurisprudence'. He died on circuit at Colesberg aged fifty-seven in 1850.

John Watts Ebden went on to become Mr Justice Ebden when he was appointed to the Cape Supreme Court in 1854. He died in Cape Town in 1886.

Porter became known as 'the father of Cape liberalism', turning down the offers of a knighthood, the chief justiceship and the prime ministership, before returning to Ireland after his lifelong companion Hugh Lynar died in July 1873. Porter then lived with his brother in Belfast till his death in 1880. He left large donations to a number of public institutions at the Cape. He is remembered among other liberal Cape politicians at the time, such as Saul Solomon, John Molteno and John Fairbairn, as a progressive force in the otherwise conservative political establishment.

And as for Tancred, a man with enough knowledge and confidence to take the powerful to court in England and at the Cape? Was it chance rather than design that saw him embroiled in events that saw his reputation established as a defender of civil liberties in the Eastern Cape in contrast to the derision he left behind in Nottingham? Did he have a penchant for challenging those in authority?

The conclusion of the proceedings in *Smith v Lindsay* marked the end of Tancred's days in the Eastern Cape. He had decided to sell up and return to Europe with the children. Once back in England he planned to make further efforts to pursue justice for Smith. Was it his intention never to return to the Cape? Once back in Europe he found he was no more welcome than he had been when he left in 1842.

Returning to somewhere else in the Cape may have seemed like the least bad option.

21

GOING HOME

Smith v Lindsay was in many ways a hollow victory. No doubt it did not look like that to Augustus, or to many others in the settler community in the Eastern Cape. When he died, obituarists across the Cape highlighted this as an important achievement. His other endeavours, as author, educationalist and farmer, having met with scant success, went unremarked.

Had he persisted at the Cape after the death of Evelina and the proceedings in *Smith v Lindsay* six months later, he might have been expected to turn his full attention to family matters, not least the care and education of his children and the development of the farm. It was not to be.

On 29 October 1847, merely a month after the completion of *Smith v Lindsay*, he offered 500 morgen (about 1,058 acres) for sale with a house and two other unspecified lots. Two months later his fellow colonists were kept abreast with what lay behind his actions in a characteristically long letter in the *Grahamstown Journal* on Christmas Day, 1847. In this he explained how he had 'been called upon to hasten to England to assume the management of certain matters devolving on me since the death of Mrs Tancred'. If money was at stake, if he could offload the children, he no doubt needed no prompting to head back to Europe, even if it meant a voyage of some 8,000 miles. His life as a settler at the Cape had not offered the comfortable, secure living he had expected. The high hopes he entertained on arrival were as dust in his hands.

Although he portrayed his return to England as a duty, he may have been glad of an excuse to turn his back on Africa. Selling up suggests permanent departure; there is no sign at this moment of any intention to return to the Cape. And yet, in the same Christmas letter, he refers to appointing an agent, Mr William Ogilvie, Jnr., to be his lawful attorney and agent 'during his absence from the colony'. Making financial arrangements while he was abroad suggests some ambivalence about a possible return to the Cape, whereas selling up, lock, stock and barrel, suggests a man with a mind made up, resolved to be gone for good. Perhaps at this stage he was unsure about his future intentions.

TANCRED THE BENEFACTOR

He had one last piece of unfinished business to attend to before leaving the colony. In his characteristically verbose style, he set out his stall in the local newspaper as a would-be generous benefactor in this address to 'The Men of the East':

> I am happy to inform you that I am enabled to bestow, and I hereby do bestow, to Graham's Town, whatever my farm in Willson's Party may realize (subject to a debt of L130) towards the erection of a Fever and Leprosy Hospital.

The women of the East are not mentioned, they are, as always, mere add-ons to the men. They exist, seemingly silent in the shadows, much as Evelina had in her short lifetime. Similarly, non-white people, the substantial majority of the population, seeing themselves as the dispossessed, and who harboured the notion that the land belonged to them, do not trouble the printer's ink.

Augustus continues along the same lines explaining that if the sum raised proves insufficient, he will cheerfully forward the remaining balance soon after his return to England. Where might this money come from? He also offers to contribute towards the proposed hospital project by adding the proceeds of his claim for losses suffered 'in consequence of the Kaffir War', as well as a claim he has made against the value of the resale of the estate of J.D. Norden, deceased, the man he charged with handling the sale of his possessions back in 1842. If J.D. Norden had died, as seems to be the case, how did Tancred stand to benefit from a claim against his estate? Presumably he claimed a debt owed to him by Norden. It is likely that his losses from the war were no more than a claim as yet unresolved.

He has long harboured a wish, he says, to see such an institution in the district and asks to be kept informed both when work is commenced and completed. Perhaps he was thinking of Evelina's illness and death? Did he believe that the facilities only a hospital could provide would have made a difference?

He had views on the proposed hospital, although, he was quick to say, it was not his intention 'to interfere or dictate in any way'. That is exactly what he goes on to do in recommending the additional erection of 'a small and separate establishment for the respectable indigent who may be afflicted with the fever' who, in their time of suffering, 'would prefer to endure the greatest privations of home, rather than be mixed up with colour and indiscriminate cases'. All this he insists is 'only a suggestion'. The racism explicit in his wish regarding people of colour is not surprising for it simply echoes the prevailing view among white settlers at the time. The man of the cloth he had once been, and the would-be civil rights activist he had partly become, might have approached people of races different from his own in a different way. Like most white people around him, he simply assumed the innate supremacy of those who were born white. He was, after all, a citizen in Victoria's Empire.

He was still not quite done with his 'suggestions': he would like the institution to be called Christ's Hospital, this in connection with Christmas Day, the day he announced his donation, and for it to make no religious distinctions, except that entry should be restricted to 'any Christian party, of whatever name'. This seems to reflect his own mobility within the Christian faith; it was certainly not a statement of the tolerance of non-Christian beliefs.

Like the school he proposed on his arrival in the colony, no evidence has been found that shows any such hospital being erected.

With a final blast of bombast and good intentions, he wishes his soon-to-be-former fellow colonists happiness in future, saying he feels no animosity towards anyone, forgives everyone who may have injured him, hopes for forgiveness from any person to whom he may have given offence or annoyance, and, finally, hopes 'that I shall meet you all with the assembled nations in Heaven'. Whether or not this final hope is reciprocated is not revealed.

In all of this he echoes many of the same sentiments, and in much the same way, as he did on leaving Christchurch thirteen years before.

Before racing off to board his ship in Algoa Bay he made two final promises: once back in England he would represent the real state of the colony (his negative view of its government), and also bring the case of *Smith v Lindsay* before the British public. He clearly still had Lindsay in his sights; to Augustus it seems to have been unfinished business. Once in England and making these representations he would be using 'whatever influence I possess with some members of the House of Commons'. What influence? Perhaps settler folk believed his tales of important connections in London.

At the same time, he continued to swat at the proverbial bee in his bonnet about the governance of the Cape. His stream of strident letters of complaint to Sir Peregrine Maitland, Governor of the Cape Colony, 'on the present Kaffir War' continued and were published in book form in Cape Town in 1846 (Part 1) and followed in 1847 (Part 2).[27] His views continued largely in accord with settler grievances.

And then they were gone, these four Tancreds, Augustus and presumably the three children, leaving

---

27 A.J. Tancred, *Letters to Sir Peregrine Maitland on the Present Kafir War*, Cape Town, Part 1 – 1846, Part 2 – 1847. Facsimile reprint by the State Library, Pretoria, 1969.

Evelina in her grave in Grahamstown. He makes no mention of the children at this point. Were they part of the agenda when he headed for Europe to deal with those unnamed matters devolving upon him since the death of Evelina? It is possible that they were placed locally, perhaps even before Evelina died, or on his departure in 1847. Although it seems unlikely, they may even have been sent ahead of him to family or other carers in Europe. Of the three children only one would ever return to the Cape.

*

December 1847 saw the end of the Tancreds' time in the Eastern Cape.

22

BACK HOME

*… the second (son), Oswald, resides in France, where he
has held a responsible situation on the staff of the Suez
Canal company; his daughter, Evelina, has taken the veil in
a convent at Boulogne.*

Obituary, *De Zuid-Afrikaan*

After the death of his wife, Augustus was faced with the
responsibility of ensuring the welfare and education of
their three children. By the time they arrived back in
Europe, Augustus Frederick was thirteen, Evelina was
twelve and Oswald was ten.

AUGUSTUS THE SOLE PARENT

The information in the 1867 obituary of Dr Tancred
in *De Zuid-Afrikaan* provides a strong clue as to the
arrangements he made for the children. Evelina was said
to have entered a convent at Boulogne-sur-Mer in France
and Oswald later worked for the Suez Canal Company
based in Paris. What of Augustus Frederick, the eldest
child? In 1895 the obituary on his death aged sixty records

that he 'received a good portion of his education in France'. At the time, Boulogne-sur-Mer had a thriving British community, and it seems highly likely that the children were taken there and placed in the care of family members or some institutional provider such as a boarding school or the Church.

THE MANAGEMENT OF CERTAIN MATTERS

Back in Europe, Augustus was now in a position to 'assume the management of certain matters devolving upon me since the death of Mrs. Tancred'. Although there is no evidence that he approached his own Tancred family, the chances are that Evelina's relatives, the Latteys or the Pittars, may have assisted with the arrangements for the children. Although Evelina's father was already dead, her mother lived until 1856, dying in London at the home of one of her sons, so may well have been there when the family returned to London in 1848. Apart from the welfare of the children, the other 'matters' referred to may have involved financial matters arising from Evelina's death. He had, after all, 'allied himself to a lady of some fortune', or so it was said (his obituary in the *Cradock Register*, January 1867).

EUROPE ON HIS RETURN

In March 1848, Augustus arrived back in the Europe he had left behind in 1841. Away from the troubled frontier in the Eastern Cape he might have expected to find peace and calm in Europe. That was not to be, for he went ashore on a continent awash with febrile political shenanigans: many were afraid that the revolutions experienced in other countries were now washing towards Britain on an incoming tide. In England, notwithstanding the extension of the franchise following the Reform Act of 1832 which mollified middle-income groups, the working classes remained dissatisfied. Although protectionist agricultural tariffs (the Corn Laws) had been repealed in 1846, the Chartists placed a peaceful petition aiming to redress the remaining grievances before Parliament in 1848, all this against a backdrop of continuing civil unrest and the accompanying nervousness affecting those in authority in the body politic. Peace is of course relative, and compared to the Eastern Cape it must have seemed very safe and secure to Augustus to be back in England.

NOT FORGETTING COLONEL LINDSAY

Once ashore in England Augustus announced two wider purposes behind his visit: the first concerned his starring role in what looked like a touring company production of the colonial drama, *Smith v Lindsay*. The Cape papers for 25 March 1848 reached the *Morning Herald* in London which gutted the contents and on 24 May 1848 reported:

'... the Rev. Dr. Tancred, who has made himself conspicuous in the colony from the active part he has taken on behalf of a burgher who, during the Kaffir war, it was alleged, was flogged by the order of a colonel of an infantry regiment recently arrived in England, is about to follow the gallant officer to this country, with the view of obtaining justice for the injured man.'

Typically, stories from the London papers were syndicated and on 30 May 1848, the *North Wales Chronicle* repeated this item which can assuredly have been of minimal interest to readers in North Wales where neither Augustus nor Lindsay, 'the gallant officer', nor his regiment had any connections.

CAMPAIGN FOR LOSSES ON THE FRONTIER

Apart from justice for Smith, a second purpose occupying Augustus' time in England seems to involve his campaign for reparations for the financial losses suffered by the settlers, himself included, in the frontier wars. He attributed these losses to the woeful state of governance at the Cape. A frequent settler complaint was that the army was too small, while such troops as there were had not done enough to protect the settlers and their farms. In September 1849, he wrote to the Colonial Office seeking compensation for the livestock losses he suffered as a farmer during the recent war. His intention was also to press for improved security arrangements in future, the ultimate key to which he saw as self-government at the Cape. From now on it was to this that he devoted most of his energies.

A MAN IN SEARCH OF A WIFE

There was another matter on which Augustus made no

formal announcement but on which his thoughts and urges pointed in a quite different direction from financial losses and colonial governance. This development might have been predicted. Helpfully, it is well documented, not least because it seems to place him back at the Cape before the end of the year of his arrival in England, 1848. Or does it?

In January 1849, he paid £15 for a 'special marriage licence' to be taken out in Cape Town for a marriage to be solemnised at Clanwilliam. Was he by then already back at the Cape? How did he identify, meet and court a bride there, and then take out a marriage licence in Cape Town unless he was back in town? Did the 'special' indicate the urgency of his wish to tie the matrimonial knot?

Surprisingly, he had not sought a bride in Grahamstown in the Eastern Cape, the area with which he was familiar and where he might even have known an eligible woman or two. Were the memories of the area too painful, or his standing there resting on ambivalent foundations? Nor did he seek a bride closer to Cape Town; Clanwilliam is 140 miles away in the North-Western Cape.

THE IRISH IN CLANWILLIAM

Why Clanwilliam? The answer may lie back in Cork from where, on 12 February 1820, an Irish settler party set off from Passage West, aboard the *East Indian* heading for the Cape. They were under the leadership of William Parker, a merchant of Cork, a man with a chequered past and turbulent future, in some ways a man not unlike Augustus. Also in the party of seventy-five was a rebellious man of

God, the Reverend Francis McCleland, a man of the cloth, another like the once young Augustus.[28]

The voyage was not a happy one with frequent quarrels among the settlers. By the time of arrival at the Cape, Parker had prepared official complaints against McCleland and one other settler. Also in Parker's sights, was Elizabeth Coyle, travelling alone, aged twenty-one and listed as a 'Governess'. He attempted to have her certified as insane.

Not content with encouraging more British emigrants to the Eastern Cape, the colonial authorities in London wanted to segregate the English and Irish contingents, the latter being seen as troublesome. On landing at the Cape, the Irish were sent to Clanwilliam rather than the usual settler destination, the Albany district near Grahamstown. The authorities may have breathed a sigh of relief, for surely they had at a stroke solved the Irish problem? Alas, Irish problems faced with solutions imposed from London rarely survive and so it was in this case. The Irish were not about to capitulate that easily. So it was that by 1825, with employment prospects and attempts at farming proving difficult in the conditions in the Northern Cape, only six families from Parker's party remained at Clanwilliam. Others had headed for the Albany district, or to work in the towns, or the more welcoming soils and climate to the south and east. There they could use the skills they had practised back home. Among those to move on in

---

28 G.B. Dickason, *Irish Settlers to the Cape, history of the Clanwilliam 1820 settlers from Cork Harbour*, 1973; D.P. McCracken and others have written extensively about the Irish in Southern Africa, for example, D.P. McCracken, *The Irish in Southern Africa 1795-1910* (1992), also *Ireland in South Africa in Modern Times*, 1996; and Donald H. Akenson, *The Irish in South Africa*, 1991.

an easterly direction was the eccentric Reverend Francis McCleland. He settled and built a fine house in Port Elizabeth with a commanding view over Algoa Bay.[29] The best-laid plans for distant lands often go adrift. Wiser authorities allow the Irish to solve their own problems. This lesson proved a long time in the learning.

Although there is no direct evidence pointing to a connection between Cork and Augustus' arrival at Clanwilliam, an Irish connection is the best possible explanation, other than random chance, of his arrival in this tiny, remote and mainly Dutch settlement in the North-Western Cape. Might he have had a contact there?

THE BRIDE TO BE, OR NOT TO BE?

His intended bride in Clanwilliam was Martha Magdalena Glendina Steenkamp, a spinster and clearly, judging by the names, from a Dutch family. Did he sniff money in the air, the prospect of another wife who came with some welcome wealth? She may on the other hand have been a lady of stunning good looks, or combined looks and affluence. How mutual the urge to tie the knot may have been is another unknown. She may have seen some cachet in the prospect of being married to a 'Dr' Tancred, an educated Irishman and a man of the world, now newly arrived amongst them in Clanwilliam.

Things were about to unravel from this high point when, for either or both parties, the prospect of marriage lost its attraction. Augustus, having identified his bride

29 Dean McCleland, www.thecasualobserver.co.za/port-elizabeth-of-yore

of choice and acquired the necessary marriage licence, found himself without a wife and out of pocket in the attempt to acquire one. If he was saddened at the loss of a bride, he certainly lamented his wasteful expenditure on the marriage licence. There was only one thing to do: he would seek a refund.

Grovelling for a refund of the cost of the special licence suggests he was short of money. The return on his expense had been disappointing in the extreme. He was not a man to let matters rest there, no, not he; Augustus would apply for a refund rather than see £15 slip through his fingers.

At this point we are brought up short by one of the most frustrating and abiding mysteries in the Tancred life story when on 14 September 1849, he appears to have been in London writing from Queen Street, Golden Square, as the 'Memorialist', and applying to His Excellency, Sir H.G.W. Smith, Baronet, Governor of the Cape of Good Hope, to authorise a refund of the £15 fee for the licence issued in Cape Town. He asked for the money to be paid over to the 'Zuid Afrikaan office' of J.J.H. Smuts, who 'will place the same to the Memorialist'.

Explaining his application for a refund Augustus described how, having paid the licence fee, and then proceeding 'to the abode of the lady's parents, he found her labouring under serious illness, and many other difficulties had been raised up, which had the effect of altogether breaking off the engagement'. That was his side of the story. Nothing is said of 'the many other difficulties'. Did Martha get cold feet at the prospect of marriage to Augustus, or realise he was not a man of means, or receive a better offer, or hear adverse reports on him from the Eastern Cape, or fear she might be expected to raise his existing children? Any or all of these would have been sound grounds for her hesitating before allowing him to make a legal leap between her marital thighs, thus transforming her from Miss Steenkamp into the second Mrs Tancred. Whether one or more of these or some other possibility was in play is another of the tantalising Tancred unknowns alongside the uncertainty as to the dates when he was in London and when at the Cape. It would of course not have been the first occasion since the dawn of time when 'the course of true love never did run smooth'.

There is no record of the Governor acceding to or denying his request for a refund, or of it ever reaching the account of J.J.H. Smuts. Which is not to say that these things did not happen.

As ever, the source of funds for his travel and maintenance costs remains a mystery.

CONVICTS FOR THE CAPE

Did such distractions cause him to miss out on the anti-convict furore at the Cape? It was the sort of cause that might have seemed close to Tancred's heart if only by bringing with it a certain celebrity status for those active in the ensuing campaign, resistance which involved violent riots and civil disorder.

The convict issue arose out of the overlap between home and colonial penal policies in London, where what to do with convicts was a perennial problem. Prisons were seen as a drain on the public funds, hard labour of little or no commercial value, and re-offending all too common the outcome on release. Costs clearly should be minimised with punishment maximised as a deterrent to crime. Transportation to the colonies was seen as an alternative to prison sentences, including the death sentence where the crime was not so heinous as to warrant execution. Convicts in England who were nearing the end of their sentences could be sent to the colonies where, on completing their sentences, they would be free to settle in the colony or return to England.

Surely the colonies would welcome the additional supply of transported convict labour both during the sentence and on release in the colony. This was not always the view when seen through colonial eyes. In the event of the implementation of such a policy, tactful and coordinated handling would be necessary. It seems that in the Cape Colony no one in authority paused to enquire into the views of the colonists.

As early as 1847 the idea of putting the Cape to good use in pursuit of this aim was floated in London. In 1848, Earl Grey, the Secretary of State for the Colonies, asked Sir Harry Smith, the Governor at the Cape, to take soundings of local opinions. It was sometimes said that Smith had in mind the Irish peasants, seen by him as having been drawn into criminal activity by the famine in 1845. Perhaps keen to curry favour with Grey in London, Smith hastened events by ignoring Grey's request to consult with the local population. This proved to be a big mistake when a public outcry in the Cape Town area soon followed word getting out about the scheme. A vigorous Anti-Convict Association sprang into life opposing the landing of the convicts and the establishment of a penal colony.

Fairbairn, journalist, editor of the *Commercial Advertiser,* and secretary of the Anti-Convict Association, encouraged a petition which attracted 450 signatures. This, together with other petitions, following numerous public meetings, was sent to the Governor who then forwarded them on to London (Parliamentary Paper, 31 January 1850).

Initially Smith, with the support of some of the settlers, particularly in the Eastern Cape, felt confident of success. However, he could not proceed without the agreement of the more powerful lobby in and around Cape Town. When the *Neptune,* carrying the convicts, arrived in Simon's Bay on 19 September 1849, with 289 convicts on board, Smith, caving in to local pressure, refused permission for the convicts to come ashore or for the *Neptune* to be supplied with fresh provisions. On 21 February 1850, after the convicts had been detained aboard ship for five months, orders from London sent the *Neptune* to Van Diemen's Land (named Tasmania in 1856).

Was Augustus in London or Cape Town at the time, and was he involved in the convict question? The man who voiced his written opinions on most matters of public consequence was mostly silent on the matter, seeming to take it as given that he and his readers were united in opposing the landing of convicts. He certainly saw the outcome as a great victory for the people of the Cape.

But was he in London at this time? In his ninth letter from England, written from Stape Hill House, Wimborne, Dorsetshire, on 23 November 1850, he assured his readers that 'Lord Grey cannot withstand you, the convict question has left him only one leg to stand on,' and continues, 'You may recollect that during the convict excitement a public meeting was got up at Cowie, and thanks crowed aloud to the Governor by the same Cock, who placed himself on the highest perch, and crowed for all the others.' This reference to a public meeting at Cowie during the convict agitation suggests that Augustus may have been present, unless he simply followed detailed reports reaching London from the Cape. It does seem to have been an issue in which a populist critic of the Governor and the Colonial Office would have wanted to immerse himself. Eventually determining when he was in London and when at the Cape would help to explain his seeming silence on the matter. That must be for future research. There are some six months during which his whereabouts cannot be established.

The agitation at the Cape and the outcome may in time have seen Augustus as one of the indirect beneficiaries. To many it now seemed obvious that the London government was out of touch with the feelings and ambitions of the colonists. Galvanising the local population against this unpopular proposal had alerted many to the power of protest and as always, high on their list of grievances, was the governance of the Cape, whether by the Governor or the Colonial Office in distant London. This combination of the awareness of citizen power and discontent added strength to the pressure from those in the colony arguing the case for representative government at the Cape.

The first Cape Parliament in 1854 was now only four years away. Might Augustus have begun to sniff a fresh opportunity in the wind?

23

OUR MAN IN LONDON

Nor need we allude to his exertions as the duly accredited representative of the large majority of the colonists in the matter of our present form of government; these are but too well known.

Obituary, *De Zuid-Afrikaan*

Unfortunately, the obituary does not spell out the nature of 'his exertions' or any evidence that he was 'the duly accredited representative of the large majority of the colonists'. If these were 'too well known' at the time, they are far from obvious a century and a half later.

All the available evidence suggests that Augustus was in London from his arrival in 1848 to his return to the Cape in 1851. But was he briefly back at the Cape at the time of the 1849 furore over the proposed convict settlement? And how does the ill-fated attempt to marry Miss Steenkamp fit into this time frame?

The *London Evening Standard,* on 18 September 1850, noted that it had 'received Cape of Good Hope papers of the 15th July' indicating that 'the colony was perfectly tranquil, and its inhabitants occupied with advancing their local interests'. This rosy view may have been how it seemed to Capetonians. In the Eastern Cape, after the seventh war which ended in 1847, and before the eighth war which began in 1850, the outlook was very different. Augustus, of course, arrived in London with an Eastern Cape point of view.

As is so often the case, the trail of the next phase of his life starts with what he says about himself. The article in the *Evening Standard* noted the inclusion of 'the only articles worth extracting' from the Cape papers they received. One such article proved to be a lengthy letter from Augustus J. Tancred, D.D., writing from 35 Golden Square, London, on Thursday 25 April 1850, reprinted in the 15 July issue of *De Zuid-Afrikaan*, and clearly aimed at the Cape readership. This shows that he was in London in the early part of 1850. Here he reminds his readers that in his earlier letters on 10 and 12 March, 'I informed you that I arrested the progress of the bill relative to the Representative Assembly until your wishes should be consulted, and the result returned to the home government. I have constantly engaged with the other points relating to the future welfare of the colony.' He then quotes four dates in April when he claims to have 'been at the Colonial Office, Downing Street'.

On one such date, Saturday 27 April, he claims to have met with a Mr B. Hawes at the Colonial Office when 'we entered upon business and discussed everything of importance, until the arrival of Earl Grey interrupted our conversation, and I have now the pleasure to announce to you that everything has been acceded to the colony that you could desire'.

What might the colonists desire? Tancred's list of what he claimed had been achieved makes it sound as if Christmas has come early to the Cape: Sir Harry Smith would be the last military Governor with 'all civil Governors for the future' with 'an assurance and a promise given to me to that effect'; he had received clarification that trial by jury in civil cases was already within the power of the colony to obtain and does not rest with the home government; Earl Grey and Mr Hawes 'entertain no limited, prejudiced or bigoted views with regard to the future form of government at the Cape' and that, on the contrary, 'they shall be ready to accede to that form which the majority of the people shall decide on and approve of'. Applauding his own achievement, he minces no words in his derogatory comments about those in powerful positions at the Cape:

> So now I sincerely hope that you will make use of the privilege and opportunity afforded you of obtaining for yourselves and your children a free and independent Representative Assembly, without the intermeddling of Montagu, Porter, the judges, the military Governor Smith, and the other paltry and worthless officials.

This is of course pure Tancred, another example of his supreme understanding of how *not* to influence people. If only these people were as clever as he!

The agenda must have been a very lengthy one, for it did not conclude at this point. Also discussed, apparently, were: the indemnifications of the losses incurred in consequence of the Kaffir War, this being a matter close to Tancred's heart and purse; the future of the territory beyond the Orange River; the law regulating the conduct between master and servant; the 'diffusion' of education; the facility of obtaining justice in the country parts; and, not forgetting, future emigration.

And that is not all! There is something totally daunting about this list of Tancred's claimed accomplishments which goes on to cover the sale of forest lands, the government monopoly of gunpowder, the salaries of clerks and others in the government offices and, perhaps the cherry on the top: if people forward their petitions directly to England, not as now through the Governor, they only have to ask unanimously for it to be granted.

'Thus far,' he concludes, 'I have laboured for you, and I hope my feeble exertions will afford you satisfaction and meet with your approbation. Hoping that the time is not far distant when you shall be all happy and prosperous, your colony free and independent, your rights and privileges secured upon solid and permanent bases'. Feeble indeed! But could it be true?

No doubt many colonists were pleased to hear Tancred's news, no doubt his stock was rising rapidly amongst just such people. Should the opportunity arise, whether by accident or design, he had now constructed the makings of a springboard into public life at the Cape. For the moment, though, speaking of 'your' not 'our' aspirations for the colony, it appears that he had not yet determined to return to the Cape.

THE EARL OF ARUNDEL AND SURREY AND EARL GREY

At first glance Tancred's claim that he attended a meeting with such distinguished people invites incredulity bordering on disbelief. But might such a meeting have taken place? In London, in July 1850, he was still strutting his stuff as a self-proclaimed colonial hero, lobbying for the interests of the folks back home, negotiating with Colonial Office officials, influencing opinion in the press, dropping words in the ears of members of the British Parliament. That was how he viewed himself but was it all no more than wishful thinking?

Perhaps not entirely, for on Wednesday 17 July 1850 the Court Circular in *The Times* (London) reported that 'The Earl of Arundel and Surrey and Dr. Tancred had an interview with Earl Grey yesterday at the Colonial Office.' On Saturday 20 July, the *Wexford Independent* repeated the same report. Why was this meeting of interest to Irish readers? The answer may lie in the career of the Earl of Arundel and Surrey. Elected as a Whig representing Arundel in the House of Commons from 1837 to 1851, in 1850 he balked at the Ecclesiastical Titles Act (1851) and then seems to have shown an interest in an Irish seat. He was elected to Limerick, one hundred miles from Wexford, briefly from 1851 to 1852, after the sitting member resigned to make way for him.

With Arundel, a staunch Roman Catholic, and Tancred back in the Catholic fold, both with an Irish connection, surely this still lacked the overlap of social status that would have allowed the lowly Tancred to be in a position to contact Arundel and, in his company, meet Earl Grey? Unless, that is, Arundel's interest in Cape affairs meant he was pleased to be accompanied by a man well versed in the issues of the colony. Tancred had, after all, been shouting from the London rooftops that he was the man who knew about such things. Otherwise, the connection between Catholicism and colonialism, and the reason why Arundel was involved with Tancred, however briefly, remains one among many intriguing unknowns.

Throughout all of this we are left in the dark as to his legitimacy as an 'accredited representative' of people at the Cape; who appointed him, how much time was spent on his 'exertions', how much did he actually achieve, and what was the source of his income?

There is evidence that Augustus, continuing to ruffle feathers in the newspapers, was in London in September 1850. On 28 September 1850, *John Bull*, a London weekly newspaper, republished a lengthy article from the London *Morning Herald* headed 'Civil and Military Governors', opening with the statement that 'The announcement of Dr. Tancred to the Cape Colonists that Sir H. Smith will be the last military Governor at the Cape of Good Hope – all civil Governors for the future...' This is followed by an almost audible hoot of derision. The *Morning Herald* is steadfastly on the side of military governors for if a civil governor:

'... had been Governor of the Cape during the recent anticonvict disturbances of that colony, martial law would have been proclaimed, and the streets of Cape Town would have run crimson red with blood. Indeed, there is no saying but that one or other Civil Governor might not have shot Dr. Tancred himself, like the Buddhist Priest in his robes, or have melted Mr. Fairbairn's types into musket-balls, and platooned that truculent editor in the middle of the Grand Parade.'

All in all, this sounds most like the views of the pro-military governor faction at the Cape.

MR C.J. LOCK'S LETTER TO P. VAN RHYN, FIELD CORNET

Once again, the next step along the road begins with another Tancred letter. In 1851, a Mr C.J. Lock in Clanwilliam received a 'personal letter' from Dr Tancred, 'our trusty friend in London'. On 22 May, Lock wrote as a 'willing servant and friend' to P. van Rhyn, Field Cornet, with a 'friendly' request to van Rhyn that he communicate the contents of Tancred's letter, which was addressed to 'Honourable Fellow Countrymen and Friends!', to the residents of his ward.

Lock referred to Tancred's letter and expressed his delight at the news, saying 'how glad these tidings made me', before going on to explain how since Tancred's departure he had 'often reflected with admiration on how a man, who has to cope with so many difficulties, can have so much strength and perseverance to overcome this unavoidable problem and be able to gain access to the Higher Government of England'.

Turning to the matters at hand, Lock pointed to Tancred's earlier letters to Lord Grey, Secretary for the Colonies, reprinted in *De Zuid-Afrikaan*, and setting out 'the true condition of our colony'. These letters included Tancred's insistence on the colony 'being granted a national representative as soon as possible, through whom we will be able to redress our grievances and maintain our civil rights'.

Lock's understanding of events seems to be that Tancred, disappointed at the lack of a response to his earlier letters to Earl Grey, had headed for London to lobby for changes to the government of the Cape. Tancred's powers of persuasion were such that, according to Lock, 'by his tireless efforts' he won the support of Members of Parliament. He had thereby ensured that the Colony of the Cape of Good Hope would now enjoy the protection of the Secretary for the Colonies who would be 'forced to accept our free institutions'. Lock saw this as Dr Tancred laying the foundations 'for how our state would be managed in future'. None of this, he believed, could have been achieved 'without the personal presence of our loyal friend in London' whose involvement enabled 'so many men of rank and stature' to speak up in Parliament for the welfare of the colony.

Tancred, in Lock's eyes, had achieved the goals for which, presumably after his failed attempt to lasso a bride, he left Clanwilliam for Europe. However, if we remember that Lock was in Clanwilliam and was not present to witness Tancred's achievements, we are led to conclude that the achievements, real or imagined, are as described by Tancred to Lock. Clearly, Tancred told a good story, but was the value inflated by exaggeration? The reception accorded to Tancred on his return suggests that his account of events in London went down well with a sizeable chunk of the Cape audience.

*

Lock, in his lengthy letter to van Rhyn, still quoting Tancred, takes up the story of Tancred's intended return to the Cape. Having, or so he claimed, nearly fulfilled all his undertakings, Tancred planned to depart from England on 29 March on the *Mary Ann* under Captain Darke and was due to reach the colony on 1 July. If, in the meantime, Lock was to gather all their legitimate grievances and claims in a proper form Tancred would, without delay on his return, investigate these matters while also indicating to the colonists, 'the direction we should take to continue promoting Right, Truth and Righteousness'. Re-branding himself in this almost Messianic guise, he would now make his re-entry at the Cape, bringing with him further messages of the possible impending arrival of self-government in the colony.

Tancred certainly claimed that he was very active in London on behalf of the colony. But what are we to make of this? Did he, as he claimed, or as Lock asserted on his behalf, address the House of Lords? The latter is ridiculous but may be the result of a misunderstanding by Lock. Was Augustus merely exaggerating both his ability to meet up with important people and the extent to which he put himself about advocating change at the Cape? Veracity was seldom his strongest suit. Although Lock refers to Tancred as 'our trusty friend' and 'our loyal friend' we do not know how well the two were known to one another. Nor do we know which difficulties Lock has in mind when he refers almost in awe to Tancred as a man who 'has to cope with so many difficulties, can have so much strength and perseverance to overcome this unavoidable problem'. What had Tancred confided in Lock about his 'difficulties' and what was the 'unavoidable problem'? He had certainly known many difficulties but a number of these might perhaps be classed as 'avoidable'.

24

RETURN TO THE CAPE

That Tancred is back at the Cape, and when, is shown by a tour of the Western Province he made between July and October in 1851 which was given publicity by him and others in letters to, or reports in, *De Zuid-Afrikaan*. These showed that he spoke at a number of public meetings which seem to have been well attended and at which he claimed that he helped draw up petitions to the government in London requesting a parliament at the Cape and, consequently, a new constitution. Letters to *De Zuid-Afrikaan* thank him for his efforts and report on his arrival at various locations and, sometimes, include descriptions of the meetings. A sideline to the tour was his addition to the series of letters he fired off to Earl Grey in London. The tour concluded with a 'monster meeting' at Clanwilliam.

His efforts along these lines continued in February and March 1852, when he held two meetings in Clanwilliam. His intention seems to have been to thank the Governor at Cape Town and the British government in London for the new constitution laying the ground for the anticipated Cape parliament. He was also busy drawing up petitions and listing people's grievances ready to be considered by the new government once it opened for business. Towards the end of March, he went to Cape Town with a deputation of Clanwilliam field cornets to present collected petitions to the Governor. Then, between May and September, he travelled around the Clanwilliam area holding further public meetings and drawing up more petitions.

That his efforts were well received is shown by the public meeting of field cornets, old field cornets, and others of the most influential men of the Clanwilliam district, held on 1 October 1852, on the farm Jan Diesel's Valley: 'to adopt measures to collect a sum of 100,000 guilders, or £2,500 sterling, for the purpose of purchasing an estate and presenting the same as a free gift to our upright and long tried friend Dr Tancred, in token of our grateful feelings towards him, as a manifestation of respect and approval of his indefatigable exertions, and as a slight offer of gratitude for the many and important services by him for so many years to this oppressed colony' (*De Zuid-Afrikaan*, 2 December 1852). The list of field cornets and others who signed the notice included one Pieter van Zyl from Langevallei. The name van Zyl would soon figure prominently in the life of Augustus.

In 1853, anticipating the constitution coming into effect, he set off on another series of public meetings between March and September. In May he was a member of yet another deputation of field cornets and other prominent men from the Clanwilliam area who journeyed to Cape Town to thank the Governor for the progress towards greater self-government and to present yet another petition.

Augustus was at this moment clearly seen through some admiring and grateful settler eyes; he had been in a similar position once before when, on leaving the curacy he briefly held at Christchurch, some members of the congregation had paid him many warm compliments in presenting him with an inscribed silver snuff box. In retrospect, with what they later learned, their estimation of his virtues had plummeted. Surely Clanwilliam was not about to witness a re-run of that episode?

For the moment at least, events in his life were once again on a rising trend. He was established back in the colony with a solid base of support, especially in the Western Cape. There was, however, an increasingly acerbic tone in his letters to Earl Grey.

Aside from his letters to Earl Grey, his tours around the countryside harvesting support for representative government, and people wanting to provide him with an estate, there was one other matter to the forefront of his mind. A familiar longing was proving restless between his thighs. His sights were now trained on the eligible young ladies of Clanwilliam. At the second attempt he was intent on securing a second wife.

25

TILL DEATH US DO PART

Dr. Tancred was twice married… His second wife, the
daughter of Mr. P. van Zyl, a wealthy agriculturist in the
district of Clanwilliam, survives him, with two children, a
daughter and a son.
Obituary, *De Zuid-Afrikaan*

What took Augustus to Clanwilliam in the first place is, apart from the possible Irish connection, as unknown as his introduction to the van Zyl family. Was it no more than coincidence that amongst the field cornets who gathered in October 1852, on Jan Diesel's farm in the Clanwilliam area to raise the money to purchase and present an estate to Dr Tancred, was one Pieter van Zyl? The van Zyls were clearly a family of some substance in the area. Had the Augustus nostrils sniffed money in the Clanwilliam air?

If it is a self-evident truth that many a widower, regardless of wealth, may find the sap rising and decide to set out in search of a wife, Augustus, a widower since 1847, was without wealth but in want of a wife. If it was true that his first wife was a woman of some financial means, he may have thought that more of the same would meet his earthly needs, a material security blanket secured beneath the bed sheets. Now, approaching fifty years of age, he was about to make a second attempt to secure a second wife. Should she be from a wealthy family, how old should she be? He left no record of his search criteria. Or was Tancred by now already a man of means as a result of the fundraising by the field cornets? Unfortunately, once again, the record does not show the success or otherwise of the size or disposal of the money the field cornets raised in gratitude to Tancred.

Even if a restless urge was stirring in the Tancred loins, he seems unlikely to have been the first choice on offer to the cream of the herd amongst the young ladies in the Clanwilliam area. On the other hand, he would no doubt let slip, as he may have done before, that he held a doctorate from Trinity College Dublin, and was a man of a wider world, at ease amongst the gentry and politicians in faraway London, at home in its smoke-laden coffee shops and the corridors of its parliamentary power. Was it all down to the Lord's will? Or the course of true love?

He set about courting the young woman he would eventually marry who, like the rejected Miss Steenkamp from this same area, was from a Dutch family. In the words of his later obituary, she was a 'daughter of Mr. P. van Zyl, a wealthy agriculturist in the district of Clanwilliam'. On this the obituary was correct. If Evelina had indeed been 'a lady of some fortune', and his second wife came from a wealthy family, it does seem that marrying money should be listed amongst his accomplishments.

*

On 22 December 1853 he and Geesje Martha Maria Van Zyl, 'Geesie', were married in the office of the NG Kerk (the Nederduitse Gereformeerde Kerk/the Dutch Reformed Church) in Clanwilliam by Erw. H.R. De Villiers. Erw. (Eerwaarde) signifies that De Villiers was one of the most senior and respected ministers in the NG Kerk. Born on 16 June 1839, Geesie was fourteen years of age at the time of her marriage, an underage spinster. Augustus was aged forty-nine years. Were any eyebrows raised on account of her age and the age difference between them? On the marriage certificate he is recorded as Dr Tancred, D.D., a widower and Doctor of Theology. Dutch, or more properly High Dutch, and subsequently Afrikaans, was the first language of his new family. Fortunately Augustus was an accomplished linguist.

26

INSULTS TO EARL GREY

In 1842 Tancred seems to have begun with a modicum of respect for those in authority over the Cape Colony, be it the Colonial Secretary in London or the Governor in Cape Town. Whenever he believed his voice was being heard, or his views finding acceptance, he was content to parley in an oleaginous manner with the great and the good. When he believed people were not listening to him, or not agreeing with him, it was a different matter and he very often became increasingly intemperate in his use of language, his emotions boiling over till he resembled a spoilt child frustrated at not being granted all his wishes.

The succession of irate letters he wrote to Earl Grey, reproduced in *De Zuid-Afrikaan*, make it abundantly clear that his campaigning in London had not been as successful as he had hoped, or had led the colonists to believe. His contempt for Earl Grey, and all colonial officials, would rapidly become blistering in tone. As usual the *non sequiturs*, a Tancred literary speciality, abound.

Henry, 3rd Earl Grey, was the Colonial Secretary from 1846 to 1852. Although of a generally liberal approach on a wide range of policy issues, the Cape witnessed him at his most intransigent, unsympathetic to the notion that the colonists' views should be given full weight, let alone that they might be given a greater say in their own governance. This was very different from his views as reported by Tancred from London. In the 1849 hullaballoo at the Cape over the convicts, Grey had proved obdurate, only capitulating in the face of the ensuing local outrage.

When faced with views divergent from his own, Tancred, the man we remember as the author of *A Treatise on Polite Philosophy, or an Easy Manner of Settling Differences Among Men*, was not the ideal person to put forward measured arguments in favour of changes to the way the colony was governed. His notions of 'polite philosophy' and 'easy manner' could so quickly go straight out of the window at the first sight of a differing opinion. Although greater self-government did come, it had not yet, and certainly not as instantly as Tancred would have liked. There was very little in the way of 'an easy manner' in his letters to Earl Grey. They all hark back to his campaigning efforts in London in early 1851 when he claimed to have met Earl Grey and the man he later described disparagingly as 'Little' Mr Hawes.

The gravest offence to Grey is of course the letter already mentioned in which Augustus praises Grey's father, contrasting this with his son, noting that the son resembles him not at all, an absence of any family resemblance which his mother can no doubt explain. Casting doubt on the Colonial Secretary's legitimacy was not a shrewd move.

Other examples abound. Status continues to obsess Augustus. He asserts that they know one another well enough for him to have no need to begin his letter with 'I take the liberty of addressing you'. This would be nothing short of humbug, for Tancred has 'a right to communicate, and that your Lordship is bound to listen'. He sees himself as equal in status to the Earl, who he sees as 'the greatest political unredeemed shuffler, and even juggler, that has been in Downing Street during the last half century'. Describing himself in contrast to Grey, Tancred makes the point, 'I speak boldly, for I speak the truth, and I am not afraid of my words, I never swallow them.' Meanwhile 'the spirit of this long-suffering Colony is so aroused, that it will require a cleverer political head than your Lordship can boast of, to keep within bounds of prudence, and the limits of the constitution such brave (underlined) and noble (underlined) people as your little (underlined) Under Secretary Hawes has since been pleased to call them'.

By September of the same year further instances of his gratuitous insults abound. In a letter from Clanwilliam which reached London on 13 September 1851, he writes 'in the hope that by the time this letter, or at the farthest the next, reaches you in England, that you may be far removed from your post at the Colonial Office, and some other Secretary in the place you now occupy'. In October he boasts that Earl Grey had 'never heard yet of a Tancred apologising'.

The point cannot have been lost on Earl Grey or his officials, who would certainly have remembered Tancred's visit to London. Long before October Earl Grey would have lost any interest he might once have shown in Tancred's ideas. The letters in all probability lay largely unread.

His visit to London campaigning for the reform of colonial government at the Cape was not, after all, the triumphant *tour de force* he had represented to Mr Lock back in Clanwilliam. Did he intend to mislead or did he actually believe in his account of what he achieved? With Tancred it is often difficult to separate one from the other. No doubt he exaggerated the number and success of his contacts with Earl Grey and the 'Little' Mr Hawes.

He sets the shortcomings he sees in London against the virtues of the colonists at the Cape. These good people, he says, are uniquely patient, loyal and faithful and 'attached to Her Majesty of England' in spite of the oppression resulting from the incompetence of the colonial administrators who are deaf to all representation in London on their behalf – representations by Tancred that is. Meanwhile colonial life goes on, the populace 'constitutionally looking for their rights', while 'kept in cruel suspense, their loyalty taken for granted', all allowed to happen in the face of 'dogged indifference' from those in authority in London.

In London his representations, barbed with insults, fell on fallow ground. This is the time when on 21 October 1851, his letters to Earl Grey were received in London, and an official wrote, 'The enclosed are a continuation of Dr. Tancred's ravings.' This was not the first time that doubts had been cast on his state of mind.

Meanwhile his stream of letters appearing in *De Zuid-Afrikaan* had the effect of raising his personal profile and that of the issues locally at the Cape. The more astute politicians would have realised that here was a man who, however worthy the cause, was teetering on the brink of a fully blown episode of mental instability at a time when no support services were available for those in need of help.

Meanwhile his tirades against Grey continued. 'Oh John! Where did you learn logic?' he asked. 'Most assuredly not at Oxford. I am sure you are not a Scotchman, and as to your theological knowledge, I have a very poor opinion indeed.'

And not content with that: 'Surely you must remember the last time I met you (all underlined) or rather the period when you did not wish to meet me. Just before I sailed from England on the 4th April of this year (1851) I demanded on a Saturday an interview for the following Monday, and Little (underlined) Mr Hawes informed me, that the time was so short, that I could scarce even get an answer to my letter. However, I received an answer full of your (underlined) political (underlined) regret (underlined) which is no regret at all, that you were unable to see me. It is all the better that we did not meet, as I intended to give it to you hot and warm, upon several things, which I shall narrate to you in some future letter. For the time you escaped (underlined).'

Augustus had by now fallen to a very low level of public discourse. It must surely have been plain to a great many people that this was not the most effective way of winning supporters to the causes he espoused.[30]

Could he ever bounce back in public or private life?

---

30 His 1851 letters from the Cape to Earl Grey in London are in the National Archives, Kew. CO 48/322.

27

THE ORANGE RIVER SOVEREIGNTY

Augustus had yet to tie the matrimonial knot and enjoy his first Christmas at Clanwilliam with Geesie when, earlier in 1853, he set off for Bloemfontein having been invited to join a committee sitting to advise on and assist in the formation of a government for the Orange River Sovereignty, a disputed political territory between the Orange and Vaal rivers. How, why and by whom had he been chosen for this role? My working assumption is that his thanks were due, for reasons unknown, to the colonial administrators in Cape Town.

BACKGROUND

As early as the 1820s white missionaries, mainly English but also some French and German, had begun to settle in the area beyond the frontier of the Cape Colony. Dutch settlers were not far behind. Other major actors in this colonial playlet were Dr John Philip of the London Missionary Society and the Griqua leader Adam Kok II whose people were invited in 1825 by Philip to settle in the area around Philippolis. The Griquas soon claimed the territory to the north of Philippolis as far to the north as the Riet River. The stage was now set for a complicated plot to unfold over the next three decades as the conflicting interests of the Griquas and the white settlers came to the surface.

In 1836 the Cape of Good Hope Punishment Act extended the reach of the law applicable in the Cape Colony to the area beyond the frontier. This made for greater British involvement in the area, as they sought to gain control over white emigrants in the area. Extending the area covered by the law was one thing, enforcing its application was a commitment of a different order. Enforcement of the law also meant a civilian administration and the presence of the British Army.

The Orange River Sovereignty began life as a quirk of colonial history when in 1845 the British government appointed a British Resident in charge of the area occupied by the tribes living beyond the north-east frontier of the Cape Colony. In January 1846, Captain (later Major) Henry Douglas Warden replaced the first British Resident. Warden purchased a farm called Bloem Fontein from a local Griqua farmer. This minor military possession of the British, with Bloemfontein as its capital, was occupied mainly by the army with its artillery, cavalry and infantry, together with some residents, farmers and traders, British and Dutch, as well as the members of the African tribes in the area. It proved an unstable amalgam of conflicting interests. Almost from the beginning the British harboured doubts as to the wisdom of the enterprise which combined relatively little commercial value with disproportionate administrative and military costs.

Somewhat precipitately, in February 1848, Sir Harry Smith, the newly appointed (1847) Governor of the Cape Colony, proclaimed British sovereignty over the area then known as Transorangia.

MAJOR WARDEN AT THE HELM

The Dutch settlers in the area had other ideas. They had left the Cape Colony with the express intention of escaping British rule. Warden, with the inadequate firepower of his small force of Cape Mounted Riflemen, plus the few Europeans attached to his staff, was vulnerable to any hostile action. Advancing on his position was a superior Boer force under General Andries Pretorius, father of M.W. Pretorius, later President of the Orange Free State. Warden had no alternative but to surrender and retire with the agreement of the attacking force to the Orange River in the direction of Colesberg. This was felt as a humiliation by the British authorities in Cape Town and London.

The British lion had been poked in the eye with a stick and it was cross, very cross. When news of this violation of the honour of Britain reached the seats of government in Cape Town and London, a force was organised to right the perceived wrong. Sir Harry Smith ordered Colonel George Buller to the area and later joined him to take overall command. With Sir Harry Smith at their head, British troops advanced on the Orange River with Warden minded to 'interview' any opponents.

Warden's 'interview' became the battle of Boomplaats (or Boomplaas) fought on 29 August 1848. The British forces were successful and Sir Harry Smith marched on to Bloemfontein, then to Winburg, to establish British sovereignty over the land on that side of the Orange River up to the 14th parallel of latitude.

The fight at Boomplaats had consequences that reverberated down the years when, not for the first time and in line with custom, the British made a public relations disaster out of a straightforward, minor military success. Captain Salis leading an advance party of troops had been fired upon, wounded and disabled, though after pleading for mercy his life was spared. Coming after the Slachter's Nek debacle, it might have proved a valuable public relations opportunity for the British. It was not to be. Two men, seen as members of the 'rebel party', De la Rey who was Dutch, and Quigley who was not, were tried by court martial and, in spite of pleas for clemency, some from the British side, were shot. The failure by the British to calm matters rather than stoking feelings of ill-will among the Dutch simply added to the increasingly long list of grievances the Dutch felt towards the imperial power. Ironically it seems that Quigley was a deserter from his regiment and not present in the vicinity of the place where the fight occurred.

INTERMISSION

With British power restored in the area of the Orange River, matters might have been regarded as settled but it was not to be. A greater authority than the Governor at the Cape controlled the purse strings in London. The decision was taken to cede the administration of the Orange River

Sovereignty to the mainly Dutch inhabitants. Although the British government had originally supported the annexation, in October 1851 Earl Grey, Secretary of State for War and the Colonies, stated the view that 'the ultimate abandonment of the Orange sovereignty should be a settled point in our policy'. At the same time a body of contrary opinion at the Cape and in England favoured retention.

In 1852, Warden was dismissed from his post as British Resident and in June the white inhabitants of the sovereignty voted to retain rule by the British. In 1853, Sir George Russell Clerk was despatched from London to the Cape to settle and adjust the affairs of the sovereignty with the British government determined to offload responsibility for the area beyond the Orange River. In July, Clerk called a meeting of delegates to solve the problem by devising a form of self-government for the area. Those in favour of the retention of British rule in the area proved intransigent until, with agreement seeming elusive, Clerk issued a threat: he would hand over the country to the local African leaders if he could not offload responsibility for the territory. Dr Tancred, 'a Cape politician' and noted critic of colonial rule and rulers at the Cape, was invited to advise and assist the Republican side, the Dutch, in the negotiations at Bloemfontein.

The pro-British rule settlers in the area sent two representatives to England to seek a reversal of British policy. In January 1854 a royal proclamation was signed 'abandoning and renouncing all dominion' in the sovereignty. On 23 February at the conclusion of the negotiations on the future of the area, Sir George Clerk and the republican committee signed the Orange

River Convention (or Bloemfontein Convention) at Bloemfontein. This recognised the independence of the former sovereignty. The journey of the representatives seeking to reverse the policy proved futile as events in Bloemfontein and London had moved faster than the vessel conveying them from the Cape. They arrived five days after the signing. In an interview with the Colonial Secretary, the Duke of Newcastle, he informed them that it was too late to discuss the retention of British rule, adding it was not possible for Britain to supply troops to constantly advancing outposts of doubtful value, 'as Cape Town and the port of Table Bay were all she really required in South Africa'. This opinion would not have gone down well among the settlers immersed in the settler wars beyond the safety of Cape Town.

In March the Dutch government assumed office at Bloemfontein.

Abandoning the area on 11 March 1854, the British predictably did things in style, firing a royal salute from the fort and hauling down the British ensign before marching out of Bloemfontein. With fewer inhabitants and a decrease in commerce after the British departed, Bloemfontein entered a period of economic gloom. Worse still was the ever-present fear of white settlers in Africa, the black tribesmen waiting to spoil the colonial party, in this case what was seen by some as 'the rapacity of the Basutos' or, more accurately, the Griquas.

OH, HAPPY MAN

If there was British settler dismay in Bloemfontein this was echoed by a vocal lobby in London whose views found expression in articles, letters and parliamentary reports in the London *Times*.

The debate in the London Parliament in May 1854 hinged on whether Great Britain should have abandoned the sovereignty. The deputation from the Cape representing the retentionist lobby, having failed to prevent abandonment, met the Secretary and the Under-Secretary of State for the Colonies as well as some members of Parliament including Mr Adderley, the member for North Staffordshire, who agreed to put the retentionist case before Parliament. On 9 May 1854, Adderley introduced a motion and Mr F. Peel, Sir John Pakington and others spoke in the debate.

Pakington's speech was reported *in extenso* in the London *Times* which included a leading article which poured scorn on the Orange River Territory and was scathing on the outcome, 'the actual finale of our dominion over the Orange-River Territory'. The dripping sarcasm continues, 'the very small sums that figure in the negotiation' include the 'moderate' initial capital of £6,000 paid to the new Government 'of what sort, what origin, what authority, we are only too thankful to be entirely ignorant'. Then there is 'the magnificent sum of £500, damages are found for half-a-dozen gentlemen illegally imprisoned, and as many widows of persons unfortunately shot'.

Amongst the payments made to individuals there was also one for services rendered by Dr Tancred. The London *Times* makes its opinion very clear: 'The Rev Dr Tancred goes off a happy man with £200; and on the strength of it, is now the centre of hospitality, the genius of improvement, and the soul of order, in the Clanwilliam district.' The writer was evidently not a Tancred admirer.

The London *Times* had only half of the story. An insider's view of events in the sovereignty was provided by Joseph Millerd Orpen, an Irishman born in Dublin in 1828 who emigrated to the Cape in 1846 and then became a land surveyor in the Orange River Sovereignty. In 1853 he was elected to stand with those who opposed the abandonment of the sovereignty and would have observed people and events at first hand.

Orpen recounted how those in favour of the abandonment of British rule 'invited a certain Dr. Tancred from the Cape Colony, a very eccentric person, to come and aid and advise them in their negotiations with Sir George Clerk'. When the negotiations concluded with the abandonment of the sovereignty Tancred 'demanded payment and the members of the new Government made up among themselves a very small subscription. He (Tancred) considered it an outrage and spoke about it at large.' When the pro-British rule side heard of this, they 'showed up its ridiculous aspect' and, going to the other extreme, voted Tancred £200 'out of the poor little funds of the country'. Meanwhile Sir George Clerk, hearing of this and bowing to public ridicule, paid Dr Tancred a further £200 'by a draft on the Commissariat chest'. The loyalists, both English and Dutch, who had wanted to retain British sovereignty over the area, noted that Tancred 'was supposed to have been a priest at some time' and vented their amusement in doggerel rhymes headed 'De Nieuwe Raad' (The New Council) ending with (translated from the Dutch):

To the help of such donkeys now,
the Priest has come,
The members of this clever Raad,
My words must well remark,
That they are nicely taken in,
By Sir George Russell Clerk.[31]

Time and again Tancred seems to demonstrate a remarkable facility for persuading people to part with their money.

*

The *SA Commercial Advertiser and Cape Town Mail,* on 2 January 1855, took a more sanguine view of the outcome than *The Times,* seeing the benefits of the 'final separation' of the sovereignty 'not only from the Colony but from the British dominions'. The writer saw it as 'a settled resolution against the taking up of any more British territory in Southern Africa'. Moreover, 'there is every appearance of the local people conducting their affairs with discretion when they can no longer rely on support from British troops in all contests with the native tribes'.

If only! As things turned out the British were not yet finished with further expansion in southern Africa and the tribe which then proved most troublesome was the other white tribe, the Boers, later the Afrikaners, of Dutch descent. When they had fanned out from the Cape into the hinterland beyond to leave behind British rule neither

31 Joseph Millerd Orpen, *Reminiscences of Life in South Africa from 1846 to the Present Day,* vols. I and II.

they, nor anyone else, knew that diamonds and gold lurked unseen beneath their feet. Southern Africa had not seen the last of British boots on the veld. Britain would come to prove more than equal to the Basutos in rapacity.

In 1910 the Oranje Vrystaat (Orange Free State) became one of the four provinces of the Union of South Africa.[32]

---

32 William C. Holden, *History of the Colony of Natal, South Africa*, 399–405, 1855; William Porter, *The Touwfontein Letters*, ed. Karel Schoeman, 1992; Karel Schoeman, ed. *The British Presence in the Transorange, 1845–1854*, 1992; George McCall Theal, *History of South Africa*, 1893.

28

THE OLD CAPE HOUSE

Augustus was soon back in Clanwilliam ahead of the elections to the new House of Assembly which was due to open its doors in 1854. He was now, and not for the first time, with one foot firmly poised on the ladder of potential success. His history to date revealed a man with an unequalled gift for choosing a ladder with faulty rungs. Would it be different this time? He was well regarded in the colony and married into an affluent farming family. Although it has not been established whether or not the attempt to raise £2,500 to purchase an estate and present it to him succeeded, it can have come as no surprise that when an election was called for seats in the first Cape Parliament his powerful local backing saw him chosen as a candidate to contest one of the two Clanwilliam seats. On election day he proved a shoe-in with a solid majority. Despite his aspirations as a civil rights campaigner, he attracted no support from the few non-white voters on the qualified roll. He never had shown an interest in the rights of non-white people.

He was now on his way to public life in Cape Town with another opportunity to put his intelligence and education to good use. Might a career of some distinction lie ahead? Much has been written about the first Cape Parliament in books, newspaper articles and reports. Here it is only possible to paint a canvas with a selection of broad brushstrokes that create a view of his parliamentary life. He never did achieve the high office which he craved, and for which his education and talents might have equipped him. But, for good or ill, he did make his mark and was long remembered after he was gone.

REPRESENTATIVE GOVERNMENT

What lay ahead for the Cape Colony? When the colony was ceded from the Dutch to Britain in 1814, it came with a gift-wrapped parcel of complex issues. At first the Governor exercised all executive and legislative authority on behalf of the government in London. Over the following forty years the administration of this large area with its heterogeneous population and myriad of problems proved to be beyond the reach of the Governor and his staff. In 1834 a new constitution established an executive council and a legislative council, with the Governor retaining the ultimate authority. The next step involved some of the power being devolved to elected representatives with greater public participation in the government of the colony.

When 1854 saw the formation of the first Cape Parliament a limited form of representative government had arrived at the Cape. Tancred of course claimed that his lobbying in the press and on the ground in London and the Cape made a significant contribution to the granting of this political development. There can be no doubt that he believed this. Perhaps in the end it hinges on the import of the word 'significant'. An egotistical man, he was apt to exaggerate his own importance. He was also good at self-promotion, and his 1851 letter from London to Lock in Clanwilliam, and Lock's letter to van Rhyn, show that, however exaggerated his claims, they did resonate with a section of the settler community. His tours holding meetings and gathering petitions no doubt added to the public's awareness of him.

Many of the problems which had previously been the responsibility of the Governor at the Cape, and the Colonial Secretary in London, now landed in the in-trays of the elected settler representatives in Cape Town. Could they improve on what had gone before?

The Cape Parliament consisted of the Legislative House which was the 'Upper House', and the House of Assembly which was the 'Lower House'. Both houses operated from 1854 to 1910. The House of Assembly came to be known affectionately by some as the 'Old Cape House'.[33]

A BRILLIANT COLLECTION

The opening ceremony took place at Government House, Cape Town on 1 July 1854, with the Acting Governor, Charles Henry Darling, seated under a scarlet canopy bearing the initials V.R., denoting Victoria Regina, none other than Queen Victoria. The Cape and all whom it did contain were indeed part of her Empire.

Assembled to the Governor's right were the members

33 J.L. McCracken, *The Cape Parliament 1854–1910*.

of the Legislative Council, and on his left the forty-six members of the House of Assembly. The *Illustrated London News* included a drawing of the scene. The individual members are indistinguishable but Tancred is somewhere in the throng of Assembly members with their backs to the artist.

Commenting on the abilities of those on show in the opening session in 1854, and drawing on his reading about and knowledge of some of those who had been present, Ralph Kilpin, later Clerk to the House, summed up the scene: 'Could anyone wish to see a collection more brilliant than this in a colony which at that time could boast of not more than 140,000 white inhabitants?' Tancred, included in this group, undoubtedly entered the House as a well-regarded member. We note also that a racist marker is already in place; in spite of the limited franchise there is no mention of a non-white member, let alone one of distinction. As for women? Certainly not. It was a typical nineteenth-century white, all-male gathering.[34]

Parliament did not lack for men of talent. Kilpin brought to mind the front benches on the Speaker's right with the four executive officers, the Auditor-General, the Treasurer-General, the Attorney-General (William) Porter, and the Colonial Secretary, followed by Fairbairn ('the father of the South African press'), Watermeyer, Ziervogel, Molteno, Meintjes, Laws, and 'on the left front benches to mention only a few, Arderne, Fairbridge, Tancred, Wiggins and White'. Behind Wiggins on a bench sat Saul Solomon, 'a dwarf in stature and a giant in intellect'

34 Ralph Kilpin, *The Old Cape House*, 1918.

and 'the brainiest man in the house'. Dr Tancred was one of two members representing Clanwilliam, the second being Advocate Johannes Hendricus Brand, one of the Speaker's sons, who served until 1863 when he became President of the Oranje Vrystaat (Orange Free State). Brand, being on court circuit during the early part of the session, was absent from the inaugural session.

*

Trapido observed that 'the introduction of parliamentary government to the Cape in 1854 is an uncelebrated and almost forgotten moment in the popular histories of South Africa'.[35]

Considering the later import of many of the policy issues raised at the time, together with the development of settler views and concerns as revealed in the debates and subsequent votes, this lacuna was regrettable. Fortunately, it has in part at least been filled by research in the decades since Trapido's assessment. In this and the subsequent chapter the emphasis is mainly on Tancred, for this is an account of his life against the background of the times.

TANCRED THE PARLIAMENTARIAN

In the early days, Parliament met in a single-storey building at the top of the road later known as Parliament Street.

Tancred may have glanced nervously at Porter, his

---

35 Stanley Trapido, 'From paternalism to liberalism: the Cape Colony, 1800–1834', *The International History Review*, xii, February 1990.

old *bête noire* from the case of *Smith v Lindsay*, heard in Uitenhage in the Eastern Cape seven years previously, when Tancred had been behind the attempt to put an end to the right of the army to flog civilians. We recall that it was Porter, normally a prosecuting attorney, who acted as the defence for the army in the person of the man who gave the order, Lindsay. Porter had seen Tancred as the man behind the prosecution of Lindsay. As Attorney-General, he now exercised his right to sit in the new Parliament. There can have been little or no love lost between Porter and Tancred, nor much by way of respect. Though no known evidence of antipathy between them exists, Tancred probably began his parliamentary career with a powerful enemy.

Tancred being included in a list of brilliant men is perhaps no exaggeration; it was neither his education nor his intellect that caused his life to repeatedly stutter, crash and burn. It was undoubtedly his mental stability that time and again hindered his progress in all aspects of his life. Now, as one of the original entrants into the new Parliament, he made a characteristically good, if erratic, beginning. He was always aware, as he saw it, of his contribution to the campaign for representative government at the Cape. Regrettably, though, it would not take long for his vexatious side to become readily apparent. His good and able side lacked staying power when, after a promising start, his subsequent progress would be punctuated by starts and stops. He represented Clanwilliam from 1854 to 1858, and then from 1862 to 1863. In 1866 he made a very brief reappearance representing Piquetberg until January 1867.

Another member joining in 1854 was John Charles

Molteno, then representing Beaufort West, and later the first Prime Minister of the Cape Colony. Molteno, unlike Tancred, had taken an active physical part in the settler struggles in the Eastern Cape during the 7th Frontier War (1846–1847). Tancred had done little more than bleat from the sidelines. Also, unlike Tancred, Molteno had been a successful farmer and businessman with consummate political nous and skills.[36]

When Tancred, aged fifty, arrived in Cape Town for the first session of the new Parliament, no one could have known then whether his best years lay behind or ahead of him. Distant from his new wife who remained at Clanwilliam, Augustus had now obtained lodgings in a boarding house on the corner of Burg and Wale Streets, an establishment owned by a Mrs Fock who charged her residents six shillings and sixpence per day. If she was a good landlady, and Augustus a good resident, and if their relationship began well, it was not to last. Things would in due course take a turn for the worse. But then, most things involving Augustus began well before taking a turn for the worse.

FIRST STEPS – STANDING RULES AND ORDERS

When the first session of the new Cape Parliament got underway on 18 July 1854, the House lost no time in appointing a select committee (Porter, Fairbairn, Fairbridge, Watermeyer, Ziervogel) to draft standing rules and orders covering procedures in the House. The rules

---

36 Percy Alport Molteno, *The Life and Times of John Charles Molteno, K.C.M.G.*, 1900.

were modelled on those in 'the mother of parliaments', Westminster, with the first statute providing for freedom of speech in Parliament and, 'remembering the Stockdale v. Hansard decision of 1839, for immunity from libel actions of all publications printed under the authority of Parliament' (Kilpin). The first to test the rules was none other than Tancred who appears to have found it difficult to distinguish between freedom and licence, this confusion leading to his eventually being committed for five days into the custody of the Sergeant-at-Arms. Indeed, testing the rules proved to be the eventual legacy by which, together with his consumption of alcohol, his time in Parliament would mostly be remembered. He had begun as perhaps he intended to continue, for this episode was followed in the succeeding years by a litany of similar parliamentary misdemeanours. He was one of only two men to be placed in the custody of the Sergeant-at-Arms.

MASTERS AND SERVANTS

At the beginning of things, on 18 July 1854, the House began to consider and report on the expediency of repealing or merely altering the Master and Servants ordinance. A select committee was appointed comprising J.C. Molteno, Dr A.J. Tancred, H.H. Loedolff, J. Collett, C. Pote and J.H. Brand. This gave Tancred an opportunity to show what he was capable of, while also advancing his reputation as a champion of civil liberties. Would he lean towards the interests of the servants rather than the masters, or default into white settler mode? It comes as no surprise to find him in the latter camp.

*

The law governing the relationship between masters and servants had a long history in Britain and its colonies. In the colonies, deviations from the norm in the mother country were adapted in the light of local conditions. At the Cape, as elsewhere, the masters were typically white, the servants mostly non-white, and the relationship between masters and servants had been codified well before the arrival of the new Parliament. Might the committee recommend a lighter touch in the law between masters and servants?

*

The 'Caledon Code' of 1809, passed predictably by the Earl of Caledon, was a foundation stone in the wall of racist policies that would endure and continue in the Union of South Africa (1910), and only become exorcised with the repeal of key aspects of apartheid legislation after 1991.

After 1809, Khoikhoi people, the indigenous population at the Cape, or the 'Hottentots' in settler speak, were required to have a 'fixed place of abode' which they were not allowed to leave without a pass. This legislation was a precursor of the infamous 'pass laws' of subsequent regimes. Khoikhoi in breach of the law were classed as 'vagrants'. The labour market intentions behind the law were transparent, and nothing less than a means of coercing the Khoikhoi to choose employment over indolence. To ensure the purposes of the law were achieved any white settler could interrogate a Khoikhoi and demand to check whether he or she was carrying a pass. A supplementary law in 1812 laid down that Khoikhoi children maintained by settlers during their first eight years would be 'apprenticed' for a further ten years. To some relatively liberal missionaries this marked the 'enslavement' of the Khoikhoi.[37]

In 1841 an ordinance reinforced the interests of the masters against those of their servants. One essential difference was the abolition of the penalty of twenty shillings for each child illegally detained by an employer. The act was 'designed to enforce discipline on ex-slaves, peasants, pastoralists, and a rural proletariat'. Furthermore, 'though it is nominally colour-blind, the penalties are invoked only against the darker workers'. (Simons and Simons.)

In 'revising' the law the committee succeeded only in setting in stone a part of the wall in the social fabric that would endure, with architectural reinforcements, down the years.

The 1854 Select Committee's report was due to appear in September.

A MEMORABLE MAIDEN SPEECH

On 11 August 1854, Tancred bamboozled the House by making an unusual maiden speech of startling originality, the substance containing little more than random gibberish. (Reported in the *SA Commercial Advertiser and Cape Town Mail* on 11 January 1855.) He notes that on this, the forty-third day of the session, 'nothing has been done to improve the deplorable and miserable conditions

---

37 Wayne Dooling, *The Origins and Aftermath of the Cape Colony's 'Hottentot Code of 1809'*, SOAS, https://jstor.org/stable/41056535

of the colony'. There then follows an almost uninterrupted stream of well over one hundred words ending in 'ions' like 'enarrations, incubrations, pollicitations, tergiveersations, scintidations, resupinations' to name but a few. This outbreak of verbal diarrhoea, partly read and partly recited, must have taxed the shorthand of the reporter and the understanding of his fellow members, for some of whom English was not their first language. To all those present it surely must have seemed a presentiment of the narrow dividing line in a man who must be either brilliant or unhinged. Mr Molteno certainly felt moved, in his calm, measured, sane voice, 'in making a few remarks in reply'. Tancred continued to interrupt. Mr Molteno noted, 'these interruptions do certainly have the effect of throwing you off your guard; at the very least it is so with me'.

Somewhere in this diatribe are traces of the issues Tancred considers important, and to which he returns, however inconsequentially, like a dog with a bone, for all the while he is in Parliament. He favours more money for education in Clanwilliam and more widely in the colony; he is against what he sees as wasteful public expenditure; he is for the reform of the law concerning masters and servants; he strenuously opposes the proposed Burgher Law requiring citizens to assist in the military defence of the colony; he supports the case for greater independence of the East from the West; he comes to regret having once supported a broad franchise. He also argues the case for the wider acceptance of the Dutch language. Throughout there is his dim view of Parliament's ability to improve the life of the people of the Cape. He had campaigned for greater independence and now he wondered if Parliament would make things any better.

Through the first sitting of Parliament he continued to lay down markers, some frivolous, some important, for those issues he thought important. He is tenacious but inconsistent, beginning well but soon spoiling his contributions when his behaviour deviates from the subject in hand like a runaway train careering off the tracks. There are times when he gnaws at minutiae, as when he points out how the District Surgeon in the Clanwilliam area was once paid £100, now reduced to £15, so no one wants the job. As is so often the case this leads him to a *non sequitur*: several murderers have got away scot-free for want of medical evidence. On the other hand he really does seem to care about education as when he points out that in all of the 63,000 square miles of Namaqualand there is only one school 'kept by an old woman'. A matter close to his heart, or purse perhaps, is the question of salaries and expenses where he is greatly exercised about the position of 'country members', those who live beyond the limits of Cape Town, or, put another way, members such as himself. In what may be an unconscious echo of his experience of the workhouse near Nottingham in England he suggests the Governor should be asked to appoint a medical man to visit the lunatic chronic sick and lepers 'until the government can without delay remove them'. But remove them to where? It is this mix of some things serious and others frivolous which reveals his scatter-gun approach to the issues confronted in the early days at the Cape.

*

On 4 September 1854, the Cape Parliament's Report of the Select Committee on Masters and Servants was printed in full. The principal recommendations included: insubordination by a servant should be punishable by up to one month's imprisonment; punishment for damaging a master's property ought to be the deduction of the value of said property from the servant's wages and an extension of their contract on half wages; masters should be able to demand the appearance of their servants before a magistrate at any point during their contract; servants should be able to inform a magistrate if they had a complaint against their master; a proposed fine of between £1 and £5 if either master or servant was found to have brought a frivolous complaint to a magistrate. The report concludes by saying that the committee did not have adequate time to come up with a full set of recommendations before the prorogation of Parliament.

As it so happened a full set of recommendations would have made little difference as the resulting act largely repeated the earlier act which followed closely on from the Masters and Servants Ordinance of 1841. Many clauses were simply repeated verbatim. It has not been possible to identify Tancred's contribution to the work of the committee.

*

As the first session of the new Parliament wound down in 1854, the House debated rules on leave of absence, a matter of some importance to Tancred who may have already been laying the ground for his own future absences. He explained to the House that, about to proceed to England, he did not like having to ask for permission to be away from Parliament. There are many instances when his words provoked, 'Hear! Hear!', as well as others causing 'laughter'. In this debate he caused a ripple of mirth when he said he was about to proceed to England, and did not expect to be treated like a schoolboy wanting to go to the toilet being required to ask, 'May I go please?'

In these early days, Parliament only met for three months in the year so that leave of absence in the other nine months cannot have been a problem for most members. But that was surely the point: Tancred was never the creature of the common herd.

The first session of the new Parliament came to an end with the prorogation of Parliament on 28 September 1854.

*

In the following year, after hearing the speech to Parliament by the Governor, Tancred responded by explaining how 'never have I yawned so much in all my life, whilst it was being read'. He quotes things which he considers 'Chateaux en Espagne, castles in the air, which would take ten years to carry out and, I calculate, would require between one and two million of money' (Hear! Hear!). He then embarked on a lengthy and provocative speech prompting some inevitable replies. Mr Pote thought Tancred must have been asleep during the Governor's speech. Tancred denied this, saying that although he was yawning, he understood it better than some other members who were awake and heard all of it. Dr Abercrombie then pointed out that he could vouch that Tancred was wide awake. This was followed by laughter.

Augustus was settling into a well-worn pattern in which he would say whatever popped into his brain without a moment's thought for the consequences. He seems to have had no mechanisms to evaluate the wisdom or otherwise of his words or actions, no sense of what was appropriate in any given circumstance.

FAMILY NEWS FROM FRANCE

On 19 March 1855, *De Zuid-Afrikaan* contained information about Tancred's sons: 'The friends of Dr. Tancred will be happy to learn that his sons, not many years ago pupils at Dr Changinon's Establishment in this town, are very successful in their studies abroad. The junior brother (Oswald, now 17) is still at Boulogne, where he has obtained no less than seven prizes and eight distinctions, while the elder, Master Augustus (now 20), is about to take a bachelor's degree at Paris. In the examination of the former year the two sons obtained 18 prizes between them. We derive these particulars from private correspondence.' It seems very likely that this 'private correspondence' came to the newspaper via the proud father.

Paris in 1855 must have been a thrilling place for young Augustus Frederick. 1848 had seen revolution in the air. 1855 was the year of the Exposition Universelle des Produits de l'Agriculture, de l'Industrie et des Beaux-Arts de Paris. London had hosted the Great Exhibition at Crystal Palace in 1851. In 1852 when the Emperor Napoleon III became the last monarch to rule France (till 1870), France was not to be outdone. The Exposition of 1855 spread over forty acres and set a new standard for advertising national industry and art (including Ingres, Delacroix, and from England Holman Hunt and Millais). Over five million visitors attended the exposition, 4.2 million to the industrial exposition and just under one million to the Beaux-Arts exposition. Thirty-four countries took part. Wines were classified according to quality for the first time in the Bordeaux Wine Official Classification. People flocked to see the new Eiffel Tower. The rebuilding of the city was underway (1852–1870) based on Haussmann's concept of what a modern city should look like. Trade and industry flourished, and it was a vibrant time for literature and the arts and crafts. To Augustus Frederick, who had known only England, Grahamstown, Bathurst, Cape Town and Boulogne-sur-Mer, this was a world view of a different order, and one likely to linger in his memory long after his later return to the Cape.

No mention is made here of Tancred's daughter, Evelina, who was last heard of, if the obituary is to be believed, 'having taken the veil in a convent at Boulogne'. Walking the streets of Boulogne in search of likely convents I found only buildings that looked like they might once have been convents. Asking around the town never yielded more than, '1847, Monsieur?' Silence. This is one of many lines of enquiry in need of research.

THE BURGHER LAW

In the second session of Parliament from March to June 1855, Tancred continued to oppose the Burgher Bill, which was concerned with a duty on civilians to serve as a local defence force and thus reduce the need for as many soldiers provided at cost to the British Exchequer. In the preceding decades this had been resented by Dutch settlers and was one reason behind their leaving the Cape and with it the British rule they hated as they headed into the hinterland.

Augustus was also becoming vociferous in his support for the separation of the Eastern and Western Cape.

EAST VERSUS WEST

Also in 1855, the simmering resentment in the Eastern Cape, directed at the more prosperous Western Cape centred on Cape Town, reached Parliament when a member from the East moved that 'Parliament be held in some suitable town in the Eastern Province'. As this would involve the records as well as the members travelling across the colony, Tancred maliciously moved an amendment instructing the Colonial Secretary (Rawson) to carry the Cape archives on his back to the chosen town and to instruct a medical officer 'to attend the Colonial Secretary and support him in his bodily and mental exertions'. Not surprisingly, no one came forward to second the amendment regarding Rawson's mode of travel and the motion was not carried.

John George Steytler (1832–1918), one of Tancred's fellow members of Parliament from 1854 to 1856, representing Paarl, provided contemporary, eye witness insights into people and events. In 1856, Steytler underwent a role reversal when he became a shorthand writer (until 1872) to Parliament.

He described an incident when, on 24 April 1856, Tancred's behaviour finally went too far. The House was debating the case for the Eastern Cape separating from the Western Cape. Tancred's support for separation would have done him little harm in his old stamping ground in the East. Ziervogel was speaking when Tancred interrupted shouting, 'Separate! Separate!' According to Steytler, Ziervogel was 'a dry pompous old gentleman who took himself very seriously'. Far from amused, the angry Ziervogel responded with, 'Perhaps the House would be glad to separate from Clanwilliam and its honourable member too – and the sooner the better.'[38]

There were now two angry members in the House. An outraged Tancred leapt from his seat shouting, 'One member is as good as another', to which Ziervogel replied, 'Yes, and perhaps a little better.' Tancred, further enraged by this remark, then challenged Ziervogel to a duel by 'throwing down his snuffy handkerchief and throwing it in Ziervogel's face', observing that he should be happy to meet his fellow member for a duel. Again, according to Steytler, 'at dinner afterwards he (Tancred) said he could not make out why Ziervogel had not taken up the handkerchief'. Saul Solomon said, 'Why, how could you expect him to pick up your dirty snuffy bandanna!'

The following morning Tancred threw his glove down, desiring Ziervogel to notice it and pick it up and accept the challenge. Afterwards, when the House met, the glove was nailed up to one of the trees outside the front entrance with the following couplet attached to it:

---

38 John George Steytler, *Remembrances from 1832–1900, IV, Return to Cape Town 1856–1900*, 146.

Whoever dares this glove displace,
Must meet the doctor face to face.
Tankard

There can be no doubt about the identity of 'the doctor' or the author of the couplet. Ziervogel, it seems, was content to observe to the House that nothing Tancred could do would offend him. Tancred then offered 'a lame apology' and the matter was laid to rest. Steytler commented, 'We often had some funny scenes which would not be tolerated now.' Steytler was right up to a point but Tancred had yet to run through the full gamut of his outlandish behaviour. Gratuitously offending those around him seemed to be his default position.[39]

Or was it so? Not entirely. Steytler quotes one further example of Tancred's contradictory behaviour when 'not until the end of the session, when the estimates were before the House and they came to the Parliamentary vote, of all men Dr Tancred, after a few words in praise of my work, proposed that the House should vote me a bonus of £100. To my great satisfaction it was warmly seconded and carried.' It was, however, abundantly clear by now that Tancred the parliamentarian would not fulfil his potential talent or make the most of his extraordinary intellectual energy and abilities.

Apart from the members representing constituencies in the East there never was more than lukewarm enthusiasm for a sitting in the Eastern Cape. The issue was raised again in 1863 when it was decided that three months of the 1864

39 *The Cape Monitor*, 26 April 1856; Die Dagboek van H.A.L. Hamelberg, 85.

session would be held in Grahamstown, at which point Tancred was not a member of the House. This was the sole occasion on which a travelling parliament met in the East.

*

On 6 June 1855 Tancred made a speech on the Burgher Bill, objecting to what he saw as an attempt to push it through before the prorogation of Parliament. This intervention proved ineffectual, for on the following day the Bill was passed into law and Parliament was prorogued.

FOCK V TANCRED

The behaviour of Augustus was now exhibiting ever more florid signs of paranoia which came to the boil in the conflict between him and his landlady, Mrs Fock. This was, perhaps gleefully, reported in the *Cape Monitor* and recounted by Hamelberg in his *Dagboek*. On 26 April, the *Cape Monitor* described events concerning 'Dr. Tancred and his Landlady again'. It was an ongoing saga. In this episode, Mrs Fock claimed that Tancred owed her some money. Augustus began by announcing that he would 'throw himself upon the protection of "His most honourable Worship"'. This proved unnecessary as Mrs Fock had not arrived in court and when her attorney requested a delay of a few minutes to allow Mrs Fock to reach the court Tancred objected and the case was withdrawn, at which point he asked what he was to do about his 'lost property'. Advised to 'institute his action in due course of law' Tancred was adamant: 'I shan't.'

The report concludes, 'The Rev. Doctor soon after left the Court with a mass of papers, which he very jealously guarded during the time he was in Court, and apparently imagining there was some design to pry into their contents.' This odd behaviour points clearly to paranoia.

On 3 May, the *Cape Monitor* reported on the latest round of *Fock v Tancred* in a 're-institution of the action for the recovery of a board and lodging account. The case occupied the attention of the court between two and three hours, during which time those in attendance were afforded much amusement by the vagaries of the Doctor.' Tancred was now a figure of fun, a source of the sort of stories that sell newspapers. When Mrs Fock proved her case Tancred immediately counter-claimed that he 'had lost two £5 notes, and £5 in gold, out of his room, and for which he considered her liable'. Surprisingly perhaps, 'the Rev. Doctor's oath was taken in proof of his loss'. His Worship seems by this time to have had enough for one day and 'reserved the point for consideration'.

Was this all a storm in a coffee cup or was there more at stake? Mrs Fock's case was that she had increased her daily rate by one shilling from six shillings and sixpence per day to seven shillings and sixpence, due, she said, to an increase in the cost of living. She had increased her weekly and monthly tariffs by proportionate amounts. If Augustus was present for dinner 'at the regular afternoon table' the cost had increased from two shillings and sixpence to four shillings and sixpence. If he brought a guest with him, he now had to pay for the guest as well.

*

A week later the *Cape Monitor* reported His Worship's judgement in favour of Mrs Fock to whom he awarded £7 9s. 4d. with costs. As to Tancred's counter-claim 'he could not find any colonial law which would make her responsible for the loss, and he was therefore of opinion that the defendant had not exercised proper prudence with the money'. At which point exit one dissatisfied and irascible Tancred.[40]

A VISIT TO EUROPE

A week later, on 14 June 1855, Augustus departed for England aboard the *Pacific* intending to proceed to Boulogne-sur-Mer to visit the children of his first marriage. He seems to have seen this as having a higher priority than spending time with Geesie, his second wife, up the road in Clanwilliam. His freedom to travel, whether involving time or money, was clearly not unduly restricted.

*

All was not lost on the marital front and Tancred and Geesie were together for long enough in or about January 1856 to conceive their first child.

THE THIRD SESSION OF PARLIAMENT, FROM MARCH TO JUNE 1856

Tancred continued to campaign against the Burgher Law, ignoring the fact that it had already been passed at the end

---

40 H.A.L. Hamelberg, *ibid.*, 87–90.

of the previous session when he and Molteno had been the tellers. He continued to support the separation of East and West, and education, as well as arguing for more to be done to stop the spread of smallpox. He criticised the government for its handling of the public finances. His behaviour continued to be erratic. He was imprisoned for a weekend by the Sergeant-at-Arms and attempted to bring his own reporter to a debate because he claimed that newspapers were refusing to report his speeches. He must have known that they rarely published full speeches.

FAMILY NEWS FROM CLANWILLIAM

On 7 October 1856, Gesina ('Geesie') Anna Maria Magdalena Josephina Tancred, the first child of the marriage, was born at Bolangvlei, in the district of Clanwilliam. For some reason, perhaps simply consistent with Augustus' way of doing these things, or his absence in Cape Town, she was not baptised until 9 March 1864 in Clanwilliam in the NG Kerk. Perhaps it was simply that she was but a girl and therefore of lesser importance, or simply waiting till she reached a greater maturity.

TANCRED AND THE DUTCH LANGUAGE

An example of his ability to attempt a positive contribution occurs in relation to the question of the Dutch language. The British had always wanted to increase the proportion of English speakers in the colony so there was little enthusiasm in official quarters for the needs of Dutch speakers.

The votes and proceedings of the House of Assembly show that at two o'clock on Wednesday 13 May 1857, the afternoon began as usual with Mr Speaker taking the chair and reading prayers. When the business reached the fourth item on the agenda Dr Tancred presented a petition signed by ninety-nine inhabitants of the Division of Albert, praying that it might be permitted for any member to address the House in the Dutch language. Furthermore, when votes were to be taken, if any member should desire to hear the question before the House put in the Dutch language, as well as in English, it might be done at the request of any such member. The motion was seconded, read and received.

Later the same afternoon Dr Tancred moved, seconded by Mr Kruger, that a select committee be appointed, consisting of Messrs Biccard, Abercrombie, Loedolff, Barry and Fairbairn, to consider the petition from the inhabitants of the Division of Albert. After discussion, and on suggestion, Dr Tancred withdrew his motion. The discussions and suggestions behind his decision are unknown. The Dutch language issue was consigned back into the slow parliamentary lane.

ANOTHER NEW VENTURE

On 9 June 1857, the *Eastern Province Herald* reported that it had received notice from Dr Tancred that he intended to start a new newspaper to be named *Briareus*. His prospectus announced that 'arrangements were being made for the publication of a new journal which will be completed with all speed possible. As a first prospectus,

Briareus, with his hundred hands, will handle all that *Argus*, with his hundred eyes, can see, and *Briareus* will also handle all that *Argus* cannot and never will see.' Not surprisingly the new newspaper would be edited by Dr Tancred.

As was too frequently the case, Tancred was showing off his knowledge of the classics with this allusion to Briareus whom he would have known as the god of sea-storms from his reading of Homer's *Iliad*. Physically the newspaper *Briareus* would be a formidable foe being one hundred-armed and fifty-headed, well equipped to see off the puny rivalry he would face in the *Argus*. If Tancred sought to impress with the name *Briareus* as a clever marketing ploy he was heading towards disappointment as very few potential readers would have rushed to buy his newspaper emerging from this classical stable.

No doubt this was Tancred in a fit of pique probably because the existing newspapers were not reporting all his words or were failing to represent views close to his own. No more seems to be have been heard of *Briareus*, which joined the list of his hare-brained schemes founded on financial grains of sand which came to nothing.

REFLECTIONS

In the following year, 1858, the final year of Tancred's first spell as a member of the House, what might have proved the sober, intellectually challenging side of the man was on public view when, on 15 October, he delivered a lecture in the Old Town House in Greenmarket Square which was then used as the town hall. The lecture, titled 'The Necessity and Advantage of Reflection', was subsequently published by A.S. Robertson in Adderley Street. If ever a man might have benefitted from a period of reflection, on his behaviour, past and current, and his circumstances, Tancred would have been a needy reflector. But no, though later classified as a 'sermon' by the S.A. Library in Cape Town, it is nothing of the sort, consisting mostly of the usual Tancred rant, just one more of his published diatribes giving an indication of the way his thinking was veering away from his original views: he now thought his early support for a relatively wide franchise had spread the right to vote too far.[41]

*

It is far from clear why in 1858 he vacated the seat he had won in Parliament in 1854, or how and why he returned as member for Clanwilliam briefly from 1862 to 1863. Or, come to that, why he sank from public life from 1863 to 1866, only to return momentarily as the member for Piquetberg in 1866. What was he up to in the gap years? Was there a tipping point when the initially respected member of the House finally descended into the drunken buffoon he later became?

---

41 'The necessity and advantage of reflection', a lecture delivered at the town hall, on Friday evening, 15 October by Augustus Joseph Tancred. Call Number: SABP.173 – National Library – Cape Town Campus – Special Collections.

29

THE JOYOUS ADVENTURER

His years amongst the early law makers at the Cape were remembered long after he was gone, seldom for the most admirable of reasons. Kilpin's description paints the picture:

> ... there was a look of anxiety in every eye when that joyous adventurer, Dr. Tancred, appeared on the scene. Shouting hilariously from the window of a cab he would drive up to the House after dinner with the express intention of "livening things up"...[42]

The 'joyous adventurer' is a more generous description than that accorded by many of Tancred's contemporaries. An example showing Tancred the parliamentarian in a revealing light comes from Limner, an acute observer of people and events in the House of Assembly.[43] He

---

42 Ralph Kilpin, *The Romance of a Colonial Parliament*, 102–103, 1930.

43 R.W. Murray, *Pen and Ink Sketches in Parliament by Limner*, Grahamstown, 1864.

remembers Tancred in advancing years looking about sixty years of age, 'stout, hale and hearty' and, though present every day, 'far more amusing to the strangers in the gallery than to the Assembly' where 'he is so full of mischief, that no party cares to recognize him. He is as likely to undermine the policy of friends, as to demolish the plans of opponents. Like a vicious horse he kicks and plunges in all directions.' Words of praise from Limner are often interrupted by a 'but' as in, 'not unfrequently, when called upon to speak to some great question, he sets out with a solemn and stately parade of arguments, and the attention of the House being attracted, he leads on in a complete and convincing train of reasoning for a short time, but all at once finding an opportunity to play upon a word, the temptation is too great to be lost. He gets himself and the gallery into a grin, and all the good he might have done is sacrificed.' His use of language is remarkable: 'proverbs and old sayings are his great delight, particularly when rendered into Latin' and 'he avails himself of every chance to adorn his speeches with them'. As is so often the case with Tancred we see a portrait of an educated man unable to put his talents to good use.

*

Although there were eight years in which he was counted a member, the total Kilpin attributes to him, it was only the years 1854 to 1858 that justified a count of four years, leaving largely unexplained the gaps between 1858 and 1862, and then from 1863 to 1866. From 1862 to 1863 he served only one year (in effect only a few months) before departing for Europe at the start of 1863, and from 1866 to 1867 he served only three months after being elected in September before dying at the start of 1867. Six years seems closer to the mark but still generous as there were the three years when he was elected or re-elected which did not include a full calendar year in service. In short, he made a lot of noise, attracted a good deal of attention, and lost no time 'livening things up' when he was there.

*

With Tancred's first spell representing Clanwilliam in the House of Assembly drawing to a close in 1858, the buffoon within him was already in the ascendant, and not only in the House. He was about to sign out with a very public demonstration of his idiosyncrasy. For a member of the House to behave in this way was bound to attract widespread attention.

The incident in question occurred on St John's Day in June 1858, when he exhibited a new line in aberrant behaviour, not in keeping with his position as a Member of Parliament, appearing in the streets of Cape Town in an outfit best described as eccentric:

> … at Kelly's Hotel, where he is residing, a white banner, with a red cross on it, was hung out, and soon after breakfast the doctor made his appearance in Hessian boots, white breeches and vest, black coat, and a helmet, with a large plume of ostrich feathers hanging from it gracefully over his back. After parading the stoep for some time, he

engaged a black boy, who paraded with the banner through the streets, followed by the doctor in full costume. Of course, this was great fun for the boys, who collected in a troop and accompanied the doctor in his peregrinations through the town.

The local newspapers and his enemies must have blessed the day he announced himself to be a Knight Templar, and his costume to be in honour of St John's Day. The Knights Templar are a fraternal order with membership open only to Freemasons who profess a belief in Christianity. Its symbol is a red cross. His claim to belong to the Masonic order was, however, quickly repudiated by the Masons. The oral history recounted in the family is that he was a Mason and, not just because he said so, for the tale is told of a descendant who inherited his pouch with gold on it. Apparently, she burnt it believing it to be evil; another descendant who inherited his gold apron gave it back to the Masons. Or so it is said.

His first spell as a member of the House of Assembly ended in style. Petrus Kotze, who entered Parliament in 1859 representing Cape Town until 1863, and then again from 1866 to 1868, recounted an occasion when after Tancred returned to his seat following a division, he complained to the Speaker that he had found a slip of paper on his table with the words 'Go to bed' on it. When the Speaker refused to take any action, Tancred declared 'with great vehemence' that if it happened again, he would shoot the perpetrator.[44]

---

44 P.J. Kotze, *Memoirs*, 30; J.L. McCracken, *The Cape Parliament*, 140.

Although Kotze does not date this incident, he overlapped with Tancred in 1862 and 1866. Steytler, meanwhile, had observed that 'we often had some funny scenes which would not be tolerated now'.[45]

Nonetheless, it is far from clear why, and in what circumstances, he vacated the Clanwilliam seat in 1858.

FALLOW YEARS

Little is known of Tancred's activities between 1858 and 1862, the years when he was no longer a Member of Parliament. We can, however, locate him on a firm date in 1860 when, at noon on Monday 27 February, Dr Tancred, the 'late MP for Clanwilliam', arrived at Plymouth, England, aboard the Union Boating Company's mail steamship *Celt* which had left Table Bay on 20 January, called at St Helena on 29 January and then Ascension on 5 February (*Cape and Natal News*, 1 March 1860). This was probably the first time Tancred arrived at Plymouth rather than London, but Plymouth was now a port advertising passages for emigrants to Canada, New Zealand, the Cape, Natal and California. On landing at Plymouth, he would probably have gone on by train to London, Brunel's South Devon Railway having reached Plymouth in 1849 before sweeping westward over his Royal Albert Bridge to Cornwall in 1850. A short-lived alternative to rail travel was also on offer with the steamship companies offering passages to London in eighteen hours. Much had changed in the country in the two decades since Tancred first left England for the Cape at the end of 1841.

---

45 John George Steytler, *Remembrances from 1832–1900*.

On 6 March 1860, he was issued with a British passport (number 15,718). Was he contemplating a long-term return to Europe, or was he now firmly embedded in the life of the colony, or simply planning one or more future trips away from the Cape?

For no known reason he was back on the tourist trail to Europe. Augustus Frederick, his oldest child, had returned to the Cape by now. Did Tancred have contact with Evelina and Oswald, his other two children still in Europe? If he did I have found no mention of it. The perpetually unanswered question hangs in the air: how did he finance these trips?

A year later, on 16 March 1861, he arrived back in Cape Town.

CLANWILLIAM - AGAIN

The *Fort Beaufort Advertiser*, on 16 March 1861, did not mince its words when informing readers that 'Dr. Tancred. – This somewhat notorious individual has again returned to the Cape from England.' It goes on to quote the *Argus* which makes interesting reading with regard to Tancred's present circumstances and likely future intentions. This time he is portrayed in a rather more favourable light being described as 'an old friend' of the Cape who has returned 'looking as well and as jolly as ever'. He is 'not only a learned, but a very witty man', the sight of whom 'brings to the minds of strangers in the gallery many pleasant evenings spent during the sittings of our first Parliament'.

The *Argus* was of the opinion that, in spite of his 'eccentricities we believe he was an acquisition to the house' such that 'we shall only be too glad to hear that some constituency, now unrepresented, had forwarded a requisition to him'. The writer then drops a heavy hint: Grahamstown, the scene of the 'early part of his colonial life' and where he 'has many friends'. He knows the Eastern Province 'as well as most men'. Furthermore, picking up on comments in the *Grahamstown Journal*, the writer continues by explaining that this would present an opportunity to get rid of Stephen Mundy (1859–1863) in the House of Assembly, an unpopular representative. Surely, in the view of this writer, Grahamstown 'could not do better' than 'take the learned and reverend Doctor in the place of that gentleman whom the Doctor himself called "Black Mundy"'. Tancred, or so the claim goes, was a better candidate and 'would no doubt do his best to carry out the wishes of the League', the separatist movement campaigning for a separate British colony in the Eastern Cape with its own political system and a policy of further eastward expansion as a bulwark against the neighbouring Xhosa areas.

Notwithstanding the best efforts of this anonymous advocate, who almost sounds rather like Dr Tancred himself, Grahamstown did not call for Dr Tancred. Stephen Mundy retained the seat he had won in 1859 until 1863.

Tancred meanwhile was shoehorned back into a Clanwilliam seat from 1862 to 1863 when he once again disappeared from Parliament until 1866.

FAMILY NEWS

On 19 December 1861 a licence was issued at Grahamstown for the marriage of Augustus Frederick Tancred, the eldest child of Augustus and his first wife Evelina. His bride, Mary Ellen Smith, was of 1820 settler stock and from Grahamstown. They were married in St Bartholomew's Anglican Church, Grahamstown on 20 December 1861. It is not known whether or not Dr Tancred, father of the bridegroom, made the long journey to the Eastern Cape to attend the wedding. This seems unlikely.

Augustus Frederick Tancred had returned to the Cape from Europe by 1859, the only one of the three children to rejoin his father at the Cape. He was at first resident in Grahamstown, where he was described as a clerk and a magistrate living in the High Street, formerly a farmer, and lately a civil servant. He had returned to the place where his mother had died. He subsequently moved on to Port Elizabeth where he became Secretary to the Union Boating Company. There he worshipped at St Augustine's Catholic Church, later consecrated as a cathedral, and contributed to the cost of a new organ.

In time, three of the sons of Augustus Frederick and Mary Ellen would become known as 'the cricketing brothers Tancred', three of whom, Augustus Bernard (known as 'AB'), Vincent and Louis, represented their country at international level in official Tests. All three played against England while Louis also played in the first Test matches against Australia. A fourth brother, Claude, also played against England but not in a Test match. Due to something of a statistical oddity Augustus Bernard was the first batsman, also the lowest scoring, to carry his bat in a Test match. It is unusual for so many brothers to represent their country at cricket and consequently they find their way into books about cricket history.

On 18 March 1862, Petrus ('Pieter') Johannes Albertus Tancred (1862–1934), the second child of Augustus and Geesie, was born at Bolangvlei, in the district of Clanwilliam, in the Western Cape.

Later in 1862, on 25 November, Tancred's first grandchild, Aida Catherine Mary Tancred, the first of the eight children of Augustus Frederick Tancred and his wife, Mary Ellen, was born in Port Elizabeth. She was baptised in St Augustine's Catholic Church on 25 January 1863. She would in time be followed by the four cricketing brothers and by three sisters, Evelina Mary, Mary Agnes and Zoe Frances Mary. Sadly, two of the sisters, Evelina and Zoe, died in childhood and little is known of the two who survived to adulthood.

As far as is known to me the two branches of the family from Augustus' two marriages, the one English speaking, the other Afrikaans speaking, met seldom if at all in the early days. The exception may have been Augustus Frederick who became an executor of his father's will and guardian of the minor children of the second marriage.

BACK AS MP FOR CLANWILLIAM

Why, after Tancred's return to the Cape from Europe in 1861, did he seek re-election in 1862, only to last in post technically until 1863, but, in effect, only till the end of 1862? 'Why?' is one of the words that recur throughout any attempt to untangle the life of Augustus.

This is not to say that he was altogether idle during his second term, for June 1862 saw the publication of the Report of the Select Committee of the House charged with considering and reporting on 'the expediency and Propriety of Altering the Present Rate of Expenses to Members of both Houses of the Legislature'. The report dealt with the expenses associated with attendance on parliamentary duties and an allowance for travelling expenses.

The committee consisted of Mr R.M. Bowker, Mr Harries, Dr White, Mr Ziervogel and Dr Tancred who was Chairman. The only change they recommended was that the £1 per day allowance to members, which was limited to fifty days, should now be raised to eighty days. Tancred it seems still enjoyed the trust of the House if only to be appointed a member as well as the Chair of this relatively minor committee. It is perhaps unkind to suggest that he had long shown a particular interest in expenses.[46]

The answer to why Augustus was soon on his way again seems to lie in a family matter, for on the 31 January 1863 the *Fort Beaufort Advertiser* reported his departure on the mail steamer *Dane* to visit his son Oswald who was in 'a very delicate state of health' in Paris. As a result Augustus' second period of service for Clanwilliam lasted no longer than the few months between his re-election in 1862 and his departure for Europe in the first month of the following year.

Did he leave Parliament and head for Paris for no other reason than his concern for his son Oswald who, according to his father's *De Zuid-Afrikaan* obituary in

---

46 *Report of the Select Committee appointed to consider and report on the expediency and propriety of altering the present rate of expenses to members of both Houses of the Legislature by Cape of Good Hope.* A.J. Tancred. National Library, Cape Town Campus, General Collections.

1867, 'resides in France, where he has held a responsible situation on the staff of the Suez Canal Company'? At that time Oswald did live in Paris and was on the staff of the Suez Canal Company, albeit briefly and in a lowly position. The Suez Canal Company records held in the Archives Nationales du Monde du Travail in Roubaix, some 300 kilometres from Paris, confirm that Oswald was employed by the company in an administrative position from February 1859 until the end of 1863. From 1861 onwards he had prolonged periods of ill health and eventually lost his job when staff numbers were reduced in December 1863. Despite an appeal to the company on his behalf by a relative who lived in Paris, and his own written requests to Monsieur Le Président (de Lesseps) to retain his position, his pleas fell on deaf ears. In the absence of other evidence, we can only conclude that it was a response to one of Oswald's intermittent illnesses that terminated his father's second tenure as a Member of Parliament. Oswald died at Boulogne-sur-Mer in 1905, living well beyond the apparent delicate state of his health in 1863 and his father's death in 1867.

Oswald left a small legacy to his sister Evelina who was said in their father's obituary to have 'taken the veil in a convent at Boulogne' on the French coast some time after the children's return to Europe after their mother's death. It is, however, much more likely that she was educated at a convent there, possibly a boarding school, unless at some point she leapt over a convent wall leaving her veil behind. The clue lies in her later life which shows that if she was in Boulogne for her childhood and education, she had moved south some time before 1891 to the very centre of

France, Saint-Amand-Montrond in the Cher region, and then to Clermont-Ferrand in the Massif Central where she was a piano teacher. She died in 1912 and was buried at Saint-Amand-Montrond, unusually, with another woman.

*

On his return from Europe Augustus' spending was clearly exceeding his income. Cash flow problems had emerged once again and it seems he was in danger of sinking in financially choppy waters. Perhaps this was due to losing his MP's expenses combined with running up debts in connection with the trip to Paris. His plight is laid bare in a letter he wrote to his bank manager:

The Manager
Bank of S.A., Ltd.

Dear Sir,

For the following reasons I regret being unable to reduce my overdraft:

I have been held up, sandbagged, walked on, sat upon, flattened out and squeezed by our... taxes, and by every society and Organisation that the inventive brain of man can devise to extract what I may or may not have in my possession.

I am drained by the Red Cross,... the Black Cross, the Double Cross, and every hospital in the town and country.

The Government has governed my business so that I do not know who owns it. I am inspected, suspected, examined, re-examined, informed, required and commanded, so that I do not know who I am, where I am, or why I am at all. All that I know is that I am supposed to have an inexhaustible supply of money for every known deed, desire or hope of the human race, and because I do not sell or beg, borrow or steal money to give away, I am cussed, discussed, boycotted, talked to, talked about, lied to, lied about, held up, hung up, robbed and d-n near ruined, and the only reason why I am clinging to life now, is to see what the … will happen next.

I am,

Yours regretfully,
A.J. Tancred[47]

On 20 August 1865, Tancred's first grandson from his first marriage, Augustus Bernard Tancred, was born in Port Elizabeth. No other grandchildren from this marriage were born in Tancred's lifetime.

PIQUETBERG

Was a return to Parliament a way of resolving his financial difficulties? He mounted a robust campaign to win a seat at Piquetberg, with strong support mirrored by equally strong opposition.

In the end it was impossible to keep a good man down.

---

47 The Standard Bank, originally the Standard Bank of British South Africa, only opened in South Africa, in the Cape, in 1862. This letter must have been written between 1862 and 1867 when Tancred died. As it is undated attributing it to 1864 is arbitrary.

Or an imperfect man? In *De Zuid-Afrikaan* of 26 April 1866, he addressed the 'men of Piquetberg and fellow colonists' thanking them for doing him the honour of 'requesting that I will allow myself to be put in nomination as a candidate to represent your district in Parliament. I cannot but feel gratified and pleased at the flattering manner in which you speak of what I have hitherto done for this now most unfortunate colony.' In truth he leapt at the offer to be put forward as a candidate, his one regret being that the colony was now in a 'fifty-fold worse state' than when he first attempted to improve conditions at the Cape. He goes on to detail what he sees as the iniquities of the colonial administration, all the while pointing out his own valiant attempts to improve matters. It is an old song, one he had sung many times before.

While awaiting the return to Parliament which he now anticipated, he occupied his time during the six months from April to October 1866 with his final series of public letters addressed to the Governor, Sir Philip Edward Wodehouse, who was in post from 1862 to 1870. Readers venturing into these voluminous letters find him covering a broad range of political, social and religious issues. Here he was often rowing back on his earlier views on the body politic. On one of these, the separation of East from West, he no longer supported separation, detaching the Eastern Cape from the western hub based on Cape Town. He was less enamoured by the virtues of total self-government, the responsible government that was a driving force behind so many of his original political enthusiasms. This was part of a pattern as he became more conservative, arguing against changes he had previously supported. It was as though he realised that change, even if well intentioned, did not necessarily lead to improvement.

He had also come to believe that the qualifications for entry to the franchise, with voting rights, had been drawn too widely. Later, in the Franchise and Ballot Bill of 1892, Rhodes would increase the income qualification and introduce an educational qualification, reducing the number of non-white electors. This proved popular with the white population as by then more non-whites had qualified as they advanced up the economic ladder.

Such consistency as Tancred did show was in his opposition to British policy at the Cape, almost regardless of what it happened to be, while his support for education in general and for the Boers remained steadfast.

*

When he arrived back in Cape Town *De Zuid-Afrikaan* reported him to be enjoying 'the most robust health'. A closer look would have shown it to be otherwise. On 28 September 1866, he took his seat in Parliament, once again a duly elected member of the House of Assembly, now representing Piquetberg. The grains of sand in the egg timer counting the days of his life had almost run their course. But not quite yet. He had begun by obtaining lodgings in Mrs Stigling's residence at 44 Burg Street. His race now had but three more months to run.

Almost immediately he became the subject of a vituperative attack in the columns of *The South African* which on 11 October carried a leading article criticising a recent speech by Tancred in Parliament. In the same issue the 'Essence of Parliament' sketch of the previous day's business contained trenchant criticism of his speech the previous day. No details of his actual words are quoted in this piece which recalls how, speaking for more than half an hour, he 'sickened, disgusted the House with the lowest, vilest, and most blasphemous scurrility ever uttered in a deliberative assembly'. Moreover, his return to Parliament was 'a standing reproach to the electors of Piquetberg'. Whereas in the old Parliament he had been 'nothing worse than a nuisance', he was now 'a polluter and destroyer of healthy social and political thought and action'. The sketch writer felt it was incumbent on Parliament to go to whatever lengths it took to remove Tancred from the parliamentary scene.

The time when such a course of action might have borne fruit was long past, for as 'Limner'[48] observed:

> He cannot be put down. No indignity that the House could offer would drive him away, for he is very far removed from the reach of insult. The House is continually snubbing him, and reproaches have been showered on him, sufficient to drive away a full half dozen members possessing any ordinary amount of sensitiveness, but its only effect has been to make the hon. member once declare that he had been ill-used, and would come no more, but after a night's sleep, he cooled down, and the insult brought him earlier to his seat the next morning. The House has given up the idea of getting rid of him.

48 R.W. Murray, *ibid.*

At this point there is no longer any possibility of changing his ways or getting rid of him. The House simply ignored his 'ridicule, sarcasm, denunciations, and accusations'. Tancred has now fallen so low that disrupting the business of the House is enough to satisfy him.

Above all, Limner sees Tancred as a snob, a man democratic in his pretentions who professes his 'love of the people', the same man who likes to trumpet his real or imagined association with those in the top ranks of society:

> … he is for ever letting the House know that he was once in the great metropolis of the world, and that certain of the aristocracy did him the honour to consult him about the affairs of the Cape. He remembers the very words that my Lord somebody, and Earl the other-body, said on every occasion, and he is extremely anxious that the circumstance of his having been talked to by big people, shall always be alive in the memory of hon. gentlemen who have not been honoured by having seen and talked to a real Lord…

In the time left to him Tancred mostly argues in favour of fiscal retrenchment as well as the importance of education. He continues his letters to the Governor. Even by his own high standards he becomes increasingly disruptive in his parliamentary behaviour. In October he threatened to sue the *South African Advertiser and Mail* for refusing to report his speeches. He had made a powerful enemy. The paper inserts this dagger into his leaky reputation by quoting Shakespeare, with Prince Hal's words to the aged Falstaff:

I know thee not, old man: – Fall to thy prayers.
How ill white hairs become a fool and jester;
I have long dream'd of such a kind of man,
So surfeit-swelled, so old and so profane;
But, being awake, I do despise my dream.

Without sight of Tancred's speech, it is impossible to judge whether this represented fair comment, or not, though he had oft-times demonstrated his facility with offensive strings of words on the border of drunken incoherence. Clearly this newspaper was no admirer of Tancred. If his performance was this dire what action did the Speaker take as a result? We know not. Tancred might have responded with some other words from Shakespeare: 'the evil that men do lives after them; the good is oft interred with their bones' (Brutus over the grave of Julius Caesar).

After all is said and done this comment by Limner may be the most damning: 'Tancred is a horrid bore… are the words most often heard from his fellow members whenever they leave the House.' Egotistical and narcissistic, he was nearing the end of his life, an educated man with exceptional talents who was unable to put them to good use.

The causes once dear to Tancred, the fight for representative government at the Cape, were now being advanced by John Molteno and others, the liberal influence by William Porter. His support for the Dutch language and the status of the Eastern Cape had seen very little progress.

30

ENVOI

In Dr. Tancred, it need scarcely be said, the colony has sustained a great loss. He was certainly one of the most able and fearless champions for the rights and privileges of his adopted country. He had many failings, it is true; but of these we shall not presume to be the judges. – Requiescat in pace.

Obituary, *De Zuid-Afrikaan*, 7 January 1867

In Cape Town he was a long, long way from his early roots in Cork. His wife and children were 150 miles away in Clanwilliam. If he had any close friends they were never mentioned. Along the road he had shaken the dust off his feet in many a house or city in Ireland, France, England, Belgium and the Cape Colony, in places where he had not been well received nor his word heard. Leaving Christchurch, he had resolved never to tarry in such a place but in the end they had all turned out to be the same as had he. He had met many a man not worthy, certainly not equal in stature to his image of himself.

The carnival was almost over. But where in the end did he belong? Everywhere and nowhere? Had he belonged anywhere? Did he retain any feelings for Ireland? He would not be the first Irishman, or Irishwoman, to leave the old sod hating much of what it stood for, only to find it forever ingrained somewhere in his soul.

Steytler left behind one clue that this might have been so:

> After dinner one night when Dr Tancred had taken too much, another member who was also in an after-dinner state, called him to order and turning to the Speaker said 'The honourable member is drunk, Mr Speaker.' Tancred at once commenced a long harangue and could not be quietened by the Speaker who called on old Major Longmore, the Sergeant at Arms, to remove him from the House. Old Longmore took him by the arm. Tancred said 'Never! Where is your authority? Where is your mace? Go and pick up that bauble.' When Longmore brought it, he allowed himself to be escorted out of the House, singing as he went along 'Rich and rare were the gems she wore.'[49]

Throughout Tancred's adult life there is little else to suggest that he retained an emotional attachment to Ireland or anywhere else. But this sentimental Irish ballad from 1808 may be the exception: a beautiful maiden, wandering with a gold ring on her finger along a bleak and lonely way, will be safe for surely 'no son of Erin will offer me harm'. Ireland's manhood can be trusted to behave honourably

---

49 Thomas Moore, *A Selection of Irish Melodies (1808–34)*; Steytler, *ibid.*

no matter how great the temptation. Was this a song with emotional meaning for Tancred that he had learned long, long ago?

In December, in the height of that summer, it must have become evident that his health, both mental and physical, was fast deteriorating. He had become overtly paranoid, shuffling down the street, muttering to himself and clutching a sheaf of 'secret' papers tightly to his chest, fearful lest someone might snatch and read them. He had hidden private papers in his room but became convinced that Mrs Stigling was sneaking in to examine them while he was out and about. He was minded to take her to court over the matter.

Perhaps it was fortunate that nature was taking its course as Christmas and the New Year drew near. Kilpin now saw his once 'joyous adventurer' as an 'insufferable, thick-skinned nuisance'. Tancred's letters to the newspapers continued almost to the end.

Before long he was confined to his bed. Ever since the debacle as chaplain at the workhouse at Basford, and as curate at Bulwell, in Nottinghamshire, he had remained committed to the Catholic faith, the beliefs of his early years when he had been a Catholic priest. Never since then had he practised as a man of the cloth. Realising he was dying, he made haste to put his relationship with the Almighty in good order. To help meet his religious needs, he was attended by Bishop Grimley from the nearby Roman Catholic Cathedral. Grimley was appointed executor of his will dated 1 January 1867. Then he changed his mind and in a fit of pique he removed Grimley from the role. He changed his mind again and Grimley was reinstated as a joint executor together with Augustus Frederick Tancred, the eldest child of the first marriage and now in his thirties. The executors were appointed guardians of the minor children, Geesie now aged ten, and Pieter now four.

Although he lingered over Christmas and saw in the arrival of the New Year, he limped out of this world and died at about ten o'clock on the morning of Friday 4 January 1867, aged sixty-two years.

In a letter home to his own family in England, Henry Hall, of the Colonial Office in Cape Town, wrote on 19 January:

> Poor old Tancred has come to an end of his existence at last – he died about a fortnight ago from the effects of erysipelas brought on by dissipation. For some time he has been making a fool of himself, appearing in the House drunk, making rows, etc, etc. and so much so that a letter appeared in the *Advertiser Mail* about him which so annoyed him that he brought an action against the writer Mr W R Thomson an MP for damages of L500. But before it had time to come on, he was dead.[50]

Death awaits one and all but dying from the effects of erysipelas brought on by dissipation cannot have had much to commend it. Was this a judgement by the Almighty, a curse placed on him and his descendants for his many misdemeanours? This was believed by some of

---

50 Cory Library, Grahamstown, MS 5713.

his descendants even when they declined to highlight their own specific sins, some of which were of course widely known. The belief, perhaps, was sufficient to remove the burden of the exercise of free will.

The undertaker, P.J. Stignant of 25 Plein Street, inserted a newspaper announcement on the day of the funeral inviting friends to attend: the cortege would proceed from 44 Burg Street at 3.30 pm on Saturday 5 January. He was interred that afternoon. As is the case with Evelina, his first wife, and his younger son, Oswald, the location of his grave has eluded all attempts to locate it. The likelihood is that it was in the graveyard on a site near the Somerset Hospital which opened in 1864. Some of these graves were later moved to the Maitland Cemetery but, when I searched to find his amongst them, either in the surviving re-erected headstones or those laid flat to form paths, his was not to be found. No newspaper reports of his funeral service, his burial, or any of the customary formal statements in the House of Assembly marking a member's passing, have been traced.

There were, however, obituaries a-plenty. Most would have pleased him. Putting together a montage of the many comments amongst them, and after allowing for the inflated value of obituary currency in the opinions voiced following a death, the resulting picture yields a ragbag of words with what were seen as his admirable qualities: a popular favourite, with wit and humour, talented, plucky, generous, good feelings, patriotic, forgiving, charitable, unselfish, sympathetic to the oppressed, foremost in asserting civil and religious liberty, fearless, outspoken, uncompromising.

That there was another side to the man was also acknowledged. Two obituaries came close to the truth in the balance sheet of his virtues and failings. The *Great Eastern* had known 'worse men with more discretion than he exhibited in his life; but there are few more forgiving, more charitable, less selfish, or more patriotic'. The *Port Elizabeth Telegraph* noted how 'his genius and his idiosyncrasies caused him to be well-known either personally or by reputation in every town, village, and district of the colony'.

The *Port Elizabeth Telegraph* may have been over-optimistic in asserting that 'the colony will never look upon his like again'. Perhaps, though, it was this newspaper that came closest to summarising his life when observing that 'with a more evenly balanced mind than Dame Nature would appear to have endowed the subject of our present notice, he might, and most assuredly would have risen to a much more enviable position among his adopted countrymen than that to which he attained'.

Surely that had been the story from the start, a talented man who was mentally unbalanced? The one positive thing he would be remembered for in many quarters, especially in the Eastern Cape, was his part in the case of *Smith v Lindsay*. His remains are now part of the dust lying somewhere unknown in the soil at the southern tip of Africa, far from his childhood and the years of his early maturity in Cork. This man from Cork had certainly made a mark of sorts on the world beyond Hanover Street. And yes, the world beyond Cork was, like Cork, mostly about men.

31

AFTERMATH

The parliamentary world moved on. There remained the task of replacing Tancred as the member for Piquetberg in the House of Assembly. No time was lost and gossip surrounded his likely successor. On 19 January 1867, the *Fort Beaufort Advertiser* noted that 'in Cape Town parliamentary circles it is said that Mr. John Ebden, the ex-judge, and Mr. Advocate Cole, are to be asked to fill the vacancy in the representation of Piquetberg caused by the death of Dr. Tancred and, should these gentlemen decline, it is thought that Mr. Advocate Buchanan, the unsuccessful candidate in the late election, will walk over the course'.

This was another example of the wheels within wheels that kept the small Cape world moving along, for Ebden was of course none other than the prosecuting counsel secured by Tancred in the case of *Smith v. Lindsay* in 1847. Ebden declined the suggestion to stand for Parliament. He had served on the Cape Bench for a very short period before going on sick leave in October 1855. Shortly after that he retired and became active in politics until ill health intervened. In 1886 he published *British Rule in*

South Africa. He lived near Cape Town till his death on 29 December 1886 at Claremont, aged seventy-seven. He was buried on 31 December 1886, in the Rondebosch Cemetery.

In February *De Zuid-Afrikaan* took up the story of the coming election noting that the Reverend Dr Scholtz, the emeritus minister of the Dutch Reformed Church at Piquetberg, had received and accepted a requisition to represent the electors of the division in the House of Assembly. In the election that followed a court was held by the Civil Commissioner to consider the nomination of candidates. Forty-eight electors were present. Dr Scholtz having been duly proposed and seconded, Mr Advocate Cole was also proposed, but this proposal not being seconded, his name was withdrawn, whereupon the Civil Commissioner declared Dr Scholtz to have been duly returned. Scholtz, as it happened, only served until 1868.

*

Augustus liked to think he might one day become Prime Minister. This was never going to happen. Five years after he died, John Molteno became the first Prime Minister of the Cape Colony in 1872.

Three years after Augustus died, in 1870 Cecil John Rhodes arrived in Africa, aged seventeen. At almost the same time diamonds were discovered between 1869 and 1871 on farms in the Kimberley area. In 1880 and 1881 the Boers and the British were at war. In 1886 gold was discovered on the 'ridge of the white waters' (Witwatersrand). From 1899 to 1902 they were once again at war.

In 1910 the newly created Union of South Africa brought together the old Cape Colony, the Transvaal, the Orange Free State and Natal into one country with its legislative capital and parliament building in Cape Town, its administrative capital in Pretoria and its judicial capital in Bloemfontein. In a little over half a century the old Cape House had served its purpose and was dissolved. Augustus would be but one of many of its members, the memory of whom lingered down the years. The all-white Union Parliament governed with ever more draconian racist legislation until the first truly democratic election in South Africa in 1994 saw the African National Congress come to power with Nelson Mandela elected President.

Appendix 1

DE ZUID-AFRIKAAN OBITUARY

De Zuid-Afrikaan led the obituary way with this lengthy account of his life.

DEATH OF DR TANCRED – On the morning of Friday, last Dr Tancred died at his lodgings in Burg Street. Since his arrival in Cape Town as the member for Piketberg, he had enjoyed the most robust health. Within the last few days, however, he was seized with ERYSIPELAS, which was succeeded by mortification, terminating in his death as above stated. The deceased, as far as we are acquainted with his history, was a native of Ireland, and the descendant of an ancient family. Born in 1802, he was in his earlier years placed under the best teachers, and at the age of 20 entered Trinity College as a student of divinity. After the completion of his studies, and obtaining his degree of D.D., he was appointed first to one curacy, then to another, and eventually held the rectorship of Christchurch, Hants, up to the period when he resigned it, somewhere between 1835 and 1840. The deceased had been married, we believe, to a near relative of the late Sir William Molesworth, and his prospects of preferment were bright; but having, by his resignation, given great offence to his relatives, he retired to Belgium, where, after a residence of three years, he determined, with his wife, to join the Roman Catholic Church. Some time after this he determined to emigrate to this colony, which he reached in 1844. After sojourning at Graham's Town for some time, he removed to a small farm which he had purchased in the neighbourhood of that place. His stay there was not a long one, when the Kaffir War of 1845-6 broke out. Dr. Tancred was one of the last to leave his home, and hardly had he left it, when it was laid in ashes. The influx of people in Graham's Town had been so great, that no decent lodgings could be obtained, and he was obliged to enter upon the occupation of a store which had been placed at his disposal. Here it was that Mrs Tancred, naturally of a delicate constitution, contracted a disease which resulted in her early death. Of his subsequent proceedings in connection with the notorious case of *Smith v Lindsay* we need not speak, suffice it to say that to his exertions chiefly are the colonists indebted for the triumph of the civil over the martial law, and to their deliverance from the vexatious and tyrannical exactions of the old commando law. Nor need we allude to his exertions as the duly accredited representative of the large majority of the colonists in the matter of our present form of government; these are but too well known. When the Constitution came into operation he was elected as one of the members for Clanwilliam. At a subsequent election he lost his seat; but Piketberg having lately erected into an electoral division he was returned as one of the members for that constituency. Dr. Tancred was twice married. The issue of the first marriage are two sons and a daughter. The eldest son, Augustus, is settled in the Eastern Province; the second, Oswald, resides in France, where he has held a responsible situation on the staff of the Suez Canal company; his daughter, Evelina, has taken the veil in a convent at Boulogne. His second wife, the daughter of Mr. P. van Zyl, a wealthy agriculturist in the district of Clanwilliam, survives him, with two children, a daughter and a son. In Dr. Tancred, it need scarcely be said, the colony has sustained a great loss. He was certainly one of the most able and fearless champions for the rights and privileges of his adopted country. He had many failings, it is true; but of these we shall not presume to be the judges. – *Requiescat in pace.*

The *Cape Argus* was content to reprint the *De Zuid-Afrikaan* obituary a day later. Many of the regional papers repeated material from *De Zuid-Afrikaan* account while adding their own spin.

On 7 January *De Zuid-Afrikaan* noted that 'The mortal remains of the deceased were interred on Saturday afternoon.'

Appendix 2

THE DESCENDANTS

AUGUSTUS JOSEPH TANCRED'S FIRST MARRIAGE

Augustus Joseph Tancred (1804–1867) and his first wife Evelina, born Lattey (1812–1847), the author's great-great-grandparents, had three children, all born in England: Augustus Frederick Tancred, Evelina Tancred and Oswald Finbar Nagle Tancred. The children went with their parents to the Cape in 1842 but returned to Europe, almost certainly to France, after the death of their mother in Grahamstown in 1847. Augustus Frederick was the only child to return as an adult to the Cape.

Augustus Frederick Tancred (1834–1895) received a large part of his education in France. On his return to the Cape he was resident in Grahamstown in 1859, living in the High Street, and described as a clerk and magistrate. He then became Secretary to the Union Boating Company in Port Elizabeth where he worshipped at St Augustine's Roman Catholic Church and is shown as a contributor to the cost of a new organ. On 19 December 1861, he married Mary Ellen Smith of 1820 settler stock. In 1863 he became insolvent in unknown circumstances. By 1870 he was honorary secretary of the Port Elizabeth Choral Society. On 27 June 1881, the family travelled almost 1,000 miles to Kimberley where he took up a post as secretary to the Griqualand West Board of Executors. Before long, in 1882, he was appointed Town Clerk and Treasurer. In 1885, aged fifty-one, he was pictured in a cricket team of 'Kimberley Veterans' sitting next to Charles Dunell Rudd, a close business associate of Rhodes. The 1889 De Beers Annual Report shows Tancred, together with H.F.E Pistorius, as an auditor of the company accounts. He was a member of the Kimberley Club. Together with Rudd, H.J. Feltham and other such notables he was described as a 'generous supporter of the game' of cricket. By 1884 he was serving solely as Town Clerk, a post he held until 1894 and the ill health which preceded his death in 1895 aged sixty.

Augustus had married Mary Ellen Smith (1839–1901), in Grahamstown in 1861. She was the daughter of an 1820 settler. They had eight children: Aida C. 1862–1894; Augustus Bernard 1865–1911; Evelina Mary 1867–1868; Mary Agnes 1869–1924; Claude V. 1870–1896; Vincent M. 1875–1904; Louis Joseph 1876–1934; Zoe Frances 1879–1890.

Augustus Frederick and Mary Ellen were the parents of 'the cricketing brothers Tancred' – see Bernard Tancred Hall, 'A.B. Tancred and his Brothers', Chapter 6, in *Empire & Cricket, the South African Experience 1784–1914*, edited by Bruce Murray and Goolam Vahed (Unisa Press, 2009). Augustus Bernard Tancred was a notable early South African cricketer, as was his brother Louis Joseph who was better known internationally. A third brother, Vincent, also represented South Africa at Test level. They are included in *Famous Cricketing Families* by Kersi Meher-Homji with foreword by Richie Benaud (Kangaroo Press, 2000). A fourth brother, Claude, played against an England team in South Africa though not at Test level. Augustus Bernard and his brothers attended St Aidan's College, a Jesuit Catholic school in Grahamstown where their contemporaries included (later Sir) Percy Fitzpatrick, author, and (later Sir) Charles Coghlan, first Premier of Southern Rhodesia.

For an account of A.B. Tancred's role in what came to be recognised as an infamous episode in South African cricket, see Jonty Winch and Richard Parry, *Too Black to Wear Whites*, Penguin Books, 2020. He is mainly remembered for his distinguished career as an early South African cricketer and lawyer. He is buried in the Maitland Cemetery, Cape Town.

Evelina Tancred (1835–1912): according to her father's *De Zuid-Afrikaan* obituary, Evelina took the veil in a convent at Boulogne. Research in Boulogne-sur-Mer has so far been unable to confirm this. However, recent research has shown that at some point in her life she became a piano teacher. Her death aged seventy-six in 1912 occurred at her home, 28 rue de l'Hotel Dieu in Clermont-Ferrand, France, some 700 kilometres south of Boulogne and 400 kilometres from Paris. She is shown as a '*professeur de piano*' (piano teacher). Though she died in Clermont-Ferrand, she is buried some 150 kilometres away at Saint-Amand-Montrond where she was living at 53 rue des Grenouillières with one servant at the time of the 1891 census. Her grave is well-kept in the tradition of French cemeteries. The grave has an impressive headstone and, for whatever reason, she shares a grave with another woman. She was the sole beneficiary under her brother Oswald's will. She did not marry. I have visited her grave.

Oswald Finbar Nagle Tancred (1837–1905): according to his father's *De Zuid-Afrikaan* obituary, Oswald held a responsible situation on the staff of the Suez Canal Company. The records of the company confirm his employment, though he seems to have had a chequered career punctuated by ill health. In January 1863, his father departed from Cape Town on the mail steamer *Dane* to visit Oswald, who was apparently in a very delicate state of health in Paris where he lived in the rue de Clichy. Later in life he lived at Boulogne-sur-Mer and died there at his home, 63 rue des Pipots, aged sixty-seven. The house still stands and is occupied. I have photographed it from the outside. The death record describes him as 'without profession' indicating, I believe, retired rather than unemployed. No record of his funeral has been found, nor his grave. His sister Evelina was the sole beneficiary of a small legacy under his will. This suggests that they kept in contact throughout their lives. He did not marry. Like his brother, Augustus Frederick, he received a large part of his education at Boulogne-sur-Mer in France.

AUGUSTUS JOSEPH TANCRED'S SECOND MARRIAGE

On 22 December 1853, six years after the death of his first wife, Evelina, Augustus Joseph Tancred married Geesje

Martha Maria Van Zyl (15.06.1839–01.07.1873) of Lange Valley, Citrusdal, near Clanwilliam. They were married at Clanwilliam. She had just turned fourteen; Augustus was forty-nine. Her parents were Pieter and Gesina Van Zyl. The Van Zyls were a successful farming family in the Clanwilliam area.

Augustus and Geesje had two children: Gesina ('Geesie') Anna Maria Magdalena Josephine Tancred and Petrus ('Pieter') Johannes Albertus Tancred.

Gesina ('Geesie') Anna Maria Magdalena Josephine Tancred (07.10.1856–23.06.1903) married Josias Marthinus Smuts (1830–1903), a lawyer, at Clanwilliam on 15 April 1875. They had eight children (Smuts). He was the son of Daniel Jacobus Smuts (1790–1870) and Helena Johanna Francina Louw, who had married in Cape Town on 15 October 1824. Josias was a cousin of General Jan Christiaan Smuts' grandfather.

Petrus ('Pieter') Johannes Albertus Tancred (18.03.1862–24.12.1934) married Anna Catharina Dorothea Schreuder (1869–1958) at Van Rhynsdorp on 6 April 1885. She was the daughter of Louis Egbertus Schreuder born in Clanwilliam in 1846 who married Johanna Sophia Christina Van Rhyn (1852–1899) at Clanwilliam on 8 February 1869. They had fifteen children (Tancred). Van Rhynsdorp was established by, and named after, Johanna's father who was a Member of Parliament. Pieter was a shop owner, bookkeeper, lawyer's agent, and Justice of the Peace.

Among the descendants of Augustus Joseph's second marriage known to have done well in life are these grandsons: Louis Egbertus Tancred (1892–1966) who owned the Eden Rose Nursery in Paarl; Arthur Francois Tancred (1895–1959) an attorney and President of the Law Society of the Cape of Good Hope; Hugo Amos Tancred (1906–1967) an accountant and Town Clerk of Tulbagh; and Andries Stockenstroom Tancred (1907–1967) who developed the Foreign Exchange Department at Volkskas Beperk (bank) where he was Foreign Exchange Manager from 1946 till his death in 1967.

After the death of Augustus Joseph Tancred, Geesie married again on 19 March 1868, at Piketberg in the district of Clanwilliam. Her second husband was Albertus Johannes Van Zyl. They had two children: Albert Johannes Adriaan, born 1869, and Catharina Johanna Jacoba, born 1872. After Geesie's death in 1873, Albertus Johannes Van Zyl remarried but had no further children.

I do hope that in time members of these branches of the family will add further information about these descendants. There are a good many as yet untold stories waiting to be told about interesting lives and successes in different spheres of South African life. They deserve a chronicler.

For full genealogical data on the descendants of A.J. Tancred's first and second marriages, and Geesie's second marriage, refer to:

https://www.stamouers.com/stamouers/surnames-r-to-u/716-tancred-moses

This contains the painstaking research into the descendants of Augustus Joseph Tancred, deceased or living at the time the tree was constructed, by Lee McGovern (living in New Zealand, born Tancred in South Africa, a descendant of the second marriage of A.J. Tancred).

Appendix 3

KNOWN PUBLICATIONS BY A.J. TANCRED

Sermons, London, 1834. There is a copy in the British Library, London. Published by James Nisbet, Berners Street, London, MDCCCXXXIV. Printed by T.C. Johns, Red Lion Court, Fleet Street.

Letters to Lord Melbourne on the Importance of Education. Date not known and no known copies.

A Treatise on Polite Philosophy, or an Easy Manner of Settling Differences Among Men. Graham's Town, 1842. Published in his own name by Dr A.J. Tancred. In 1847, William Porter, Attorney-General of the Cape Colony, alleged that Tancred was not the author but simply published another man's work under his own name. No known copies.

Letters to Sir Peregrine Maitland on the Present Kaffir War. Cape Town, Part 1 – 1846, Part 2 – 1847. Originally published in Cape Town, at the office of *De Zuid-Afrikaan*, 92, Wale Street. Available as a facsimile reprint, State Library Reprints No. 45, Pretoria, 1969.

The Necessity and Advantage of Reflection. A lecture delivered at the Town Hall, Cape Town, 15 October 1858. A.S. Robertson, Cape Town, 1858. Available in the SA Library, Cape Town.

His 1851 letters from the Cape to Earl Grey in London, the National Archives, Kew, London, Reference CO48/322. He also wrote numerous letters to many newspapers and individuals.

The Pocket Companion, or Man's Best Friend, by the Reverend Augustus J. Tancred, D.D., 'may be had of Mr. R.H. Caffyn, Graham's Town, and of Mr. A.S. Robertson, Cape Town, Price-3s'. Undated. No known copies apart from a photocopy of the title page.

Appendix 4

PUBLICATIONS ABOUT THESE TANCREDS BY B.T. HALL

Bernard Hall, *AJT: The Search for Augustus Josephus TANCRED, 1802–1867* (Private circulation), 30 January 1995.

Bernard Hall, *AJT: The Search for Augustus Josephus TANCRED, 1802–1867* (Private circulation). Revised edition May 1995 (second printing with minor amendments).

B.T. Hall, 'Dr Augustus Joseph Tancred DD', chapter 10 in Donal P. McCracken (ed.), *Ireland and South Africa in Modern Times*, Vol. 3 in the Southern African-Irish Studies Series, University of Durban-Westville, 1996.

W.G. Schulze and B.T. Hall, '*Smith v Lindsay* – A legal *cause célèbre* from the Eastern Cape in 1847', in *Fundamina*, published by the South African Society of Legal Historians, Pretoria, Vol. 4, 1998 (appeared in 1999).

Bernard Tancred Hall and Heinrich Schulze, 'The Cricketing Brothers Tancred, Part 1', *The Cricket*

Statistician, the Journal of the Association of Cricket Statisticians and Historians, Autumn 2000, No. 111.

Bernard Tancred Hall and Heinrich Schulze, 'The Cricketing Brothers Tancred, Part 2', *The Cricket Statistician, the Journal of the Association of Cricket Statisticians and Historians*, Winter 2000, No. 112. [See also reference to this article in the book by David Frith, *Silence of the Heart: Cricket Suicides*, 2001, p. 102.]

Bernard Hall, 'All Roads Lead to Boulogne – or do they?', in *French Ancestor, the Journal of the Anglo-French Family History Society*, No. 28, December 2000.

Bernard Hall, 'Dr Augustus Joseph Tancred, DD', in *U3A Dacorum Digest*, Issue No. 33, Summer 2001, pp. 22–24.

Bernard Tancred Hall, 'The Meddlesome Dr Tancred, Part 1', in *Basford Bystander*, Nottingham, Issue 89, Dec. 2001/ Jan. 2002.

Bernard Tancred Hall, 'The Meddlesome Dr Tancred, Part 2', in *Basford Bystander*, Nottingham, Issue 90, Feb./Mar. 2002.

Bernard Tancred Hall and Heinrich Schulze, 'A Last Word on the Tancred Brothers', *The Cricket Statistician, the Journal of the Association of Cricket Statisticians and Historians*, Spring 2005, No. 129.

Bernard Tancred Hall, 'Daltons and Tancreds; Ireland and Austria', in *The Journal of the Dalton Genealogical Society*, Vol. 46, July 2007, pp. 31–35. ISSN 0141-2655

Bernard Hall, Richard Parry, Jonty Winch, 'Chapter One, More than a Game'; Bernard Tancred Hall, 'Chapter Six, A.B. Tancred and his Brothers', in *Empire and Cricket, the South African Experience 1884–1914*, edited by Bruce Murray and Goolam Vahed, UNISA Press, Pretoria, 2009. Shortlisted for the Cricket Society and MCC Book of the Year.

Bernard Hall, '"Dr" Tancred', in *The Coelacanth, the Journal of the Border Historical Society*, Vol. 57, August 2022.

About the Author

Bernard Hall grew up in South Africa before graduating in Economics and Economic History at the University of Edinburgh. After working as an investment analyst in Edinburgh he taught Economics at Glasgow and Durham universities. When later employed in London his role involved regular visits to Dublin and Cork and the opportunity to spend off duty time confirming details of the life of his Irish great-great grandfather, Augustus Joseph Tancred. Things though proved not as they seemed and eventually the trail led him back to South Africa. Four decades later he believes he has approached an approximation to the truth. He now lives near Brighton in England.